G. Esra Bulbul

12 May 2011

Cambridge, MA

The beautiful ...

An American Woman's Letters to Turkey

YES, I WOULD

Love another Glass of Tea

An American Woman's Letters to Turkey

YES, I WOULD

Love another Glass of Tea

Katharine Branning

Published by Bluedome Press
244 Fifth Avenue #2HS
New York, NY 10001

www.bluedomepress.com

Library of Congress Cataloging-in-Publication Data Available

ISBN: 978-1-935295-06-8

Printed by
Numune Matbaacilik ve Cilt San. Ltd. Sti., Istanbul - TURKEY
www.numune.com.tr

TABLE OF CONTENTS

I AM ON A LONG AND NARROW ROAD

Aşık Veysel (1894–1973)

I am on a long and narrow road
Walking all day, from morning till night
Knowing not where I am or where I am going
Walking all day, from morning till night

From the very moment I was born
I started walking
On a journey in this han of two doors
Walking all day, from morning till night

I keep on walking, even in my sleep
Ever seeking a reason to keep on going
Always seeing those who are departing
Walking all day, from morning till night

Forty-nine years on these roads
On these plains, these mountains and deserts
Banished to these strange lands
Walking all day, from morning till night

If you really think about it
When you get there it will still seem far away
The path is but one minute long
Walking all day, from morning till night

Veysel is confused by all of this
Sometimes crying, sometimes laughing
On this road to reach his destination
Walking all day, from morning till night

FOREWORD

I have always admired two periods in history above all others. The first is the Age of Enlightenment Europe, in many ways due to its many sparkling women of letters. The second is the era of the Turkish Ottoman Empire of the sixteenth century, with its search for refinement and grace in the arts. So it was only natural that when I first read the "Embassy Letters of Lady Montagu," they struck a particular chord in me.

Lady Mary Montagu (1689–1762) was one exceptional woman. She was one of the many astounding women who shone like bright stars in the Pleiades of eighteenth-century Enlightenment Europe. She made a name for herself through her provocative letter writing, which showcased her exceptional intelligence and erudition. Her perceptive wit shone in the comments on everyday life that she included in the many letters she wrote from abroad to her family and friends. She also made a name for herself through the events of her troubled marriage, her courage in the face of smallpox, her difficult relationship with her children, her numerous voyages, her outspoken feminism, her political activities and self-imposed "exile" from England, and her unbridled lifestyle in her later years... all of which is documented in the hundreds of letters that have come down to us.

She was born Mary Pierrepont in 1689 in Nottinghamshire, England, in one of the 224 rooms of her father's stately eighteenth-century home, Thoresby Hall. As the daughter of the Duke of Kingston and thus a child of privilege, she received an outstanding education. Her natural intelligence was noted at a very early age: it is reported that she learned Latin before the age of eight. While still a teenager, she met Sir Wortley Montagu, a noted lawyer and politician. The two fell in love over a courtship of seven years. The Duke of Kingston rejected the proposal of Sir Wortley for his daughter's hand – not financially stable enough for his tastes – and found a fiancé for her more to *his* taste, rich, but unfortunately, a bit too loutish of character for hers. In a first display of the astonishing independence that was to characterize the rest of her life, she defied her father and arranged for Montagu to kidnap her on the road to her wedding. The two eloped and married in 1712.

Sadly, the events following this fairy tale beginning did not feed the dreams of her highly-demanding imagination. Married life proved difficult for Mary, and her letters provide many insights into her increasing disillusionment. As an outlet for this unhappiness, she embarked on a literary career, writing essays and critiques. When the couple moved to London, Mary became the darling of London high society, which appreciated the combination of her great beauty, wit, and writing. This was a period of relative happiness for her, despite her continuing marital difficulties. Her son Edward was born a year after her marriage.

The next year, in 1716, the Montagu family left for Turkey, where Sir Wortley Montagu had been appointed as ambassador. His charge was to negotiate peace between the Ottomans and the Austrians and to safeguard British commercial and naval interests in the Levant. Lady Mary was 27 years old at the time. Her second child, Mary, was born in Turkey in January, 1718. During her 13-month stay in Turkey, she wrote 25 letters home to friends and family. These letters, published posthumously, are now known as the "*Embassy Letters.*"

And here is where her story and mine begin to cross…

* * *

I would like to thank Muhsin İlyas Subaşı for his continued support and encouragement to my writing and research efforts. And much love to my husband, Stephen Eibe Gottlieb. His eternal kindness and understanding for everything that I do are what make him the most beloved of men on earth to me. And of course, I especially thank the people of the Republic of Turkey. Despite what I say about talking stones, they were the real reason I fell in love with this remarkable country.

SECTION 1

TWO LADY AMBASSADORS, TWO BRIDGES

LETTER 1

A thousand glasses of tea

My dear friends and family,

One day, my friend, the Kayseri poet and historian Muhsin İlyas Subaşı, said to me: "You remind me in many ways of Lady Montagu, and I think if you wrote down all the things that you have seen here over the past 30 years, it would be of great interest to both Turks and the rest of the world. All would be curious to see how Turkey is perceived by a foreigner who has come here so often."

At first I thought it was a preposterous suggestion, for I couldn't imagine that my experiences in Turkey would be of any interest to anyone. Yet the more I thought about what he said, I decided that he did have a point, and that I needed to write down some of my travel experiences. In doing so, I can try to explain why I have continued to travel there for all these years.

And so I decided to enter into an imaginary correspondence with the great Lady Mary herself, and to write my impressions and personal reflections in letters to her, as if I were updating her on the country she grew to love. The following letters are addressed to her, but also to you, my family and friends, to anyone else who cares to read them and to the Turkish people. I am not writing a guide for foreign travelers to Turkey, and in this way, these letters will be very different than most of the travel pieces that have been written by visitors to Turkey over the past 400 years, and especially those written in the last twenty years.

These letters will not constitute a travel journal, because a traveler usually ventures through unfamiliar places, whereas everywhere in Turkey is familiar to me in some way. I also do not wish to bore the reader with travelogue stories of the petty absurdities and pesky frustrations of travel: the gippy tummy, the missed planes and busses, the lost money or camera. You will not find here the racing explorer stories of Richard Burton, Alexandra David-Neel, and Fred Burnaby.

I do not wish either to write a guide book describing scenic spots that can be discovered in the many travel books now being published or blogged on the internet. These letters are not to serve as a primer on the country of Turkey, providing historical facts and fillers that can be found in any serious guide book. My readers do not need to hear about all that Atatürk has done, mysterious stories of the harems, customs of the hamams, or what the Hittites did at Çatalhöyük.

In the same vein, these letters will not be a sociological study of Turkish lifestyle patterns. Turkey is changing so rapidly that it would be impossible to encapsulate it. Nor are these letters to be a political analysis. Although I do not wish to close my eyes during the bad parts of the movie or to gloss over problems, I cannot pretend that I, as a foreigner, could ever understand those thorny parts of Turkish society. I cannot demystify this land of contrasts and contradictions; I will let the sociologists and politicians take on that one.

And I certainly do not want these letters to serve as my memoirs or my autobiography: my life is certainly not that interesting and my travel stories not all that adventuresome that I should indulge myself in boring you all with it.

Most importantly, I do not want to poke fun at the Turks. Western eyes have always been upon them, and not always in a kind way. Such celebrated authors as Lamartine, Nerval, Gide, Loti, Gautier, Twain, Stark, Burnby and others have taken turns describing the customs of the Turks. My major criticism of these travel writers, especially the great nineteenth-century travelers who crossed through the "exotic Levant" with their overblown heroic tales of difficulties surmounted, is that they seem supercilious, uncharitable, and downright disdainful towards their subject. I do not wish to relate lengthy and boring stories that lead the reader down a circuitous route to make a mocking point about how odd the customs of the land are, nor do I want to skewer Turkish pride by telling contemptuous or comical stories. I just want to relate some of the stories that have happened to me and what they mean to me.

No, these letters will include personal experiences about everyday life, some of which I don't always understand. My years of travel and my entire professional career in cross-cultural relations have taught me much, the biggest lesson being that one must tread very lightly when walking in or talking about foreign lands and people. I have learned that your viewpoint onto the world is always tainted by the perspectives that you carry inside of you, inherited from your native land and from your upbringing. When you are confronted by an unexplainable situation, you must take a deep breath and stand back from it, and then remove your Western hegemonic eyeglasses. Then, and only then, can you start to analyze what is theirs, yours, and the truth. Opening your eyes to the value of other people and other countries and societies unlike yours has a reward beyond price. And no other country in the world makes this encounter so gentle and as colorful as Turkey.

I have been on the road with Turkey and her people for a long time now. I have grown to love this land and its culture as much as my own or as much as France, my other adopted country. But I know all of you do not understand how I can feel so strongly about this "Midnight Express" country and its "Terrible Turks." I would like only that you give Turkey a chance, and I write these letters to try and establish, in my simple way, a greater understanding between Turkey and the rest of the world. And so, when you all ask me why I continue to travel to Turkey year after year, going back to the same dusty places instead of dashing off to discover the four corners of the world like Phileas Fogg, I hope I can provide you here with some form of an answer.

However, as I said previously, I am not just addressing these letters to you, my family and friends and any potential readers, but also to the Turkish people. In doing so, I hope they will constitute one long and simple thank you letter to Turkey and her people, a simple expression of my respect and love for a country and its citizens. They are to be my way of paying them back for the thousands of glasses of tea that have been offered to me over the past 30 years: which is a lot of tea, indeed. Yes, I would love another glass of tea.

Love,
Your Big K

LETTER 2

A pen of poise and perception

Dear Lady Mary,

I hope you will not receive this letter as an intrusion, and that you will forgive my forwardness in writing to you. The wish to express my admiration for your writing has emboldened me to address you directly. I also wish to express the affinity I feel with you after reading the letters you wrote home during your in Turkey from 1716 to 1718.

Please allow me to introduce myself. My name is Katharine Branning, and I am an American woman, a librarian by profession. I share many things in common with you: we both left home when young to live in a foreign land, and we both chose to make our lives abroad for many years. I am married too. We both believe in the power of education. But most importantly, we share Turkey, as I have spent much time traveling in Turkey over the past thirty years.

Like you, I am a letter writer. They are a joy for me to create: I love to see the page cover up with lines like a bathtub filling with warm water, and I love to sense the slight tension as the pen nib slides over the paper. I choose my epistolary armory with attention: only the finest dense paper or colorful card, a gracefully-designed pen of fine manufacture that balances perfectly in my hand, and carefully-selected postage stamps full of colorful references to history or subjects I favor. Writing a letter holds such promise and excitement, and in preparing one I feel as if I am showing the same devotion as when I cook a fine meal for loved ones. I imagine the whole chain of people who touch the letter along its way, the expression on my friend's face when the letter appears in his box, his curiosity as he deciphers those stamps, his expectancy as he picks up the letter opener and slits the envelope seal, and then, hopefully, his delight at reading what I have to tell him. But above all, I suppose I savor most the intimacy that letter writing allows between two people, the possibility of standing as far back or as far forward as one wishes to convey a sentiment. I appreciate how you can hide secret thoughts behind words, or how you can step out in the spotlight with them. Nothing can replace the intimacy that the distance of a letter permits. And you unquestionably had that distance, Lady Mary, between Constantinople and England, between your uncertain new life and the familiar, old one you left behind. On the other side of the coin, writing a letter offers great liberty, directness, and energy. Writing a snappy-toned letter also allows me to dispel the melancholy that often plagues me.

You wrote twenty-five letters home from Turkey during that year you were there: which is quite a few, considering you were busy setting up your new household, managing a 4-year old toddler, and preparing for the birth of your second child. Ever since you wrote those few letters, you have managed to capture the imagination of countless readers and artists, and especially mine, as both a traveler and a writer. Along the way, you have earned the reputation of being one of the finest letter writers of the English language: some 900 of them have come down to us in print since you first wrote them. Those letters from Turkey, published only after your death, are still read today, serving as a quote-mine for travel writers, and feeding much fodder to the post-modern, orientalist, and feminist academic paper mills.

I have a Turkish friend, a writer himself, who says I remind him of you – quite a flattering comparison for me, indeed! I do not think he meant to assume that I had your same gifts of wit or talent, but I think what he meant to say was that I strive to have the same open and unprejudiced eye to my surroundings as you showed. For that, in my opinion, is what makes your letter writing so distinctive: not for all those insightful glimpses into the history and daily life of the era that you provide, but for the ease and poise with which you entered into the situation of being a stranger in a different culture. I admire how you reported incidents and facts openly and honestly, never negatively or critically. You were an appreciative tourist, and always acted as would a guest in someone else's home. You were never a ruthless scold in your tone, looking down on the Turks as their moral superior. You allowed yourself the liberty to question your own social structure, not that of the Turks, and you never passed prejudiced judgment on them. You understood the true meaning of cross-cultural exchange, especially in discussions with your tutor Achmed (or as he would be known today, Ahmet). You sought out the contrasts between Western Europe and Turkey, and contrasts as well within Europe and within Turkey.

I also enjoy imagining the personality of the woman I perceive behind those words. You sought with eager curiosity to learn all you could about daily life, from religion to stoves to food. You immersed yourself in your new world, and let nothing get in your way of discovering it. I sense that you are a bright and high-spirited woman, whose wit and charm always shine brightest in the upbeat endings to your letters. Your letters provide indications that you can be both strong-willed and warm-hearted, depending on the situation.

And such exciting letters you wrote home from Turkey, Lady Mary! I am always surprised that so many travelers to Turkey, at centuries distant, encounter and grapple with the same issues, misunderstandings, and frustrations. We seem all to be struck by the same things: whether it be you, the bumbling military adventurers of the nineteenth century, or the moderns of the late twentieth century. Some things just never change, some conflicts never find resolution; so many questions still remain unanswered. When I look at my experiences and see how much they echo in your own, I feel a connection with you. You were determined to make the best of every situation, to enjoy life, and to get the most from every personal encounter. I try to imagine how you reacted to everyday incidents, how you dealt with all the misunderstandings and confusion while keeping such a clear, non-judgmental head. But you did, with ease and grace, never simpering or complaining, and I have always admired that in you. I have tried to adopt the same open-eyed approach in both my work and in my travels, but as both an insider and an outsider it is impossible for me to see anything truly clearly. The insider in me wishes to be included and thus has a tendency to gloss over any difficulties, and the outsider in me is full of potential prejudice and imperialism. And so in the end, when I travel, I try to apply the same strategy that guides me in my profession as a librarian: I collect information, I organize it, and I diffuse it. I try not to interpret it, I do not edit it, I just diffuse it. Or so I try. As you yourself said in your letter from Ratisbon, "*tis prudent to remain neuter.*" Or once again, from Vienna:

"*Gallantry and good breeding are as different in different climates as morality and religion. Who have the rightest notions we shall never know till the Day of Judgement.*"

I am certain you are nodding your head and smiling at many of my comments, already felt by you 290 years before me. But long live this continuum, this constant eternal search for understanding, the comparison, and the challenge. The cultures of the world have much to share and to gain from each other. And in the end we can perhaps learn how to better participate in this unchained movement of humanity, towards a society of understanding, respect, and peace. It can all start with writing a letter, don't you think?

So will you allow me to write you? It would give me much pleasure to share with you of my impressions of a country that is mutually dear to both of us. I hope that you will enjoy hearing details about Turkey of the late twentieth century. You will be reassured to know that so many of the values and sights you so admired have remained unchanged, but you will also be pleased to see how the country and its people have evolved and grown. It is perhaps people like you who have helped to promote that growth, by showing Turks that the West and its citizens can be as generous and kind as they are.

Sincerely yours,
Katharine Branning

LETTER 3

X marks the spot: a place in the
world called Sivas

Dear Lady Mary,
Ah! my Lady Mary, you never had to deal with one very thorny question in your letters. In many ways, you had only the charge of sharing your impressions of this country that you were visiting, and what a wonderful job you did of that, I may say. But you never had to justify *why* you were there, which, believe me, is not always an easy topic to treat. You were "posted" to Turkey; that is, you went there to follow your husband, and thus you really didn't have a choice in the matter. I suppose you could have stayed *at home* around the hearth in your English countryside great house, but that would not have been an option for someone as curious as you. But it was different for me: I went to Turkey to quench an obsession. To the question, eternally asked of me, "*Why Turkey?*" I am often very embarrassed to provide the real reason why I first went there. Sometimes it is easier to stammer a bit and say that I have Turkish friends, or, more specifically, that I have a Turkish sweetheart (which seems to be the answer that everyone wants to hear), or that I enjoy studying rare languages, or that I am a rug collector, or that I do business in Turkey. But no, the truth of the matter is that I first went to Turkey to see a building.

Yes, a building. But not just any building: a thirteenth-century building, older than anything an American could conceive of existing or seeing in our own land. It is hard for non-Americans to understand the fascinating power that history holds for many of us in our young country. When I first encountered this building, projected on a grainy slide during a univer-

sity lecture of an introductory course to Islamic art history, it planted a
seed in my head that kept growing until it took over the entire garden of
my imagination.

I was 19 years old, a Midwest girl from Ohio, gone far from home to
attend university in France. The day of that encounter was in wintertime
Paris, and as usual for Paris in the winter, it was grey, it was rainy, it was
bone-chilling damp. Sitting in class in a darkened, vast university amphitheater one day during my first few months there, I was feeling a bit lost.
Lost because I had yet to make friends, frustrated because my French
wasn't as polished as needed to completely understand everything, and dis-
couraged because I was finding the format of the French "*cours magistral*"
so unfriendly. Those huge master classes seemed so impersonal, as compared to the small, participatory classrooms I was used to in the American
educational system. I missed the tug of war between student and teacher,
the commotion and civility of an American classroom. I was even starting
to doubt whether I had chosen the appropriate course of study, for everything I had encountered up until then had seemed so detached from any reality between art and life, much less suited to my interests. For months in
my art history classes I had studied the famous French archaeological digs
in Ancient Mesopotamia, with hours of class lectures filled with endless images of amulet rolls and clunky statues from confusing, co-existing, and
very dead cultures. It seemed all so uninteresting, pointless, and boring.

Yet on that grey winter day, right in the middle of an introductory
course in Islamic art history, the *deus ex machina* appeared: without warning, up popped on the screen an image that shook me from my pessimistic
doldrums. It was a picture of a building that seemed built of golden stones.
As if by magic, the sun suddenly came out on that dark afternoon, yellow
light poured out from the screen to light up that gloomy room. All at once
it seemed as if I were standing outdoors on a late spring day, under a sky
as blue as the ceramic tiles I saw decorating the building's walls. These
golden stones were deeply carved with dancing animals, stars, plants and
trees, cursive writing, and birds, all framed by lace arabesques. They were
as beautiful and magically expressive as the sculptures on the Romanesque
abbeys in France that I admired so much. The professor said, "...*Et main-
tenant nous voyons ici le Gök Medrese de Sivas*".... I had never before
heard the words "medrese," "Gök," or "Sivas" (and much less had the

slightest idea where it was), and as I scribbled them down in my notebook as best as I could, I knew these words were going to become the starting vocabulary of a new language for me.

Just what was it in that building that captured my imagination so? I will tell you about that in a later letter, but many of your own letters are filled with descriptions of buildings you have seen, so I am sure you can understand me on some level. Suffice it to say that it was just like the first time you gaze into the eyes of the man you will marry: you just *know* it is for real. Yes, stones can translate warmth and life; architecture can render tangible the most hidden emotions: yes, I was now certain of it.

I ran to the library after class to find a book that could spell out those words to me and explain their meaning. I found a book with a map, showing the location of that place called Sivas, a town dead center in the country of Turkey. That dot on the map became a compass point for me, like the "X" on a treasure map that marked the spot where laid buried the hidden pot of gold. I knew that I just had to go to see firsthand the country that could produce a building like that.

Its image continued to haunt me, overtaking my mental garden like Virginia creeper, popping into my thoughts at all times of the day and night. I soon realized that I needed to either weed that garden or to fertilize it. Thus I decided to go to Turkey, to travel to that place called Sivas, and to find that building. For you see, I *would* be able to find it, for it wasn't a buried treasure, it was there for all to see! I wanted to stand in front of it and touch those warm stones. I was convinced they would talk to me. I was certain that they would have the power to continue to turn my dark days into sunny ones.

Now when I think back on this incident that led me to Turkey, it seems a bit silly, the stuff of adolescent dreams. And yet, my favorite story in the Bible is the one of Paul's dramatic conversion on that road to Damascus, so I would never be one to deny that startling incidents can happen, strange things that can alter your life forever. And once in Turkey, standing in front of that building, I knew that I had found the pot of gold on those streets of Sivas. It wasn't a disappointing wild-goose chase, for I had found a treasure chest booty even richer than the building itself. I had found a perfect example of the translation of artistic aspirations into daily life. This architecture and those stones were talkers.

From that day forth, I made a pact with myself to become friends with this place in the world called Turkey. I wanted to find more buildings like this one. I wanted to discover how such a building could have been built, and by what kind of people. As I came to know Turkey better and better over extended yearly visits of travel, research, discovery and many, many more stones over the next 30 years, there was never a doubt in my mind that I would remain forever linked to this magnificent country, filled with people with hearts as warm as those stones.

Respectfully yours,
Katharine Branning

SIVAS

Tourist brochure and hotel envelope, Sivas, 1978

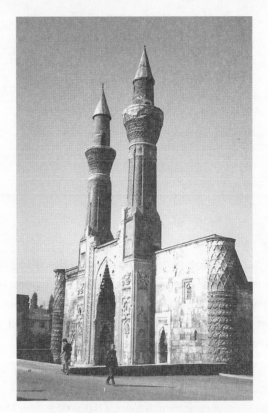

Gök Medrese, Sivas, 1271

LETTER 4

Building a bridge

Dear Lady Mary,
In the letter you wrote to Abbé Conti describing the last leg of your overland journey through Europe to Constantinople you mention staying overnight in Silivri and Büyükçekmece. Those two towns are famous for their fine Ottoman bridges, which impressed you as much as they do travelers today:

> "*The rest of our journey was through fine painted meadows by the side of the Sea of Marmara, the ancient Propontis. We lay the next night at Selivria, anciently a noble town. It is now a very good seaport, and neatly built enough, and has a bridge of thirty-two arches.... We lay the next night at a town called Buyukcekmece or Great Bridge, and the night following at Kucuk [sic] Cekmece, Little Bridge, in a very pleasant lodging, formerly a monastery of dervishes, having before it a large courtyard encompassed with marble cloisters with a good fountain in the middle. The prospect from this place and the gardens round it are the most agreeable I have seen, and shows that monks of all religions know how to choose their retirements.*"

Both the Büyükçekmece Bridge over the Marmara Sea, with its distinctive peaked arch, and the Silivri Bridge had been commissioned from the court architect Sinan by Sultan Süleyman the Magnificent, right before his death in 1566. Most certainly the troops of Sultan Ahmet III that you saw in Adrianople (Edirne) had crossed over them earlier on their journey to the battle fields of Austria, on their way to fight in the very war for which your husband was trying to broker a peace treaty.

The persistent dream of the Turks to expand their influence in Europe has never let up since the glorious days when those two arched bridges were built. I am curious about your impressions of those bridges because Turkish bridges have played a particular role in my life. At the same time I encountered those talking stones in the university amphitheater, another incident happened that could not have been a mere coincidence, and served as one more signpost on the road leading to Turkey.

When I first moved to Paris as a young student, I needed a job to pay for my living expenses, and I had the good fortune of finding one in a firm that did translations for the top French civil engineering corporations. I worked with teams of engineers cranking out French to English translations of such highly demanding documents as industry codes, calls for tenders, building standards, bids, construction documents, and the like. It was all very cut and dry, but I liked the precision of it, the exactness, and the clarity: in many ways I think this experience fed into my decision to choose librarianship as a profession. When I started off with this firm, I was still very green: new to France, to the French language, and to the adult world of work – and a little scared. The first translation project I was assigned was thus a major step for me to prove my capabilities. When I was told that I would be working on bid documents for the construction of a bridge, I felt an immediate sense of identification with the project and my own need to build bridges to France and to adulthood.

But this was not just any bridge. It was to be a bridge across one of the most famous waterways in the world, the Bosphorus Strait in Istanbul, Turkey. Not the first, momentous one built in 1973, but a second one, farther to the north. Of course I knew my geography, but that night I took out my map and looked closely at the spot where it was to be built. Certainly the coincidence of its location, there in that land of the talking stones I had just seen in class, was not lost on me.

Over the next months we worked hard on those bid documents, which constituted the submission portfolio by one of France's leading construction firms for this major international construction project. The millions of dollars involved in the project staggered me; the scale of the construction, the amount of metal, the bearing loads, the savant calculations were all dizzying for me. Even though I come from a big country used to building big things, I had never encountered firsthand a project of such an overwhelming scale.

At night when I returned home after hours of translating stress factors and load bearing equations, I would pull out books and study images of this Bosphorus strait, and tried to answer some questions that kept nagging me about my involvement in the project: What impact was "my" bridge going to have? How would it change the lives of the people on each side of it? Was I stomping on these people just like the huge pylons were going to trample the Judas trees on the banks of the Bosphorus? Was it going to be respectful of the history and the natural setting in place? What were the leaders of the country trying to say with this project? I looked at old and new photographs, as well as the famous late eighteenth-century series of etchings by Melling and tried to make some sense of the history and the context of the area. The old lithographs depicting calm waters and lazing wooden *caique* boats and the modern world of rushing cars full of people and rumbling trucks full of goods could not have been more dissimilar. Yet, the more I read about the country of Turkey, its history and its dreams, the more I began to understand that this bridge was more than a channel for cars and people: it was to be a conduit of ideas and values. It symbolized progress for this country; it was to be the golden spike of this transcontinental road linking Asia to Europe. And so I began to associate the ambition and vastness of this bridge project with the land in which it was to be built. I suddenly felt a part of something very momentous, the birthing of a powerful country, and that my little participation would have an impact on the lives of the people who would cross this bridge daily, on the country in whose pylons it sat, and for the world of ideas that would travel over it from the East to West and vice-versa. I eagerly read about the history of this people and especially about the man for whom the Bridge was to be named, Sultan Mehmet "Fatih," the Conqueror of Byzantium in 1453. I realized how this bridge was destined to continue the vision of greatness and expansion that he had started. It was also the fulfillment of the aspirations of other great men to follow, namely Süleyman the Magnificent and Atatürk, as well as those of the leaders of the modern Turkish Republic. I understood that its people are still identified, 260 years later, with Fatih's same spirit. As a daughter of the pioneer Midwest, I could understand and admire that ambition. I wanted to know more about these eager builders. I began to dream of crossing the bridge with them.

So you can see, Lady Mary, how I lived the story of this Fatih Bridge on a very personal level. I felt a kinship with this country, so eager to modernize itself, just as my own continually does. I was rooting for them. I felt connected to those people who would one day cross "my" bridge, and I imagined how they would feel at that moment when they could turn their heads and look at both the Eastern and Western horizons, as well as at the ribbon of blue watery silk beneath them.

All the while I was working on those documents, I began to think as well of the construction project of my own life. This project became a touchstone for the questions I was starting to struggle with in my passage from a young taker to a productive adult giver. Did I want to be a bridge builder to connect cultures? Did I want to help people cross from one place to another? Did I want to physically build things like my builder father had? Did I want to be a translator of other people's creativity or to be an artist myself? I suppose you asked yourself these same questions, Lady Mary, when you started out on your career as a writer. What was the catalyst that made you pick up the pen in the first place? What gave you the courage and impetus to forge ahead with your literary endeavors, despite the social stricture in which you lived? Well, whatever that catalyst was for you, it appears that for me, it was a Turkish bridge.

Unfortunately, the French company in question did not win the contract to build the Fatih Bridge. But they, and I, went on to build other ones, as well as hospitals in Africa and universities in Saudi Arabia. Yet no translation documents ever thrilled me, satisfied me, or affected me as much as those for that bridge over the Bosphorus. When all the bid documents were completed and sent off, I knew I had accomplished more than a translation. I had found the yardstick to measure the rest of my life. Yes, I wanted to build things and feel that resulting power and sense of accomplishment. Yes, I wanted to help people cross from one bank to another over a bridge of understanding. Most of all, I knew that Turkey would somehow be a significant part of my life.

Much has been written since about this Fatih Bridge and its obvious symbolism for the many elements of the bilateral tug of war that has played in the heart of every Turk for centuries: East/West, old/new, secular/Muslim, Europe/Asia, Ottoman heritage/Atatürkian vision, peasants/savants, poverty/wealth, and urban/rural. This symbolism still preoccupies them today, and this bridge keeps asking the same nagging question, "Which side do you stand on?" The double steel cables that suspend this bridge are strong and flexible at the same time, much like the various geographic, linguistic, political, economic, and religious issues currently exerted on the Turkish Republic. In the end, however, bridges are symbols of power: he who commands access to a bridge exerts the prevailing strategic hold. In this fashion Istanbul has positioned itself, via this bridge, to become the central pinion of the European and Asian chain.

And so you see, Lady Mary, why I asked you about your impressions of those bridges at Silivri and Büyükçekmece. You were then, like me, and like the country of Turkey at the time those Ottoman bridges and the Fatih Bridge were being built, at the start of a new life. You did not know what was on the other side of that 32-arched bridge, or to where the road on the other side would lead. But you did know, by the very fact that a bridge had been built there, that the other side was worth reaching. And that is what makes crossing a bridge so thrilling.

Sincerely yours,

K. A. Branning

The 9-arched Büyükçekmece Bridge, 1567

The 33-arched Silivri Bridge (now, as in Lady Montagu's time, only 32 are visible), 1568

The Fatih Bridge, Istanbul, 1988

LETTER 5

Crossing bridges

D ear Lady Mary,
And so I headed off for that land of talking stones and bridges in the summer of 1978.

My impressions of that first visit are not sharply described in my *carnet de voyage*. I have a feeling that I was so overwhelmed that it was difficult for me to document it all. However, I do distinctly remember being very excited when I saw my first pencil-minaretted mosque ·from the airplane upon arriving in Istanbul (as your Constantinople is now known). What was your first impression of this pearl of a city, Lady Mary? You describe your first encounter with Constantinople, 259 years before mine, as follows:

> "...we arrived the next evening at Constantinople, but I can yet tell you very little of it, all my time being taken up with receiving visits... Our palace is in Pera, which is no more a suburb of Constantinople than Westminster is a suburb of London. All the Ambassadors are lodged very near each other. One part of our house shows us the port, the city and the seraglio and the distant hills of Asia, perhaps altogether the most beautiful prospect in the world. A certain French author says that Constantinople is twice as large as Paris..."

One of the strongest first impressions on me was of course, the Bosphorus Bridge, the "first" one, which stood alone at the time, because "my" Fatih Bridge had yet to be built. It was a glorious thing to behold, its dramatic siteing and span so similar to the Golden Gate or Brooklyn Bridges in my country.

It was only later that I experienced first-hand the pride that the Turks themselves felt towards this bridge. On a subsequent visit to Turkey, I stayed in Suadiye on the Asian side with the family of a friend I had made. One day, they announced that they had a big surprise for me. Back in those days, my comprehension of Turkish was not all that strong, so I was not quite sure what was in store for me, but I was game. Uncles and aunts, a few young cousins, my friend, and I all piled into an old Chevy and headed out. It was a snowy and freezing cold winter day, so I was glad for the warmth of the 8 people piled into the car. This was a time of penury and extreme difficulty for Turkey, during the martial law winter of 1980, so I knew that spending gas for this trip meant that it had to be something very special. After starting off, they announced to me: "*We are going to drive you across the Bosphorus Bridge! We want you to soar above the strait like a bird, so that you can see the ferry boats from on high and you can feel what it is like to cross from one continent to another!*" They were so very proud to offer their guest this experience, and I was fairly speechless, for they had no idea of my personal relationship to the Bosphorus and bridges. And if you thought, Lady Mary, that the vista from your house was "*altogether the most beautiful prospect in the world,*" you should see those Asian hills from atop the Bridge at 105 feet in the air.

And so I crossed my first bridge in Turkey.

In that rattletrap car with a bunch of enthusiastic Turks, I made a significant, symbolic step towards the rest of my life. I experienced the thrill of being a part of something bigger than myself, something that pulled me as if by magic strings. After crossing that bridge, things were never the same. I started off on one side as a visitor, a tourist, and got off on the other side as something more.

When I was first living in France, I walked home one night in the raking late October evening light. On that fall day in Paris, the tone of that dusk light on the rue du Bac distilled in me a moment I will never forget. Suddenly I saw things very clearly, and I knew that I belonged in that place. I felt a sense of ownership, I felt accepted, I felt that I could find my place there, I knew I could grow there, that I would be accompanied along that journey, and that I would be invited to participate in its life and allowed to give of myself. I knew that I had somehow a right to be there, a right to finding my happiness there. I loved Paris, and it showed its love for me in return. I felt the very same affirmation when I crossed that Bosphorus Bridge.

Much like myself over the years, Turkey is always questioning itself, growing and stretching. Turkey has been a bridge for me, a safe place above waters both calm and turbulent. It serves as a constant reminder that I am crossing to somewhere and that I am always between two banks: the one I am, the one I could be or am becoming. Crossing bridges teaches me to organize my own path through culture, both there and at home, and to research my own character against the different backgrounds of others. My life has been touched by Turkey and I have touched Turkey by mine, and I keep traveling there and crossing bridges to understand this constant emotional connection that binds my shore to that other one.

To this day, crossing a bridge is still a thrilling moment for me. And there are many bridges in Turkey to cross. Not just those two outside of Adrianople that you crossed, Lady Mary, or the two Bosphorus bridges, but hundreds of other ones, built over thousands of years, by Romans, by Byzantines, by Seljuks, by Ottomans – all built to link together the arteries of this crossroads of communication, cultures and trade. I make it a special point on my travels to seek them out and walk over them. When I cross them, ever so slowly, I absorb the strength of their stones through my feet. I reflect on all the people, famous and infamous, plain and fancy, that have taken the same steps: donkeys, peasants, travelers, warriors, kings, sultans, and dervishes have all crossed over them before me.

I have crossed some remarkable bridges: the bent Eğri Köprü on the outskirts of Sivas, where Kangal dogs frolic on its banks; the thirteenth-century Ak Bridge in the middle of bustling Ankara; the long, thirteen-arched Kesikköprülü Han; the twelfth-century Artukid Malabadi Bridge, big as a dam; the sixth-century Byzantine Dicle Bridge outside the city walls of Diyarbakır that can be seen from outer space; and my all-time favorite, the tiny Seljuk Bridge over the Yeşilırmak River in Tokat. That bridge inspires me by its beauty, setting, simplicity, and its message. Three competing brothers for the Seljuk throne managed to put aside their feuding for a moment, for the time it took to build this small gem linking the new north-south trade axis of their kingdom.

So let us too, as rulers, citizens, and nations, take time from our feuding to build some bridges to cross together, one foot in front of the other.

Sincerely yours,
Katharine Branning

Hıdırlık Bridge in Tokat over the Yeşilırmak River, 1250

Bosphorus Bridge, Istanbul, 1973

SECTION 2

A COUNTRY

Letter 6

A home away from home

Dear Lady Mary,

The United States of America did not exist at the time you wrote your letters. You knew, of course, of a British colony to the west of the Atlantic, where many of your countrymen were emigrating to set up businesses, settlements, and farms. Many of your compatriots, including urban and educated shopkeepers and tradesmen, skilled craftsmen and farmers, sought new life in these colonies. The descendents of the Quakers of the North Midlands area near your ancestral home of Thoresby Hall founded a city which became an important part of America's history: the city of brotherly love, Philadelphia.

Dutch, Swedes, and Germans came along as well, and these pockets of settlers, after a hundred years of living together, all learned to tolerate each other and their differing traditions and religions. In an effort to maintain the property and independence they already enjoyed, and to resist the "taxation without representation" imposed by your good King George III, son of the King in power when you went to Turkey, these "Yankees" banded together and won a hard-fought battle for their independence, creating the United States of America.

I tell you all of this, not to gloat over the fact that your all-powerful king could not hold onto this colony, but to tell you that a magnificent country was created from it; indeed the first democracy in the world. Its founding principles were the fruit of many fine men, many of whom descended from your English shores. When I first went to Turkey in that summer of 1978, a very strange thing happened to me. I felt as if I had not gone away to a foreign country, but that I had come home, to my America, this country of varied traditions, peoples, and religions.

Since you don't know this America, I am sure it is hard for you to understand what I am talking about, so let me try to explain. I remind you that at the time of that first visit I had been living in France for several years. You, too, were familiar with France and the French, as you spent some time in Lyon and Paris on your return trip to England from Constantinople. You make some very amusing and pertinent remarks about the French society and culture, and you state that you *"think Paris has the advantage of London in the neat pavement of the streets, the houses being all built of stone, and most of those belonging to people of quality beautified by gardens."* You had little patience, however, for French women, *"absurd in their dress and unnatural in their paint"* and for the *"nauseous flattery and tawdry pencil of Le Brun."* I admire this country and civilization immensely, but I have to admit that sometimes it is not an easy place for a foreigner to live. You are often made to feel excluded from this society by your foreign birth, heritage, religion, or language skills. In addition, Parisian culture relentlessly pursues refinement and perfection. Even as a foreigner, I was expected to play by those same exacting rules in this demand for excellence, and at times, it was hard to bear.

In comparison, Turkey is a merciful and accepting country. When I went to Turkey for the first time, I sensed a freedom from this guarded societal structure. I did not feel like people were looking at every move I made and waiting for me to make a false step. People were forgiving and kind, like those in the America I grew up in. It is perhaps difficult to explain to you, Lady Mary, but when I discovered this land and met its friendly people, I knew I could make myself understood here, for we spoke the same language. You felt as if you were going to an entirely different culture. I, on the other hand, felt that I had somehow oddly returned home.

And the more I got to know Turkey, the more I was convinced that it resembled my own country of America on several levels.

Firstly on a personal level. I come from a family of preachers and teachers, and I have never let go of that Midwesterner's goggle-eyed perspective on the city and certainly on foreign places and other cultures. Those great fawn plains I saw outside of Sivas were just like the great corn and wheat fields of the United States. The rumbling of their tractors, and the smell of their mud and manure transported me back to the prairies of my uncle's farm in Kansas. Iznik seemed like a small Ohio village with its main street lined with sycamores, while Tokat reminded me of a western cowboy town. Life in these towns resembled life in small Midwestern towns, with grain co-ops, tractors and coffee shops. You can substitute a tea garden for the coffee shop, but the conversation revolving around crops and taxes and the feeling of camaraderie is still the same. People in both countries pepper their conversations with snippets of Scripture, and my Midwest and my Turkey are unapologetic in their defense of the same shared values: religion, family and children, the good earth, community, sharing, simplicity, faith in God and service to Him, love of nature, animals, daily life, love and marriage, combat for survival... and, above all, a love of homeland.

Did I come on that first trip with any prejudices against Turks? I don't think so, because I am an American and not a European, and so I was not branded with the stigma of the Terrible Turk knocking at the doors of Vienna. I only had images of Turks fighting shoulder to shoulder with my countrymen in Korea and standing by our side in NATO.

Looking at the geography of both countries alone is enough to establish similarities between the United States and Turkey. America is a huge country, and compared to Europe, Turkey is a big country, too, bigger than France and Germany combined. Both are lands with geographies of strong personality, each having seven distinct and varied regions, very similar in their makeup. The Northeast, the Atlantic, the South, the Great Lakes, the Great Plains, the Northwest, and the Southwest of the United States compare to Turkey's very similar seven divisions of the Anatolian Plateau, the Eastern Highlands, the Southeast, the central Lake Region, the Black Sea Region, the Mediterranean and the Aegean, and the Thrace and the Marmara. Like the United States, Turkey has bountiful coasts, plains and mountains, some deserts, and a varied climate. Both are bounded by two seas, experience wide and extreme climate changes, as well as some frightening dangerous natural phenomena, such as earthquakes, tornados, hurricanes, floods, and avalanches. The United States has two major mountain ranges that run north to south, and Turkey has two running east to west. Both are lands of great rivers: the Tigris, the Euphrates, the Mississippi, and the Ohio. Both are lands of impressive peaks (Ararat, Erciyes, Uludağ, McKinley, and Rainier); of midland chains of lakes (the lakes of the Eğirdir region and the Great and Finger Lakes); of impressive natural wildlife and birds; of rich natural resources (water, coal); and of varied crops of tropical fruits (bananas, citrus) and every possible type of grain.

When one looks at our social structure, there are similarities, too. Turkey is a country like America, based on meritocracy. It has a society made up by citizens who have earned their fame by hard work, not what they inherited by class and birth like in France and your England. Both offer its citizens the potential of great social mobility. The Turkish business community is as dynamically entrepreneurial as America's, ready to tackle the twenty-first century on equal footing with the rest of the world. Turkey is full of headstrong, determined, positive, can-do people, not afraid to make mistakes: just like my fellow citizens.

But it is perhaps in the makeup of its populations that I feel that the two countries resemble each other the most. There are so many different types of Turks! All cultures have left their mark in the DNA of the children now born there: Romans, Byzantines, Persians, Armenians, Arabs, Greeks, Georgians, nomads from Central Asia, Great Seljuks from Persia, Mongols from the East, and the Ottomans. Just like its wide regional variations, it has a rainbow of peoples. To be a Turk means to be a citizen of the Turkish Republic, and that represents a national rather than an ethnic identity. They are heirs to the cultural traditions of the Ottoman Empire and the modernization ideals of Atatürk and the West. We, the People of the United States of America, understand this, for we have all come from somewhere else, with different languages and religions and educations, united in our pursuit to build a great country.

It is not just the similar physical makeup of our lands and our peoples that made me feel at home here. Our problems are similar, too. I have seen destitute villages filled with hungry children, ramshackle houses, and poverty in both Eastern Turkey and in Appalachia. Like America, the discrepancy between the rich and the poor is staggering. Both countries have recently suffered cruel natural disasters: the Izmit earthquake of 1999 and the Hurricane Katrina in New Orleans of 2005. We are both societies riddled with internal problems, violence, and strife. And yes, unfortunately, we both have issues with some population groups that are not entirely integrated into the democratic dream. Yet we are free to fulfill the promise of that dream.

Upon your return home you wrote to the Abbé Conti that *"I cannot help looking with partial eyes on my homeland."* You state that all we get by traveling is *"a fruitless desire of mixing the different pleasures and conveniences which are given to different parts of the world and cannot meet in any one of them."* I do not return home from my travels to Turkey and compare how much finer my country is to it. However, travel there does help me to feel proud of both my country's achievements and those of this country I have just visited. The similarity between the two countries points out to me even more vividly the lessons we can learn from each other in order to better build the community of nations in which we live. These similarities have made it possible for this outsider to become an insider. In any case, one that always feels in a home away from home, an Ohio Yankee in Sultan Osman's court.

Sincerely,
Katharine Branning

Letter 7

Türkiyem!

Dear Lady Mary,

On the face of a mountain outside of Erzurum, there is a huge sign composed of painted white rocks forming individual letters. Maintained with loving care by army recruits, it can be seen from miles away. It reads of only one word: "*Türkiyem.*"

"*Türkiyem*": "My Turkey." Such a simple phrase to express pride in one's homeland. Nothing more needs to be said, as every citizen can interpret their own meaning of the word. As I gazed upon it, I realized that it had significance for me, for I have constructed my own personal concept of the country. "My Turkey" is not the one that is known by 99% of visitors to Turkey (and I would say 95% of Turks). It is not the Turkey of the sophisticated, wealthy, and urbane cities of Istanbul, Antalya, Bursa, or Ankara. No, it is the Turkey of the Anatolian plains. My heart lives east of Ankara.

You, like most tourists, traveled in the inclusive, multinational, cosmopolitan, and heterogeneous world of Constantinople and Adrianople (now known as Edirne). You state in a letter written in Edirne that "*the Manners of Mankind do not differ so widely as our voyage Writers would make us believe,*" yet you did not venture forth much from that cosmopolitan and wealthy realm to know the difference, or to discover the rural populations surrounding these cities. How I believe you would have enjoyed it had you done so!

Most tourists know Turkey only from Istanbul and the southern beaches, but my Turkey is different. It is the Turkey of a life lived on the land, of a life lived by sweat and hard work; the one of dry plateaus, not lush seaside beaches. It is easy to be seduced by Istanbul, pearl of the world, city of Man's desiring, but I fell in love with empty plains. To me, much like the fields of my Midwest, they prove the eternal power displayed in nature and the hope of man to push farther and harder. Most people see these plains as bleak and monotonous, but I find them open, free, endless like the sea, and full of mirages.

When I first went to Turkey, few foreigners traveled to these regions. Now everyone is dashing off to Istanbul for 36 hours, a weekend here and there; foreigners have invaded its market spaces and are working and living the expat life to the fullest. They are mostly in Istanbul, which, if truth be told, is as sophisticated an urban center as Paris or New York. I have always thought Istanbul to be a cross between New York, Algiers, and Venice, but whatever individuality it takes, it is still a very urbane place.

Not so for "*Türkiyem*" – "My Turkey." I love traveling to small towns where there are local markets and few restaurants or teahouses. I believe that when Americans hear the word Turkey, they think of it as being very mysterious and exotic and can mention only two cities: Istanbul and Ankara. Yet you would be surprised at how little those two cities really represent the country, just as I would never associate the America I grew up in with New York or Boston. The countryside outside the major urban centers is a whole other country. People are curious as to why I always choose stucco villages, dusty and brown plains over the mountains, the sea or the turquoise waters of the Caribbean, the Riviera, or even southern Turkey. Perhaps I am a bit odd, but the wealth of experiences I see "out there" is unbounded.

"My Turkey" is a place where there are festivals of every kind and imagination: besides the numerous prestigious cultural arts festivals held in many cities (the "Golden Orange" film festival of Antalya, for example), there are numerous festivals that honor local folklore and heroes (Nasreddin Hoca, Yunus Emre, Hacı Bektaş) or celebrate local produce and particularities, such as Camel Wrestling in Selçuk and Denizli, pelicans in Birecik, "Powergum" candy in Manisa, cirit (a type of rugby-style polo) in Konya and Erzurum, snakes in Mardin, roses in Konya, cherries in Tekirdağ and Isparta, grease wrestling in Edirne, strawberries in Bartın, tea in Rize, apricots in Malatya, tomatoes in Tokat, hazelnuts in Ordu, honey in Çankırı, master chefs in Mengen, ceramics in Kütahya, grape harvesting in Cappadocia, watermelons in Diyarbakır (last year's champion weighing in at 98 pounds), bullfighting in Artvin, figs in Germencik, coal in Zonguldak, and whirling dervishes in Konya. These festivities can compete with the Ohio State Fair any day.

In "My Turkey," neither sea, spas, chic clubs, beautiful bikinied people, discothèques, nor ski slopes await me. The lure is other. It is one of wooden houses, mountain meadows, votive ribbons tied on trees, bubbling roadside water fountains; of troubadours and dervishes, humpbacked bridges, cisterns, woods, running rivers, *saz* players, singing birds, pilav days and circumcision celebrations, windows and porches full of flowers planted in empty olive oil cans, clock towers, restaurants with private rooms for women customers, tea gardens under pergolas of strung vines, women in fields tossing grain or sorting apricots or onions, timbered houses, lush green valleys, washed kilims set out to dry, lace curtains, headscarved women, carved stone portals, low voices, windows shaded by pierced wooden shutters, fawn plains, jumbles of tiled roofs, walled gardens scrambling up hillsides, village busses filled with kids, animals, bags of potatoes, spare tires or machinery parts; harsh salty lakes in the middle of dry plains, meat grilled over vines and bay leaves, a lonely worker walking on the edge of the road with his bag of supplies in his hand, carved and painted wood ceilings, horse carts, hot springs, caves, farm workers bouncing in the back of trucks on the way to the fields, boys and girls droning recitations of the Koran to fix them to memory, waterfalls, loud drums announcing circumcision or wedding feasts, reed marshes, tractors and donkey carts, fields of watermelons and tomatoes, cities crowned with castles and fortresses themselves topped with fluttering Crescent flags, silences so thick one can touch them, buzzing flies, rainbows of bright-colored kilims on mosque floors, old men with canes walking to the village square to meet their friends, the wild and angry nature of moving tectonic plates, sidewalks littered with sunflower shells, the red-hot burning soil of the southeast, tragic family events and gentle weddings, low brushwood and yellow dust, scurrying inter-village jitney vans, roaring rapids, endless visual feasts at the bend of mountain roads, sheep shorn or slit, snow falling so hard and fast that it blocks roads within the space of a few hours, dervishes and Alevis, men spending hours drawing verses from the Koran in swirling calligraphy, half-timbered Ottoman houses, cobbled streets trod by Hittites, Persians, Greeks, Romans, Persians, Seljuks and Ottomans and Atatürk's patriots, golden plains running off the horizon of the world, hot springs, earthquake tremors, history peering at me from every stone, bustling weekly market places, snow-covered mountain peaks, candy and nut shops, dense fir forests and mountain passes, conical tomb towers filled with green-shrouded cenotaphs, open vegetable markets, covered bazaars, backstreets filled with woodworkers, tinsmiths, saddle makers and tinkerers; Kangal shepherd dogs the color of the plains chasing dusty sheep, bird sanctuaries filled with pink flamingos, heat-warped horizons, bleating herds of fat-tailed sheep, diving swift swallows, deserted ruins, views of sparkling blue lakes from the crest of the road, women observing the street from their perch in deep-set window frames, cemeteries filled with tipped-over ancient tombstones, scrubby plains and semi-arid chaparral, chattering Kurdish women dressed in giddy wildflower colors, meadows where horses and their colts run wild, rose bushes everywhere in bloom, fresh white mulberries, the smell of blood, fresh bread, dust, manure and watermelon rinds, houses of wood and stone and mud brick, close-hewn hills of green, black tents and white sheep, nomads and shopkeepers, low-leveled steppes that run forever off to a ridge of hills, houses with floors of tamped earth, flocks of waddling geese or sheep blocking the roads, a sky that comes right down to the earth, the yellowed, coarse paper of small press books, fresh apricot juice, climbs up mountain passes and the 360 views over the quilt of green and fawn patchwork plains below, the smell of dung fires, water sipped from a cup straight from a bubbling spring by the side of the road, full moons twice as large and bright as in the rest of the world, towels set out to dry in front of barber shops, caparisoned horses with fine tapestry weavings and blue beads, ancient bridges and fallen column capitals, mysterious caves and traces of civilizations gone millennia ago, a high decibel nature with loudly sounding frogs, insects, birds and flowing water, hard-working farmers, brown fields lit up by yellow sunflowers and yellow melons; dust devils, towns with one street lined with a string of 800-year-old structures and modern concrete apartment blocks, one-room schools, grain elevators and agricultural co-ops, and plains so vast they can't fit into a wide-angle camera lens or even into my eyes.

Such is "my Turkey," the one I have come to love so, the one far from sophisticated and elite Istanbul. How could blazing beaches and discotheques filled with foreigners match the thrill of any of this? Ah, Lady Mary, if only I could have been your guide to "my Turkey": I am sure you would have come to love it as much as I do.

Sincerely,
Katharine Branning

Olive oil cans

Çakır Ağa Ottoman house, Birgi, 1761

Ottoman bedesten, Amasya

Maternal prides, Çay

Taş Han, Akşehir, 1250

Street scene, Bursa

Crossing the Kuş Bridge in Amasya

Tomb guardian, Alanya

Street scene, Iznik

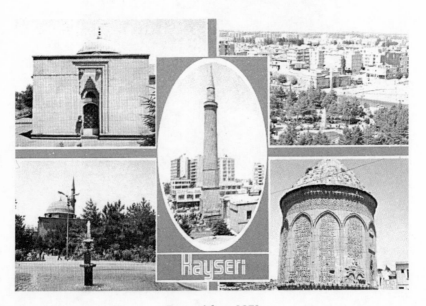

Postcard from 1978

Kastamonu street of doctors   *Market day, Çay*

Sunset over Lake Beyşehir

Street scene, Kütahya

Source of the Euphrates river, near Erzincan

LETTER 8

I have been adopted by a Turkish family

To Saadet Subaşı Hanmefendi

Dear Lady Mary,

There is one thing you learn very quickly in Turkey: the country is not run by the politicians of government, the turbines of business, or by muftis on pulpits high. No, Turkey is run by the family.

You will not encounter another society where the family bond is so strong and so cohesive. The unity of the family is a symbol of what is best in any society, no matter where it is on the globe, but in Turkey the bonds of family structure are more solid than most, with each family run as a mini-corporation. Family values are a way of life, not just a political or religious discourse for politicians, as it appears often to be in my country, where families are freer and looser.

You see, Lady Mary, I have known both types of family structures. I come from a good, solid, Midwestern Christian family. Although both my parents were orphans, my numerous aunts and uncles and cousins created a joyous and bonded group. Every Sunday after Church, we were at least a dozen around one of our tables for the big "Sunday meal." Yet I have many friends who are emotionally distant from their families. Lady Mary, you defied your father to run away and elope with Wortley. I left my family at a very young age to live abroad. We both grew up in cultures where children were encouraged to be independent at an early age. I now live in a city that is 1,000 miles away from my nearest relative. So perhaps in some ways it is difficult for us to understand the cement-hard devotion that bonds Turkish families.

I have had the good fortune to be "adopted" by several Turkish families, which has allowed me to make some important comparisons between Turkish and Western family circles. You never were fortunate enough to experience this, Lady Mary. You were received with great ceremony into the courts and the homes of Sultans, harems, and ambassadors. Yet you never sat around the breakfast table with a Turkish family, you never joined in their circle to sip tea and share stories, and you never got to hold their babies on your lap. You missed a great part of Turkey in this way. In many aspects, I received the same level of ceremony and honor in a small one-room home as you were shown in the salons of Topkapı. All the attention Turkish families shower on you can be overwhelming at times, but it is something quite marvelous.

Why is the bond of family so firm in Turkey? I suppose it comes from their strong sense of the *ulus*, the tribal confederation inherited from their Turkic ancestors. The *ulus* is the societal organization that determined all the functions of the Turkic peoples: administration, structure, function, politics, transhumance and migration patterns, the military, succession and power. It is what allowed them to successfully migrate into Anatolia and set up the Seljuk state, the basis of modern Turkey. Today's *ulus* takes the form of the individual family, and its leaders take the form of the Turkish father, otherwise known as "*baba*." The landmarks of life – birth, circumcision, marriage, and death – are all organized as in the *ulus* of yore and are marked with elaborate and extensive ceremonies. The modern Turkish family, run by the father, is deeply rooted in the *ulus* tradition.

The absolute veneration for parents seen in Turkey is as sacred as any law of the Koran. The family father, or "*baba*," is accorded enormous respect and deference. Next in the power line is "*abi*," the oldest boy, who serves as deputy father. This child may have a name, but he is never called it by his brothers and sisters: he is always known by his title, "*abi*." There are other names for various family members, depending on if you fall on the paternal or maternal side of the family. No one is called merely "aunt" or "uncle" or "brother-in-law" here: every family member is pegged with a precise exact title, defining his exact position in the family. This elaborate terminology of kinship is one of the toughest challenges in learning the Turkish language and culture. There are four terms alone for sister-in-law! So, you can see, Lady Mary, that this is not an impersonal society.

The glue of these families is a very simple one: love and respect. In fact, these two keywords, learned at home, form entire basis for the Turkish culture in the largest sense. All families strive hard to instill moral training in these two basic values: respect for elders and kindness and love for the young. There is much hand kissing of parents and elder relatives. The ceremonial kiss of an elder's hand, comprised of a bow, kissing the hand, and then bringing it to touch the forehead is one of the most poignant gestures I have ever witnessed.

Turkish families, as in many cultures, strive to provide every opportunity for their children, often taking very elaborate proportions. I am pleased to say that the strongest driving motivation for Turkish parents is to ensure that their children receive a solid education. They will do almost anything to provide this opportunity for them. They work multiple jobs and all hours to earn the money to buy books, knapsacks, costly private tutors for exam preparation, tuition in private schools, and even – the ultimate dream – to send them to America to study. *"Abi"* pitches in as well to help his little siblings and considers it an honor to pay for his sister's tutor, rather than to buy himself personal items with his spending money. Turks believe very strongly in post-graduate degrees, and families – especially upper class ones – will send their children abroad to be educated. If a child does not have the capacity or skills to attend the university, his family will ensure that he has every opportunity to set up his own business.... and even set out to find him a suitable life partner. The whole village participates in this educational encouragement. Once when I was visiting a mosque in Bunyan, a man approached me and we had a little chat. He then went over to a group of curious children nearby and said: *"See! She is American AND she can speak Turkish! What are you doing to become as accomplished? Now scat and go home and do some studying!"*

Turkish families stick together like glue. They call each other numerous times each day on their cell phones, just to hear the voice of the beloved family member. They camp out in hospital rooms when one of their own is sick, tending to the patient in many ways overworked nurses cannot, such as monitoring, bathing, and dispensing medicines. This is healthcare with a heart, and they certainly would never understand the concept of support groups or out-patient treatments, as this role in the healing process is assumed by the family. Another happy tradition I enjoy witnessing are circumcision festivals. Two years after you left Istanbul, Lady Mary, the Sultan in power during your stay, Ahmet III, held what is considered the most opulent festival in Ottoman history. It was a joint circumcision celebration for four of his sons. It lasted 15 days and comprised parades, fireworks, boat races, musicians, dancers, and floats. What a pity you could not have been there to see them! Although today there are elaborate circumcision galas held in fancy hotels, the ceremonies I enjoy are the modest ones, held in the family circle. Every boy at about the age of 8 undergoes this rite of passage, and the family makes it an event that the child will never forget, dressing him in a traditional fancy costume and showering him with sweets and gifts. If a family is too poor to ensure one for their son, either a local wealthy man or the city itself will pay for the ceremony. Summer Sundays are full of honking cars and visits of local holy spots by gaily-costumed boys and their families *en route* to the ceremony itself.

Never are the bonds of the Turkish family more apparent than at the breakfast table. You provide a description in one of your letters of dining with the Sultana, but I can ensure you that breakfasts in Turkey are celebrated with equal attention and ceremony. Breakfasts in Turkey set the tone for the day: all the family is there, all the love is there, and each olive is a promise of the goodness for the day to come and the joy to unfold once the table is left. No one eats alone, grabbing a coffee and a piece of toast on the run. No one starts the day without love. No one starts the day without community. The ornate breakfast buffets seen in Turkish hotels are nothing more than an extension of this family custom. Even in the most modest of hotels, in the poorest of regions, breakfasts are presented with utmost care, attention, and love.

Baba may give the orders to the family, but it is the children who are truly the ones in charge. Turks are absolutely besotted with children and allow them every type of indulgence. The first question you are always asked as a woman is *"How many children do you have?"* Ottoman female tombstones are decorated with carved flowers, one for each child the woman bore. Trees are planted in villages when a child is born. Turkey is the only country in the world which has a legal holiday for children. Every year on April 23, Turkey hosts numerous festivals and activities to honor them and to protect their future, freedom, and well-being.

There are kids everywhere in Turkey, a country with 70% of the population under the age of 35. They are generally enchanting, with the big eyes and sweet smiles. They are constantly cuddled, fussed over, kissed, picked up, and bounced. Turkish boys are like playful puppies, with their flat shaved heads and dirty faces; Turkish girls are like little coy kittens. A Turkish gardener told me once that he chose that profession because he thought that flowers were like children, each one different and beautiful and needing love and attention and that he could not think of anything more joyful to do in life.

Turkish children on the whole are very well-behaved. I have been on 8-hour bus rides with a 3-year-old child behind me and not heard a peep the entire time. They do not fuss in public but sit quietly with their parents, and they do not need toys or games or gadgets to keep them quiet and entertained. They learn complete self-reliance, one of the greatest of all Turkish traits, at a very early age. You cannot go through one day without seeing a pack of them playing a game of soccer. Just give them an open space and a ball and they are on their way – and this ball can be nothing more than a stone or a ball of rags if need be. I have seen village kids play with a stick, a piece of string, two walnut shells, and a stone, devising an imaginary game that kept them diverted for hours.

Turkish teenagers generally retain much of the sweetness of children. It is rare to see Turkish youths laughing loudly, making rude jokes, swearing, pushing, shoving, or showing public displays of affection. The word in Turkish for a young person is "*delikanlı,*" or "crazy-blooded," but my experience with teens in Turkey is that they are a very well-behaved lot. There is, however, one particularly impertinent group: the young teenaged boys who follow you around all day, insisting that they be your guide so that they can improve their English. They can be quite pesky and never take "*NO!*" for an answer. It is usually very hard to refuse this zeal for self-improvement, so I usually cave in and spend a bit of time with them, but it is very tiring and bothersome when it goes on and on. No sooner do you finish with one when another one pops up, yet it is always harmless. An encounter with some teenaged boys I once had in Istanbul sheds much light onto the Turkish youth and how they are raised by their families. I boarded the Tünel at the bottom to ride up the hill, and there was a group of boisterous teenage boys sitting together in the car, laughing, joking, and playfully pushing each other. The only available seat was in the middle of them. I went to sit down and my traveling companion said, *"No! I am not going to sit next to those pests!"* but I went ahead because I was hot and feeling faint, and quite frankly, they just seemed like boys being boys to me, nothing more. And after I sat down, one of the boys spoke out in a low voice to his friends: *"Hey! Quiet down, will you?! Look at that foreign blonde woman sitting next to us. We had better behave lest she get a bad impression of us!"* Of course, they did not know that I spoke Turkish and could understand their comment or understand how pleased I was to see that those boys knew how to behave in public, and especially in front of a foreign guest.

Turks want to make friends more than anything, and the way they do that is by inviting you to become a part of their family. I have been a guest in many Turkish homes, and in each one, I felt that I had been adopted into their circle. Perhaps it was for an afternoon, a day, or for a week, but I was always made to feel that I was a part of their lives. Tea, glasses of tea, endless glasses of tea pave the way always for this feeling of fraternity. I have spent an afternoon looking at photos with the family of a caretaker of an Amasya dervish monastery. I have spent a day shelling walnuts in the courtyard of a 200-year-old Ottoman home outside of Kastamonu with a farmer and his family, and then, at the end of day, I helped his daughter drive the cows home from the field into the ground-floor enclosed yard of the house. I have spent an afternoon with an opium-sniffing grandmother in her home outside of Kırşehir, where I was served freshly fried flatbread along with the tea. I have been invited to the home of a museum keeper in Safranbolu, whose wife plucked me fresh figs from the garden for my tea.

Upon taking leave, the ritual is always the same. Addresses are exchanged, for they want to be remembered, to exchange letters, gifts, news and photos, or to be remembered in thoughts and prayers. I have had people cry when I have left, women have poured water over the doorstep to ensure that my trip will flow smoothly, and I have been offered presents and flowers when I get on busses. My very own family does not shower me with this type of love and attention, does yours, Lady Mary?

I have even been invited to be a part of a Turkish family in New York when once I was asked at the airport by a Turkish woman, a total stranger, if I would take care of her 16-year-old son on his first flight to Turkey.

By far my closest family in Turkey is the one that has adopted me as their "*abla*," or older sister: the Muhsin İlyas Subaşı family of Kayseri. They have baptized me with a Turkish name and treat me with more respect, consideration, and fuss than you had ever received on one of your official diplomatic visits, Lady Mary. I am one of theirs, I am a friend to them. I met the head of the family via a letter, similar to this one. I wrote him to compliment him on the book he wrote on the history of Kayseri, and when he answered me back, we embarked on an epistolary relationship that led to me being received as a guest in his home. It is a home of peace and beauty, sitting high up in the hills outside of Kayseri to catch the cool breezes, with a view over the volcanic peak of Mount Erciyes. It is a home of quietude, with no loud voices, blaring music or televisions. It is the home of an *efendi* who owns 7,000 books that are kept immaculately in place in his third floor study. It is a home set in a garden of lush cherry, apple, apricot fruit trees, and vegetable patches bursting with tomatoes and peppers. It is a home of comfortable furniture, airy spaces, much light, and flowers in vases. It is a home of strong women, with his wife and three daughters looking over everything and running the home like an efficient, well-oiled factory. It is a home with 30 pairs of shoes at the entry awaiting every conceivable size of guest; it is a home where neighbors drop in for visits to share tea, coffee, gossip, and news. It is a home where his married daughter has built her own family home next door and where the son-in-law brings over special food gifts he prepares, from freshly-ground spices to a pot of stew big enough to feed the Janissaries. It is a home where original poetry is read in the family circle after dinner, where neighbors feel welcome enough to cut through the garden on their way home. It is immaculate, with not one item left unattended or misplaced, one dish unwashed. It is a home where elaborate meals, notably the famous Kayseri *mantı*, are prepared in a finely-appointed kitchen and served on delicate trays with great finesse by the daughters of the house. It is a home where breakfasts of 15 dishes are laid out under a vine-covered pergola in the garden in the freshness of morning. It is a home finer than any castle in England you could imagine, Lady Mary, or any Sultan's palace you visited. It is a home that beats with the heart of a loving family. It is a dream home, and now it is mine to share, thanks to the kindness of a Turkish family who had adopted me as one of theirs.

Sincerely yours,
Katharine Branning

Boys and Kangal puppies, Niksar   *Breakfast with Saadet Hanım in Kayseri*

Wedding ceremony, Tokat

Family celebration of circumcision, Ankara

Painted wagon, Pazar

Yörük Köyü

First day of school, Eğirdir, September, 1991

LETTER 9

It is all in a worthy name

Dear Lady Mary,

You are an officially titled Lady, to the English manor born and by marriage confirmed. When you went to Turkey you brought with you a bearing confirmed by your birth, your heritage, your upbringing, your wealth, your education, and your connections. All closed doors were magically opened to you because of your high-born status, your husband's political introductions, and your diplomatic passport. All the heritage of your Ladyship distinguished you even before you crossed the border and made people attentive to you once you were there. You were called "*Lady*" everywhere you went, just as you were in England. Yet perhaps you do not realize that your ladyship did not make you all that special in Turkey, for every woman there is a "*Lady*."

I, too, am a "*Lady*" in Turkey. A Lady a bit different than you, perhaps, but a lady nonetheless. Not one high born of the manor, but one born into the nobility of womanhood. Turks consider all women, since the time of the Mother Goddess of the Hittites, to be an exceptional class. When they address you, they call you "*Hanım*," which translates as "Lady." They put this term after your first name if they know it, and you instantly have an automatic title. In Turkey I am not just Kathy, but rather "*Lady Kathy*" wherever I go. Being called a "Lady" makes me look at myself differently, and I somehow feel a bit more distinguished, lucky to have been born in the noblest class of all: the sisterhood of women.

Turks have a very special relationship with the titles of Lord ("*Bey*") and Lady ("*Hanım*") and apply them every time they use your name. You are not "Mr. David Jones" or "Mrs. Sarah Hart," but "Lord David" and

"Lady Sarah." Last names are not commonly used in Turkey, and despite the trends of Westernization over the last years, people still refer to each other only by first names. The use of a last name seems odd to Turks, who find its use too formal and an impediment to proper communication. When you were in Turkey, it was the same: you were on a first-name basis with your acquaintances Fatima and Achmed, a liberty of familiarity that you never would have taken at home in England.

In fact, no one at all had a last name in Turkey until very recently. Turks lived for centuries operating with one name only, or, as is the traditional custom in Islamic countries, with a nickname, such as *"One-Armed Ali"* or *"Mehmet the Hawk."* That was all before the arrival of the tornado known as Mustafa Kemal Atatürk, who took it upon himself to enact a reform that would change forever the way Turks were called. The Name Law of 1934–36 was a deliberate step towards Westernization, along with many of the other politically-directed social reforms that he instigated in the first years of the Turkish Republic. This Last Name Law enacted legislation requiring every citizen to register a family name, which set the Turkish people scrambling to come up with names for themselves. Although urban Turks had little problem with this new law, the rural population had some difficulty understanding the necessity for his move. In the end, they adopted several patterns for name selection, designating what was important to them. These chosen surnames tell legions about the societal values of the times, which perhaps in some ways still hold true today.

One of the first surname types chosen was to designate a family relationship, which showed the well-grounded respect for elders that I spoke about in the previous letter. This usually took the form of "Son of" (*oğlu*), tacked on to the end of the name. Yes, here in Turkey, you can truly be named *"Son of a Gun Maker."*

Turks know who they are and where they come from. They are very proud to be from their area, often picking names to reflect this pride, such as *"Ahmet from Konya"* (Konyalı). They are also very proud of their glorious ancestors and chose patriotic names of the great heroic tribes, be it of the canon of the Central Asians, Seljuks, or Ottomans: *"Ali, Son of the Seljuks"* (Selçukoğlu), *"Mehmet, Son of the Karamans"* (Karamanoğlu) or the nicknames of the famous Ottoman sultans (*Yıldırım, the "Lightning-bolt"* or *Yavuz "the Resolute"*) or eventually perhaps the name of a specific nomadic tribal lineage, such as the *"Sworded Ones"* (Kılıçlılar*)* or the *"Big Belly"* (Karnıbüyük*).* On a simpler level, the Turks often picked pleasing or inspiring common object names like *"Lion"* (Arslan) or *"Greywolf"* (Bozkurt), *"Black Knife"* (Siyahbıçak) or *"Pure Cream"* (Özkaymak).

I especially like the last names that were picked just because they sounded pretty, poetic, or for their pleasant evocations: *"The One Who Smiles"* (Gülen) or *"Let You Be Exalted"* (Yücel), *"The One from the Rainy Valley"* (Yağmurdereli), *"Sky of Steel"* (Gökdemir), *"Big Full Moon"* (Büyükdoğanay), *"Silver Belt"* (Gümüşkemer), *"Black Smoke"* or *"White Smoke"* (Akduman, Karaduman), *"Son of a Good Friend"* (Dostoğlu), *"Former Wrestling Champion"* (Eskipehlivan), *"Well-Cooked Milk"* (Pişkinsüt), *"Beautiful Voiced"* (Tatlıses), or *"Piney Pass"* (Çamlıbel).

Especially creative are the names that were chosen because the person had a distinctive physical characteristic, such as *"Son of the One-Armed Man"* (Çolakoğlu), *"Son of an Orphan"* (Öksüzoğlu), or *"Son of the One Who Wears Tassels"* (Püsküllüoğlu).

My all-time favorites are the last names chosen to designate an occupation. To me, this symbolizes the great pride of Turks for their chosen trades. Names such as *"Coffee Maker"* (Kahveci), *"Son of an Archer"* (Okçuoğlu), *"Son of a Scrambled-Eggs Maker"* (Menemencioğlu), *"Son of a Chickpea Roaster"* (Leblebicioğlu), *"Son of a Candlestick Maker"* (Mumcuoğlu), *"Son of a Quiltmaker"* (Yorgancıoğlu), or *"Son of a Hazelnut Grower"* (Fındıkçıoğlu). These names will always serve to remind Turks of a way of life at this period in their history. Today, a chosen last name would probably take the form of *"Ali, Son of a Computer Programmer,"* but in 1934, things were different.

Even some seventy-five years after Atatürk's last name law was enacted, first names are still the coin of the realm. Everyone is on a first name basis immediately after being introduced, which creates an intimacy and a familiarity that is oftentimes surprising to our more reserved culture. I was raised not to call anyone by their first name unless invited to do so, but here, you are intimate at once, and this informality takes some getting used to for Westerners. Despite all the will of Atatürk, Turks to this day still prefer to call each other by first names and have not universally adopted the practice of last names. The Istanbul phone book only started listing last names in 1950, long after the Name Law was passed. I work as a volunteer with a Turkish charity group here in the United States, and I was given the task of updating the database of member names... which I discovered was entirely organized by first names.

First names, too, are as creative and interesting as the surnames. In the past, the names used by the Ottoman Turks were in essence Arab and Muslim in origin. There is a trend now to pick baby names that are more Turkish-based (Aslan, Orhan, Özer, Turhan, Kubilay, Timur, İlhan) and less influenced by Persian or Arabic traditions. In addition to this growing preference for traditional Turkish names of Central Asiatic origin, European and more exotic names are starting to make an appearance: "Tayfun" is one I found exotic, if not odd. There are definitely fewer Ahmets and Mehmets appearing on classroom rosters today.

Like the surnames, these first names are often inspiring, poetic, and beautiful. Boys tend to be given strong and stirring names such as Cengiz (Genghis), Timur (Tamerlane), or Yılmaz (The Dauntless). My favorite male name is "*Tarık*," the brightest star in the heavens. Girls are given sweet and dainty names, often after the most lovely things in nature or to describe poetic thoughts, such as Silk, Pearl, Dream, or Honey Spring. My favorite is "*İrem*," Garden of God.

When you add a colorful first name to a flamboyant last name, this can often evoke an entire epic: *Mr. Lightning Whitecloud* (Yıldırım Akbulut), *Mr. Pure Iron Son of a Fur Hat maker* (Özdemir Kalpakçıoğlu), *Mr. Mongol Rock of Steel* (İlhan Demirkaya), *Mr. Rock of the True Earth* (Kaya Öztoprak), and *Mr. Everblooming Wild Rose* (Dursun Deligül) are some examples that have caught my fancy. Can you imagine going through life known as Lord Lightning Whitecloud? How I wished I could have grown up being called "*Silken Rose*" or some other such name! If I had a brother named "*Tarık*," perhaps he would have grown up to become an explorer or a space traveler.

Yet, I have a very pedestrian first name. One day, my Turkish poet friend asked me: "*Kathy, just what does your name mean?*" I was embarrassed that I could not tell him, for in truth, I have no idea what Katharine means or why my parents chose it. I then realized how poor we were in my culture, to give our children names detached from any meaning, to deny them the inspiration to grow up to resemble their name. It made me appreciate how creatively Turkish people attributed such characteristics as hope, strength, and poetry to their children.

As a result, my friend, being a take-charge Turk, decided to rebaptize me with a Turkish name. He came up with one sounding similar to my real name and at the same time with a meaning that he thought suited me well: *Kadriye*. It means "*honorable one, she who has esteem and value.*" It turns out that this is a very old-fashioned name, yet, whenever I introduce myself as *Kadriye*, Turks respond to me completely differently than when I give my real name. It is of course easier for them to remember and pronounce than my English name, but above all, it sets me apart as one who has been considered as worthy of esteem and consideration. For that, I am eternally grateful to my friend for rebaptizing me, for it has made me feel more welcome and a part of the Turkish culture. Now, I am known as *Kadriye* to any Turk who meets me and to all of my Turkish friends.

Besides this given name, I have been given other nicknames as well, always used with my "Lady" title. I have been called the "Swimming Lady," "Caravansarai Lady," "Lady Yellow Rose," "Lady Smiling Eyes," and "Lady Blue Eyes." You can be sure that I never forget those creative and heartfelt gestures of friendship expressed in a simple name.

It is all in a name, indeed, as the old expression goes. So what do their names say about the Turks? Their names say that they are proud of their heritage, their families, and their trades. They indicate their deep love for nature and beauty. They show how the Turks like to dream and how they wish to create a strong identity for their children. They show their creative and playful side. They let us discover a people that are respectful and friendly at the same time. Yes, something as small as a name tells legions about this people.

Have you ever thought what last name you would choose if given the chance, Lady Mary? Indeed, it would be hard to choose one above all others. I probably would have been known as "*Lady Keeper of Books*," and you would have been baptized as "*Lady Flowing Pen.*" Yet in the end, I agree with the Turks. Who needs a last name after all? I think being called "*Lady Yellow Rose the Worthy*" suits me just fine.

Sincerely,
Kadriye Branning

LETTER 10

Good mornings!

To my Turkish teachers past and present

Dear Lady Mary,
One of the most touching comments I have read in the *Embassy Letters* is the one you wrote to your sister from Vienna:

> "*A chosen conversation, composed of a few that one esteems, is the greatest happiness of life.*"

Indeed it is. It is one of the main reasons I have always been so interested in languages, for they permit you to have those chosen conversations with "esteemed ones" in many lands. This was my primary motivation to learn Turkish, for I knew that if I wanted to truly get to know this country and its people, I needed to speak their language. Little did I know, however, the challenge that it would prove to be!

You, too, knew that learning the Turkish language would be the key to mastering your environment, but also that it would allow you to read their literature, which is something that interested you more than other pursuits. Engraved above the entrance to the humanities building at the university in Ankara is a quote by Atatürk: "*Hayatta en hakiki mürşit ilimdir*" (The truest guide in life is knowledge). You share this conviction, and it drove you to embark on a very disciplined and rigorous program to learn Turkish, even before you arrived in Constantinople.

It would seem that you learned the language relatively easily (you had, after all, learned Latin before the age of eight), and I must admit that I am a bit jealous that you were able to learn so quickly! It helped that you had an excellent tutor: after leaving Vienna, you stayed for three weeks in Belgrade where you were tutored by Achmed effendi: *"He has explained to me many pieces of Arabian Poetry, which, I observed, are in numbers not unlike ours, generally alternate verse, and of a very musical sound. Their expressions of love are very passionate and lively..."*

He opened the world of Arabic, Persian, and Ottoman literature to you, and you must have been a phenomenal student, for a few weeks later, you shared with your friend Alexander Pope some observations on the language, stating in your letter that *"the language of the court is an entirely different language than the one of the vulgar Turk."* You illustrated this style of poetry by sending him a poem written by a nobleman, and you show off your literary erudition to him by stating, *"You see I am pretty far gone in oriental learning."* I must admit I have trouble believing that you could be this far gone in your learning in so short a time, but by the time you meet the *"handsome as an angel"* Fatima for the second time in Constantinople one year later, you are able to maintain the conversation with her in Turkish. Impressive indeed. You write to a friend in April, 1718, a year after you arrived, that *"I speak the language passably and I have had the advantage of forming friendships with Turkish ladies and of their liking me, and I can boast of being the first foreigner ever to have had that pleasure."*

Upon your arrival in Constantinople, you continued your program to educate yourself, setting up a rigorous daily routine for language learning. You describe to your friend Pope your weekly disciplined schedule of activities, which you considered superior to your occupations in England, as follows: *"I endeavor to persuade myself that I live in a more agreeable variety than you do, and that Monday setting of partridges, Tuesday reading English, Wednesday studying the Turkish language (in which, by the way, I am already very learned), Thursday classical authors, Friday spent in writing, Saturday at my needle and Sunday admitting visits and hearing music, is a better way of disposing of the week than the perpetual round [in London]."* Indeed, learning a language can be a passionate and engaging enterprise.

Yet you are not the only one who has a gift for languages: Turks are wizards at this game. Perhaps this is due to their natural cleverness or to the fact that they have always lived in a linguistic crossroads. You remark on how knowledgeable they are with languages in a letter dated March 16, 1718:

> *"... I live in a place that very well represents the Tower of Babel; in Pera they speak Turkish, Greek, Hebrew, Armenian, Arabic, Persian, Russian,*

*Slavonian, Walachian, German, Dutch, French, English, Italian,
Hungarian; and what is worse, there [are] ten of these languages spoke
in my own family. My grooms are Arabs, my footmen French, English
and German, my nurse is an Armenian, my housemaids Russians, half a
dozen other servants Greeks, my steward an Italian, my janissary Turks,
that I live in the perpetual hearing of this medley of sounds, which pro-
duces a very extraordinary effect upon the people that are born here.
They learn all these languages at the same time and without knowing any
of them well enough to write or read in it. There are very few men,
women or children here that have not the same compass of words in five
or six of them... This seems almost incredible to you and is, in my mind,
one of the most curious things in this country, and takes off very much
from the merit of our ladies who set up for such extraordinary geniuses
upon the credit of some superficial knowledge of French and Italian."*

To this day, there are many "different" languages spoken in Turkey:
Arabic in the Hatay, Kurdish in Eastern Turkey, and the European languages of the old Levantine families of Pera (French, Greek, and Italian
mostly). I have discovered another language all to its own in Istanbul: Bazaar speak. I am constantly amazed at how masterful the shopkeepers and
dealers to the tourist trade can manage to shift gears so effortlessly between
Russian, English, French, Italian, and even Japanese with the greatest of
ease. Not only can they speak these languages, but they have multilingual
currency converters in their heads and can compute the price of any object
with the rapidity that would challenge an electronic board.

I wish I could brag to you of my prowess in Turkish like you could
boast to your friend Pope. Despite having had many outstanding tutors
myself, I have never developed an ease with Turkish. I can pretty much say
anything I need to, but when I speak, I can see in people's eyes that they
are either struggling to understand what I am exactly trying to say, or else
their eyes twinkle with amused charm at hearing my fractured phrases. I
have spent many years promoting and teaching foreign languages and have
run one of the largest language schools in the world, and I am thus very familiar with the challenges, frustrations, and joys of learning a new language. I can attest that Turkish has provided me more than a fair share of
challenges. Not just linguistic challenges, but also cultural ones.

I learned very early that the first rule of order for families in Turkey is
the same one that rules all communication interchange: Respect. Turks are

very careful to communicate to a person in a fashion that reflects the proper degree of respect. This respect depends on factors such as age, wealth, contacts, or the position the person holds in his profession or in society. Shame to he who fails to show the correct amount of respect. In communication Turkish-style, this respect is shown principally by allowing your partner to speak at length without interruption and by looking attentively while they are speaking. One must never contradict the other person, which is interpreted as a declaration of aggressive hostility. Turks are very sensitive to this, and it has proved a hard lesson for me, for in my culture, especially in the bullet-speed pace of New York City, many conversations go on at the same time. In France, contradiction in conversation is an expected way of life, for if you do not contradict a person's remarks, it means you are not paying attention to him. It is just not so in Turkey.

Other than pure language exchange, it is necessary to understand the little formalities that go into every successful communication encounter. For example, it is bad form to approach a person and ask a question directly, without first prefacing it with a *"Hello, excuse me, I am sorry to bother you,"* etc. In fact, Turks always start off an encounter with the sweet little word *"Acaba"* which means *"I wonder if... would you mind... could you possibly...?"* You discover quickly that if you don't observe these little rules and formalities, your relationship will be skewed, and you will be the one coming off as rude. For example, when someone approaches you and asks if they can direct you anywhere, you must accept it as a genuine offer, and not refuse it, even if you know perfectly well where you are going. To do so would be extremely rude. You must *always* accept the offered glass of tea. Perhaps one of the greatest linguistic misunderstandings for foreigners in Turkey is over the simple word *"no."* When a Turk wants to express *"no!"* it is not said, but merely gestured with a very serious and dour raising of the eyebrows, clicking of the tongue, and tilting the head back. Sometimes you get one or all of these gestures, and they are almost imperceptible. Yet they are there: *"no"* is rarely said, but gestured, and you must look for the signs. Foreigners who meet silence to their questions often think that they are being ignored when in reality, they are being answered in this silent code.

The universal rules of communication are perhaps more important in Turkey, due to the heightened awareness of respect. The way to avoid misunderstandings is to think not of what is apparent on the surface but what is lying beneath. For all types of communication, there are three different messages on the table: the message you wish to convey, the one that actually comes out of your mouth, and the one the other person actually hears and interprets according to his framework. Every person in the room with you, whether in a village or in a shop or in an urban center or in a business meeting in a town, is acting according to the likely effect the discussion will have on them or on their relations with others. And in Turkey, foreigners who are sympathetic to this way of thinking and careful to show respect where it is due will be more readily accepted.

It also helps to try and find humor in the communication absurdities that happen on a daily basis. Nothing should be taken for granted in any encounter or situation, and you must accept that you cannot always make sense of everything. Even when things get explained to you, you still sometimes can't understand them because, well, you are just not Turkish. So many things may be normal or commonplace, but because I cannot understand the background of motivation, they appear puzzling. I was once told that I resembled a horse, a comparison which had me upset for days, for in my culture this is a resounding insult. It was only a long time later, when I learned of the absolute veneration of the Turks for horses, did I realize that I had actually been paid one of the highest compliments possible.

In the first years I went to Turkey, it was very rare to come across a foreigner who spoke Turkish, especially in the rural areas where I tended to travel. It was not at all uncommon for a simple *"Hello, good mornings, I wonder if you can indicate where I might find the Ulu Cami"* would create a sudden stampede of Turks upon me like locusts in a field of grain. You, too, ran into the very same type of incident. In your letter to your friend Lady Bristol on April 1, 1717, you talk of how you and the French Ambassador's wife drew a crowd on an outing:

> *"I went with her the other day all around the town in an open gilt chariot, with our joint train of attendants, preceded by our guards, who might have summoned the people to see what they had never seen, nor ever would see again; two young Christian ambassadresses never yet having been in this country at the same time, nor I believe ever will again. Your Ladyship may easily imagine that we drew a vast crowd of spectators, but all silent as death. If any of them had taken the liberties of our mob upon*

*any strange sight our janissaries had made no scruple of falling on them
with their scimitars..."*

Drawing such crowds could often be quite intimidating, and on many
occasions I would be somewhat afraid, until I realized that it was only out
of pure curiosity that these people clustered around me. When I finally understood that it was not me, but my Turkish mistakes and accent that were
the star attraction, I was put to ease. For you see, I am convinced that for
many of these people, it was the first time they had ever heard their language spoken by a foreigner, and they just wanted to hear how I cobbled
sentences together, what words I chose, and most of all, to hear my accent.
I have found that having an accent in Turkish has proved particularly helpful for getting good service in restaurants, for as soon as I would sit down,
five waiters would bustle over to take my order, adjust my napkin and pour
water for me, just to be able to hear me say anything in my off-key accent.

Yes, when I first went to Turkey, there were few language schools to
learn Turkish, only a handful of grammar books, and virtually no textbooks
for teaching Turkish to foreigners. Now Turkish is taught in universities
and schools throughout the world, Turks are churning out TSL textbooks,
there are language competitions for young students of Turkish, and the
Turks have adopted the European Common Framework for Language in-
struction guidelines in their language schools long before I did in my own.

Yet learning Turkish has still proven difficult and elusive. The worst
has always been telephoning, for I get lost and make terrible mistakes, caus-
ing very pregnant pauses on both ends of the line. Telephoning is so stress-
ful that I often write the script out ahead of time and hold it in my hand
while telephoning. I have found that if I want to make sure I understand
something, I will usually ask a woman, as their Turkish is easier to understand (or is it perhaps because women all over the world tend to speak the
same dialect?) Often during long conversations I become so frustrated, so
drained and exhausted by the mental effort of trying to pick out under-
standable words and to build them into meaningful sentences, or by the
constant attention and challenge of trying to understand everything, that I
burn out. The shutter comes down, and I just have to decisively walk away
and hope that I do not come off as impolite or disrespectful.

As hard as Turkish may be to learn, it is made tenfold easier by the
help that Turks give you when you are trying to express yourself. They are

like cheerleaders, rooting for you to get that phrase out and to express your thought. When you speak bad Turkish, they never stop your flow; they just keep talking to you, which is such a change from the French, who are so ready to correct any minor invasion to the propriety of their language. Turks applaud you like a horse thundering down the racetrack and provide continuous ego boosts by congratulating you when you cross the finish line of a sentence. Above and beyond my tutors, the whole country is dedicated to my language acquisition.

Furthermore, the attention to respect that the Turks show during communication is particularly welcomed and appreciated by foreigners. Turks wait until you have finished speaking, even if they haven't a clue about what you are going on about. They nod their heads often. They *never* correct your Turkish (that would be a contradiction, you see), nor do they ever look at you with furrowed brow as if they don't understand what you are trying to express. They repeat your name constantly when they talk with you to keep you pulled in and so as not to lose you. And when they see that you are lost, they will stop and totally re-paraphrase the thought into words and sentence structures that they know you will grasp. They have infinite patience. It is hard to make bloopers in this language, for the Turks just won't allow you to; the minute they sense something is not going right, they will gently help you along. It is just as difficult for them to understand what you are trying to say as it is for you to understand them, but they never show it. They are true communicators, for they nurture you along. The nature of the Turks comes out when they communicate with foreigners: the traits of respect, kindness, generosity, patience, and humor are all in full evidence.

So if this language is so devilish to learn, why do I persist? Besides the anticipation of those "*chosen conversations*" and reading the poems of Nedim, there are many things that attract me to the Turkish language. Linguistically, its agglutinative structure is fascinating: one adds suffixes to words one after the other like freight cars on a long coal train. Like German, I love finding the verb at the end of the sentence, where it acts as the final, declarative defining caboose to all those noun/adjective train cars. I am intrigued that it is feasible to create an entire clause in mid-sentence based on one word. I am challenged by these sentences that, compared to English, seem structured inside out and backwards. I love the fact that Turkish has a "maybe" tense for reporting things you have not seen or heard first-hand, so as to delicately distance yourself as the bearer of news potentially not correct. I love that they have a tense that can be present, past, and future depending on the situation (and good luck figuring it out). So you see, "The post office in the front of which the-red-sweater-wearing ready-to-pull-out-her-hair foreigner stands... maybe" is not gobbledygook: it is a perfectly-structured Turkish sentence. In this fashion Turkish keeps me on my toes because I never quite know where I am in a sentence. In those rare times when my mind can cut through the linguistic Gordian knot of a train car sentence, I feel as if I have deciphered the code of a secret document.

I love the sound of the Turkish language: when men speak it, it sounds like the flowing water in a wooded brook. When women speak it (especially the ones from Istanbul), it sounds like little chittering bird speak. I appreciate that the Turks have borrowed so many words from French in the realms of administration, fashion, and the arts, which has made my life much easier, for I can oftentimes find one to fall back on. In addition to creative borrowing, I also enjoy how the Turks are artistic in inventing new words to accompany the march of civilization, like "knowledge counter" for computer and "pocket phone" for cell phone. I love the strength and power of some of the imperative commands that can stop a rocket in space: "*Yapma! Var! Ayıp! Dur!*" (Don't do that! Yes! Shame on you! Stop!) And a true joy in Turkish is the thousands of proverbs that pepper their speech. Turks love to use common-speak folkloric expressions, and their collection is quite colorful. "*An ass does not appreciate fruit compote,*" "*A defeated wrestler is not tired of wrestling,*" "*The buyer of the rotten beans is the blind man,*" "*Who enters a Turkish bath will sweat,*" "*There lies a lion in every heart,*" "*The shroud has no pockets,*" and "*The cock that crows too early gets his head cut off*" are some examples of this homespun fun. Whole dictionaries have been devoted to them.

I love the sweet things Turks say to each other in daily life, such as "*Health to your hands*" when you cook or make something excellent, "*May it pass*" when you find out someone is sick, "*May it go easily*" when you pass manual workers, and the touching "*May the worst of our days be like this one*" said on happy occasions. There are also some magnificent particularities in Turkish, notably the "YOK!" with its many meanings, ranging from NOT! to "You've got to be kidding" to "Don't you dare!" And my all-time particular favorite is the peculiar habit of wishing someone "Good

Mornings" and "Good Evenings." When I ask for an explanation to this, I get blank stares, for it seems inconceivable to them in their infinite generosity that they would chose to wish someone only one measly "Good Morning!" rather that a whole lifetime of them.

I have spent much time translating Turkish stories and poetry into English, and I find it a challenge that goes above and beyond the normal ones imposed on translators. You, too, shared with a friend an amusing Turkish love letter that you translated yourself. It is often very, very difficult to render this bubbling flow into smooth English, perhaps because the sentences are conceived in a circular and not linear matter as are ours. Lady Mary, you confessed after translating a poem: "*I cannot determine, upon the whole, how well I have succeeded in the translation, neither do I think our English proper to express such violence of passion, which is very seldom felt among us and we want also those compound words which are very frequent and strong in the Turkish language.*" Translations are like the reverse side of a rug: you can see the colors, you can read the fineness of the knot count, you can see any knotting imperfections the weaver made, and you can directly determine the skill of the weaver. In translations, carpets and communication, you need to look at both sides of the rug to judge the quality of the effort and to appreciate the total beauty.

After months of studying Turkish, even you, Lady Mary, the gifted polyglot, hit a wall. You feared you were losing your English by trying to cram in too many other languages into your head: "*'tis as impossible for one human creature to be perfect master of ten different languages as to have in perfect subjection ten different kingdoms, or to fight against ten men at a time.*" However, this fistfight with Turkish is worth the struggle, because it has allowed both of us to live there as foreigners, not as tourists. It has allowed us to make friends and share our lives. As you state about your Achmed, "*You cannot imagine how much he is delighted with the liberty of conversing with me.*" And we with them.

In one of your very last letters, you write to tell a friend that you regret to leave Turkey now that you have learned the language. Yet surely you must know, Lady Mary, that one may leave a country, but one never leaves behind a language learned. The first of all republics is the one of language.

Good evenings to you,
Kadriye Branning

*Sayings of the folk hero Nasreddin Hoca, in his supposed
birthplace in the village of Hortu*

Ottoman scribe as depicted by Bellini

*Karaman; the protection of Turkish from foreign influence is emphasized by
Atatürk on this plaque honoring the first formal recognition
of the Turkish language in Anatolia by the Karamans*

The sayings of Hacı Bektaş-ı Veli

LETTER 11

I am easy here

Dear Lady Mary,
Another question I get asked continually, by Turks and non-Turks alike, is why do I *continue* to travel to Turkey year after year after year (it comes in second to the question, *"why did you go to Turkey in the first place?"*). Travel in and of itself can be both a challenging and exhilarating thing, especially in Turkey. As you put it in one of your first letters, Lady Mary, travel there is like an opera performance: *"this country is certainly one of the finest in the world. Hitherto all I see is so new to me it is like a fresh scene of an opera every day."* After my first trip in 1978, I began to truly understand the rewards of travel. I discovered that I could receive my nourishment from the differences of others, but that it would take an investment of effort to discover them and to break the wall of stereotypes. And that type of investment meant repeated visits.

We are very similar, Lady Mary, and we would have made excellent traveling companions. I, too, became interested in the social life and Islam, have strenuously self-studied the language and poetry, visited mosques and ancient monuments, and I travel there alone without my husband. I, too, am very interested in the lives of women and their issues of education, health, equal opportunity, and marriage. Like you, I question my own religion by looking at another one. We both were able to gain insight into various issues because we were women and foreigners and people of a certain standing.

Traveling, especially alone, demands a motive resilient enough to withstand all the diverting influences of heat, fatigue, appetite, worry, anxiety, inertia, and natural laziness. When you are in a foreign place, such simple incidents as mutual incomprehension, melancholy, and too brief encounters provide as much insight into yourself as they do about the country you are in.

There are the simple, indulgent reasons why I love to travel in general. It allows me to meet new friends, taste new dishes, discover new games and sports, rediscover friends that I only see once a year, and discuss all kinds of topics for hours on end. I can take photos, draw and paint, write, read, eat three meals a day, have time for tea breaks and refreshments, and view natural and man-made wonders. Travel allows me to walk, to be on my feet all day, to sleep soundly at night. Travel allows me to be outdoors in nature, to look at trees, listen to birds, and breathe deeply.

Yet traveling in Turkey allows me something more. It allows me time to daydream, especially on those long bus trips. It allows me time to catalog the books in the library of my life into a classification system that works for me. Those rides across the endless plains help me do that, as they give me the time to sit quietly with myself and provide me the opportunity to listen to my own voice. Traveling in Turkey helps me heal when I am wounded. In those moments when you feel your strength has left you, when you are afraid to step out from behind the curtain into the spotlight of the stage of your professional life, when you think there is no life after love, when the suitcase full of your insecurities becomes too heavy to tote around, when you yearn for that intangible lost part of your life, when your life is filled with loneliness or fear – well, at that moment, the empty fawn ribbon road comforts you, for you can see, that even in that barren Anatolian plain, that all kinds of beauty can grow. On that road, estranged from all that is familiar, you more clearly see from what you are isolated in your life. This challenging unfamiliarity is for me, oddly enough, both a pleasure and a source of strength of travel. When I confront fear, loneliness, isolation, and self-doubt on the road, I subdue it, and then conquer it. I take pride in these tiny victories. They are the mortar that repairs the chinks in my battered walls.

In Turkey, even when traveling alone, one can feel safe doing these simple things, and one can truly relax, something I certainly cannot do in New York, where I must be constantly on guard. On a trip through Turkey, in that happy interval between home and the resolution of the unknown, I have found a country meant for a traveler, full of gentle hands, refreshment, and havens from weariness or worry.

One of the things you admired most in your friend Fatima was her engaging spirit: *"She is very curious after the manners of other countries and has not that partiality for her own so common to little minds."* I, too, do not wish to have a "little mind," and so I travel.

Yes, there are so many joys particular to travel in Turkey. Your first letters from Adrianople show great enthusiasm and zest, and I can sense your excitement and delight at discovering not only Ottoman society, but the world of travel itself. You experienced a wide range of travel and tourist experiences similar to mine. You stayed in one of the Sultan's palaces, and I have stayed in the Çırağan Hotel, a former sultan's palace. You were escorted in Adrianople by a troop of 500 Janissaries, whereas in my case, the flocks of helping hands that surround and engulf me when I travel can feel like an army of personal guards. You describe with rapture the pleasure of the Turkish hot baths, the sight of over 200 half-naked women and their curiosity towards you; and I can attest that being a blonde Western woman in a hamam in a small town used to draw quite a crowd around me. You express rapture about the lush decoration and furniture of palaces, but how I wish you could witness the extravagance of the Dolmabahçe Palace built after you left! You relate how you watched the Sultan pass by in a parade, and I, too, have seen political royalty and have shaken hands with Prime Ministers Mrs. Tansu Çiller and Mr. Süleyman Demirel during my travels. One of your most famous letters tells of the meal you shared with the former Sultan's wife: I have eaten with semi-royalty too, with the Mayor of Istanbul during the festivities of the 1995 congress of the International Federation of Librarians Association. Another letter reveals how you dressed up in Turkish clothes to more easily visit religious sites; and I too, have a special outfit specifically for the road, which covers my arms and legs and head, and which allows me to pass discretely through streets and into any building I wish. I have also enjoyed purchasing babouche slippers, fezzes, scarves, and woolen socks at a bazaar to play dress-up in my hotel room. Your description of the Selimiye mosque in Edirne would shame descriptions by the leading art historians today, as you depict it perfectly down to the last detail. I was happy to see how you made a Turkish friend, the beautiful Fatima, for I, too, have known the joy of making Turkish friends and visiting them again and again. You took carriage excursions to the surrounding countryside, much like I have hired a driver to embark on an adventure to find the ruins of Kubadabad or a lost *han*. After you arrived in Istanbul, you found a rhythm to your life that sounds much like mine when I travel, falling into a pleasant routine of reading, writing, studying the Turkish language, listening to music, visiting markets, streets, old neighborhoods, baths, mosques and dervish monasteries, and enjoying boat excursions up the Bosphorus. You see, we share the same delights of travel in Turkey: I am indeed in your footsteps.

Your joy as a traveler/tourist especially shines forth in your letters written from Istanbul, passages of which would shame the attempts by modern travel writers to capture the essence of this pearl of a city. Your boat ride up the Bosphorus, with its gardens, forests, and mosques stacked like a *"curio cabinet adorned by the most skilful hands,"* your description of visits to the Topkapı sectors, Hagia Sophia, Süleymaniye and Sultan Ahmet Mosques, the Hippodrome, and a whirling dervish lodge still ring true today.

Like you, I have enjoyed many thrills during my travels in Turkey. I have trod the same roads as did Paul before writing many of his Epistles; I have walked in the shadow of the ghosts of Alexander the Great, Santa Claus, Justinian and Theodora, Rumi, Herodotus, Julius Caesar, and Mother Mary. I have swum, like Cleopatra, in Side in the shadow of an antique Roman theater. I have prayed in the same mosques as did sultans, attended performances in the same amphitheaters as the Greek emperors, and I have set out to discover the world from the same town as the famed geographer Strabo.

A particular joy for me in Turkey is discovering ancient trees. I have taken shade in the many 500–600 year old plane trees planted by sultans and which have weathered storms, famines, and wars. They still stand tall today, inspiring us by their resilience. I understand why Turks believe that *"every tree is a soul"* and why wedding parties stop to tie votive ribbons on them. Many of these venerable trees have impressed my memory as vividly as the interior of any historic mosque: the giant trees of the mystic Muradiye cemetery of Bursa, the twin courtyard trees of the Taş Han in Merzifon and the Beyazit II complex in Amasya, the tree standing guard outside the Çile Han in Karaman, the sprawling old tree in Bursa on the road up to the Uludağ, and the tree planted by Sinan in the mosque courtyard of the Atik Valide Mosque in Üsküdar. I have even eaten in a hotel restaurant in Eğirdir built around a tree. Whenever I see one of these giant souls, I imagine how they grew along with Turkey during its march of history, from Süleyman the Magnificent to Atatürk through to our present day, where an impressive program of Turkish national forests protects them for future generations.

I have traveled in many towns, both famous and unknown, in bustling metropolises and in ten-home villages. I have been in villages and towns where I was the only woman with my head uncovered. It would be impossible here for me to give you my personal and individual impressions of the over 250 cities, towns, and villages I have visited in Turkey. My list of favorites is too long. From these places I have gained a wealth of experiences and visual joys and pleasures for all of the senses, much like you did.

As exciting as it is to read your travel descriptions, Lady Mary, what a regret it is that you never knew the joys (and frustrations) of traveling alone on the road. I have traveled in Turkey both in rented cars and by intercity busses, each with their own pleasures and frustrations. The excellent network of busses that links all of Turkey today should be a model in transportation efficiency for the rest of the world. Years ago, however, things did not run as efficiently. The ritual of a trip with the chaotic bedlam of the bus stations, freely-interpreted departure and arrival times, hawkers, the constant game of musical chairs to ensure that no woman sits next to a man, stops all along the way to pick up three passengers and ten horseflies, dreadful heat, travelers with cardboard boxes with string, burlap bags, sports bags, provisioned with every conceivable snack for the long-haul was an experience of humanity in motion. Travel by automobile allows greater liberty to investigate out of the way sites otherwise inaccessible, but Turkish roads are notoriously full of dangerous drivers. I have known the trepidation of being pulled over by the side of the road by a grim machine-gunned soldier, only to have him smile at me and say, "*May the road in front of you be open and clear, Lady Visitor.*"

There are other travel frustrations that you did not get to experience, Lady Mary, as you were always in the company of guides, interpreters, and those 500 Janissaries. The infamous tourist office, for example, was always a rich source of perplexity. Tourist offices thirty years ago were very meager affairs. They were grey and dusty places, with torn plastic chairs and a low coffee table and some vague travel brochures scattered on top of it, always in the one foreign language version that was of no use to you. You were invariably the only customer there, and despite their every intention and will to be of service, the clerks were of limited help. You often did much better asking for information in pharmacies, which proved to be excellent places to get instructions.

Particularly aggravating when traveling alone are the carpet touts that follow you all day long, dog your every step, jump out at you from behind every turn, oftentimes forcing you to flee the street to the haven of your hotel room to escape their badgering. I think it would even defy those 500 Janissaries of yours to disperse this relentless group. In the days before automatic cash machines, changing money in a bank was a half-day event, with multiple copies of forms to fill out, lines to stand in, and questions asked.

Simple things also can be risky during travel in Turkey. Marble sidewalks may be beautiful, but they are deadly slippery. Concrete sidewalks, on the other hand, are often full of potholes and loose tiles that pitch you forward into some spectacular falls. There are rarely side rails along precipices. The worst threats come from the packs of small children that descend upon you like a circling school of sharks sensing blood. In the town of Siirt one year, children started to follow me in ever-increasing numbers. When I became disoriented and asked a man for directions, he took pity on me and decided to accompany me to help find the mosque I was looking for. It was in a poor section of town, and by the time we got near it, we were surrounded by over 60 children aged 4 to 9, mostly boys. The horde of children became more and more intense, screaming, hopping, pushing, grabbing, pulling, pushing, and throwing things. For the first time in my life, I was afraid that I was going to be pulled apart by the limbs. The man was even more afraid than I was, which heightened my panic all the more. It was then that I decided to become my own Janissary, and bellowed out a large "*YETER!*" (Enough!), which broke the spell, and we were able to push our way through. I fear that is the last time that man will be so kind as to help a tourist in need. How ironic it should be that the only time in Turkey I felt threatened should have come from children!

One other particular danger is unfortunately all too frequent in Turkey. I will never forget the two earthquake tremors I felt in southern Turkey, the one in 1998 left 110 dead and which was a foreshadow of the horror to come the next year.

Despite the frustrations of the road, the views of the stunning Turkish countryside are worth every bit of it. The dirt road coming out of İncesu to Ürgüp is particularly dramatic: a spiral climb to the top of the hill which opens up to the surprise of a breathtaking view over the entire Göreme Valley of Cappadocia. The drive from Niğde to Çiftehan through the Aladağlar and the Bolkar Mountains through the famous Crusader Cilician Gates, one of the rare passes through the Taurus Mountains, offered some of most beautiful scenery I have ever seen in Turkey and perhaps in the world. On the drive to Artvin through the Ardahan fields of green grass and wild flowers, I saw wild mares galloping freely, with their colts dancing behind them. One of my favorite drives is the stunning climb from Tokat to Sivas over the Çamlıbel pass, which offers a 360 degree vista over the whole country: and if you look closely, you can see the Kangal sheepdogs at work in the brown fields below. I relish the hours spent on these roads, with the sound of the wind in the car window being the only sound to break the silence. I take many of the recollections of that silence and harmony back with me in the suitcase of my memory, and I unpack those luminous moments on the nights when I feel a captive of the concrete city where I live. I recall those perfect drives and that enchanting solitude as some of the most beloved and long-lasting of my travel memories.

You were happy in Turkey, Lady Mary, I can feel it. As I said in a previous letter, to this day, I will never be able to find the words to express the natural feeling of happiness and contentment that I experience when I am in Turkey. I especially feel it in your final letters from Istanbul which are tinged with great sadness at having to leave too soon. "*I am now preparing to leave Constantinople, and... 'tis with regret, but I am used to the air and have learnt the language. I am easy here.*" You took a suitcase full of imperishable memories home, like I do each time, didn't you, like a fountain of remembrances to drink? I have cried at the airports; I have had people cry at my departure, even though I had only met them for a few days prior; I, too, have had women pour water over the threshold upon my departure so that my voyage would go smoothly; I, too, have had a passport agent, seeing my tears, speak softly to me and say, "*but you will come back to us again, promise?*"

Yet you did have to leave, and upon your return, you experienced the full circle of what being a traveler means. You were glad to be home. For despite our love of travel, or the consideration we hold for foreign countries, there is no place like home. Understanding that and rejoicing at homecoming are some of the sweetest rewards of crossing bridges. I can taste your ale and pippins along with you, in this, one of your most touching letters:

"... I cannot help looking with partial eyes on my native land. That partiality was certainly given us by nature to prevent rambling, the effect of an ambitious thirst after knowledge which we are not formed to enjoy. All we get by it is fruitless desire of mixing the different pleasures and conveniences which are given to different parts of the world and cannot meet in any one of them. After having read all that is to be found in the languages I am mistress of, and having decayed my sight by midnight studies, I envy the easy peace of mind of a ruddy milk maid who, undisturbed by doubt, hears the sermon with humility every Sunday, having not confused the sentiments of natural duty in her head by the vain enquiries of the schools, who may be more learned, yet after all must remain as ignorant. And, after having seen part of Asia and Africa and almost made the tour of Europe, I think the honest English squire more happy who verily believes the Greek wines less delicious than March beer, and the African fruits have not so fine a flavour as golden pippins, and the becafugas of Italy are not so well tasted as a rump of beef, and that in short, there is no perfect enjoyment of this life out of Old England. I pray God I may think so for the rest of my life, and since I must be contented with our scantly allowance of daylight, that I may forget the enlivening sun of Constantinople."

Yes, to come home tempers the sadness of leaving Turkey. Yet, this country became a home to you, as it has for me, and we are all the richer for it. Dashing around the world to discover a million countries holds no interest for me, nor do I think it makes me a more interesting person. It is not a point of honor for me to notch countries and continents visited on my belt. I wish to savor my version of the process of travel: I want to feel perfectly happy in a place where I have made a home, a place that makes me appreciate returning once again to my real home. Travel to Turkey allows me that savoring.

So in the end, how can I answer that question of why I really like to travel to Turkey so much? Exactly what is it that pulls me back there every year, like a pilgrim to a holy site? I suppose, if truth be told, it is not just a question of talking stones and bridges and 500-year-old trees and the open road. It is, quite simply, because Turkey is full of Turks.

Sincerely,
Katharine Branning

Hand-drawn map of Afyon, 1983

Newspaper report of a thou-
sand-year tree near Erzincan

Bursa Uludağ Tree

On the road near Erzurum

Bursa Muradiye Cemetery

Konya Tram

İLLER

01 Adana	26 Eskişehir	51 Niğde
02 Adıyaman	27 Gaziantep	52 Ordu
03 Afyon	28 Giresun	53 Rize
04 Ağrı	29 Gümüşhane	54 Sakarya
05 Amasya	30 Hakkari	55 Samsun
06 Ankara	31 Hatay	56 Siirt
07 Antalya	32 Isparta	57 Sinop
08 Artvin	33 İçel	58 Sivas
09 Aydın	34 İstanbul	59 Tekirdağ
10 Balıkesir	35 İzmir	60 Tokat
11 Bilecik	36 Kars	61 Trabzon
12 Bingöl	37 Kastamonu	62 Tunceli
13 Bitlis	38 Kayseri	63 Şanlı Urfa
14 Bolu	39 Kırklareli	64 Uşak
15 Burdur	40 Kırşehir	65 Van
16 Bursa	41 Kocaeli	66 Yozgat
17 Çanakkale	42 Konya	67 Zonguldak
18 Çankırı	43 Kütahya	68 Aksaray
19 Çorum	44 Malatya	69 Bayburt
20 Denizli	45 Manisa	70 KARAMAN
21 Diyarbakır	46 K. Maraş	71 Kırıkkale
22 Edirne	47 Mardin	72 Batman
23 Elazığ	48 Muğla	73 Şırnak
24 Erzincan	49 Muş	74 Bartın
25 Erzurum	50 Nevşehir	75

License plate numbers of Turkish provinces

Check-in counter, Turkish Airlines at JFK New York

Sinop port

Haliç shipyard

Bus station ticket office, Malatya

Ünye on the Black Sea

Eğirdir

Karaman

Rainbow near Erzincan

SECTION 3

A PEOPLE

LETTER 12

Ne mutlu Türküm diyene

Dear Lady Mary,

I have noticed that you do not spend much time dissecting the Turkish character or passing judgments on their behavior. You describe things without analyzing them, and I like that, for I try to do the same thing in my professional and personal lives. The fact that you refuse to be condescendingly critical towards the Turks is the greatest legacy of your letters. You understood that it would be extremely arrogant for a foreigner to come along and categorize the citizens of a country without this falling-into-rude generalizations and stereotypes. You spent more time analyzing yourself and your very own social structure, rather than the Turks. About the only comment I read that you make about the Turkish character is that they do not lie: "*'Tis a degree of generosity, to tell the truth, and 'tis very rare that any Turk will assert a solemn falsehood.*" You also tell Abbé Conti that "*I can truly inform you, sir, that the Turks are not so ignorant as we fancy them to be in matters of politics or philosophy or even of gallantry.*"

It is actually we in the West who are the ignorant ones in matters of politics, and especially in matters concerning the Turks. I think that still today, years after the image of the "Terrible Turks" beating at the doors of Vienna and the curse left by the film *Midnight Express*, there remain many misconceptions and misunderstandings about the true nature of the country of Turkey and its people. Over many years of travel to Turkey, I have noted some Turkish attitudes that are different than the ones in my own culture. In observing these tendencies, I have tried to remain as objective as you, viewing neither through rose-colored glasses nor lenses of scorn. You can understand, however, that my outlook is through a corner of a window smudged by the personal baggage of my upbringing and culture. As you state so clearly: "*Human understanding is as much limited as human power or human strength.*"

As I mentioned, there are many basic and egregious misconceptions about Turks that prevail to this day, and it is hard to imagine that in our globalized world, people still hang on to fusty images inherited from the past and kept alive by prejudice and apprehension. Turkey is not in the Middle East and the Turkish people are not Arabs. They are not Bedouin camel riders who live in the desert. They speak the Turkish language, not Arabic, and this language is written in the Latin alphabet. The country is predominately Muslim, but all religions, since the times of the Seljuks, may practice there and you can see churches and synagogues throughout the country, just as when you were here, Lady Mary. There is freedom of religion, and the country is not governed by Sharia or Islamic laws. Turks are proud to be a part of the only democratic secular nation in the world with a majority of its population being Muslim. In as much as is possible in our world today, where women still face the same uphill battle as they did in your times for the same equality and independence as men, women in Turkey enjoy the same legal freedom as men and are not forced to cover their heads in public.

Turks are not terrorists.

While the rest of the world may still hold false perceptions of Turks, I often wonder how the Turks would describe themselves. Perhaps this is not so strange, as there are many types of people in Turkey, and it would be difficult to encapsulate the diversity of the many races, religions, origins, classes, and social strata of this country.

The Turks, on their own scale, are as culturally mixed as Americans. The lesson that America gives to the world is that a profusion of cultures leads to a vibrant social force if it is allowed to breathe and grow, and the same diversity prospers in Turkey. There is no real Turkish ethnic norm, as Turkey has a mixed population: Laz, Kurds, Arabs, and the descendants of the Turkish tribes from Central Asia that came here starting in the tenth century. These ethnic types provide a startling diversity of physical types among the Turks: there are Turks with big Black Sea noses, tall Balkan blondes, and short, strapping Asians with high cheekbones and slanted eyes that seem to be stepping right off the page of a Persian miniature. There are the fair-skinned blonde or red-headed descendants of the Circassians who came to populate the harems of the sultans (those "*skins shineingly white*" that you referred to when you went to the baths), lean, olive-oil skinned Mediterranean types, Kurds with long noses and striking vibrant eyes, and the solid, pointy-head, chunky Anatolian peasant with facial features as if carved by a knife. There are women with delicate, almost Far-Eastern features and those with broad Slavic faces; there are the red-haired Crusader babies of the Black Sea, the hatchet-nosed Lazes, and the burnished-skinned Arabs of the Hatay. This diversity fosters as well a wide variety of clothing styles, from the designer fashions of the glossy-lipped Istanbul fashion plate, to the knotted cummerbunds, tunics, and checkered head wraps of the people of the southeast, to the baggy trousers of Central Anatolia worn by both men and women, to the flashy, gay-colored clothes with sequins and ribbons running down the backs of Kurdish women. Turks wear flat cloth caps, white skull caps, highly-colored silk women's scarves, or simple cotton ones bordered in crocheted little flowers. Many of these styles are probably still very similar to the ones you must have seen, Lady Mary. However, today's globalization is starting to erase this diversity in favor of tee-shirts, jeans, and sports shoes, now worn quasi-universally by the youth of Turkey.

I was on the lookout from my first day in Turkey for the stereotype that I had inherited from other people's eyes and which proved in some ways true. In French, to describe someone as stubborn, you say, "*He is as mule-headed as a Turk!*" I would not call Turks as stubborn as much as I would call them authoritarian and obstinate. Turks are assertive and will always decide what is best for you, even if it is not what you had in mind. You are not allowed to order a dish on the menu if the waiter doesn't think it is in your best interest, and you will be brought dishes you did not order or have any interest in, just because he thinks they are what you should have. You are not allowed to buy an orange sweater if the shopkeeper does not think the color suits you, no matter how green is your money. I have begged hairdressers to cut my hair short, only to have them slam down the scissors and say, "*NO! I will not cut it that way! A woman like you must always be able to toss her hair!*" I once went to have a manicure, picked out a discrete color of beige and then dozed off in the chair. When I awoke, I looked down to see fire-engine red polish on my nails! When I protested, the woman manicurist said, "*No, I am sorry, you are a woman born to wear red nails, not boring pink ones!*" In the end, it is always best to give in and smile, and enjoy that someone is making your decisions for you that day.

Turks have a built-in personal radar system that is very sophisticated. They are aware of everything going on around them: nothing escapes their purview, and they make it their business to look out after yours. They have eyes everywhere. They do not miss a trick, and nothing gets by them – and don't even try to pull anything past them. This is not the secret police-type of surveillance though. It is rather a discrete way of making sure that you are being taken care of, that children do not fall down steps, or that a lady who is about to faint will be given a stool, for example. Turks are very protective and want no trouble or problems for people in their immediate territory. It can take an official form like traffic checkpoints on the Malatya road, but for the most part, it is more like an informal angel watching over you. It is done thoroughly and so discretely that you are taken off-guard when you discover it. There is a Turk behind every tree, in every corner, aware of everything, ready to spring into action if need be. It is the hotel clerk in Van who calls his colleague in the next town you are traveling to, in order to verify that you arrived safely because he sensed you were not feeling well. It is the shopkeeper in Kayseri who says, "*Good morning Miss Kety*" when I step into his store (how ever did he learn my name?). It is the grocer in Sivas during the days of political difficulties, who puts down his gun to serve me a cherry juice, pulls out a stool for me, and then picks up his pistol again and stands at the door. It is the carpet shop in Van in eastern Turkey where I was greeted with an enthusiastic: "*Welcome! I have been waiting for you to show up!*" When I asked him how he could have known of my existence, he said, "*Oh yes, I know all about you! I heard you were in town and was waiting for you. The entire town is talking about the tall blonde statue of a woman walking down the streets!*"

Turks love flowers: it is a national passion. They are on all curtain fabrics, women's silk headscarves, and tea pots. Florists spend hours making large, ornate floral wreaths for weddings. Turks create complex bouquets of plastic flowers with artificial resin dew drops on them which outsell cut flowers, they layer petals on salads and scatter them on dining tables, and they plant flowers in empty olive oil cans and then stick them in every conceivable spot. They are just crazy about flowers, but one flower is beloved above all others: the tulip. I will talk to you about the famed Iznik gardens of paradise in another letter, but this story will give you some indication of their passion. There is a tale about the Lale (Tulip) Cami in Kırşehir, built in 1272. The name supposedly is derived from a tulip of great beauty that a student in the nearby Cacabey Medrese gave to the builders. This one flower was sold to finance the reconstruction of the building as a mosque. But I do not need to tell you about this passion for tulips, do I, Lady Mary? Ahmet III, the Sultan in power when you were in Turkey, left his mark on history by fashioning the "Tulip Era," a period of gaiety and enlightenment, centered around a passion for tulips in art, literature, and social life. Tulips were popular even before the craze that swept Turkey when you were there. Busbecq, the Austrian ambassador who came to Süleyman's court in 1554 wrote in his letters: *"We saw everywhere an abundance of flowers... the Turks are so fond of flowers that even the marching troops have their orders not to trample them."* He brought them back to Europe, and by 1630 the "Tulipomania" craze swept through Holland. Turks fully enjoy each season of the year, and tulips are a symbol of the rebirth and joy of life. Tulips are seen everywhere today: in pots on the Turkish Airlines counters, on every brochure published, on key chains. It has become the semi-official symbol of Turkey. As for all those thousands of glasses of tea? They are served in little glasses shaped like a tulip, of course. However, the tulip has a serious rival in the rose, symbol of the Prophet. Even in the dustiest and most modest village in Turkey, there will always be an attempt to create some sort of a public garden (it may take the form of a grassy patch in the middle of a traffic circle), always planted with rose bushes. There are often lush rose gardens around neighborhood mosques, lovingly tended by a local gardener. In my eyes, the sweetest roses in Turkey are the pink ones that grow on the banks of the green river in Tokat. Once I was in a shop with a friend, who wanted to buy a teapot, and the shopkeeper kept showing her model after model, but she did not care for any of them. He finally brought out one that had bright red roses painted all over it, and a clutch of ladies standing nearby and observing us cried out, *"Oh! Yes! That is the prettiest one! She definitely must take that one!"* However, my friend left without a purchase, and I felt obliged to stay behind to explain to the shopkeeper that he shouldn't be offended, for it was not reflection on the quality of his merchandise but simply because my friend just really didn't like flowers. I will never forget the look of total disbelief on all of their faces, for such a thing is just inconceivable to a Turk.

Besides flowers, Turks love nature more than any people I have ever met. It is sacred to them, for the green of nature is also the color of the Prophet, and its verdant vibrancy is reproduced on door and window frames, on dome tops, on rugs, and in basil pots. The network of national forests covering the entire country of Turkey is extensive, with the Ilgaz Dağları National Forest being one of the most beloved. Turks love nothing better than to climb to high mountain plateaus for picnics, and failing that, to stop by the side of the road to sit under trees and share fresh fruit and tea or to barbecue on the grill. The country of Turkey has been blessed with an extraordinary natural bounty, which is not lost on the Turks who venerate and savor their seas, mountains, forests, and lakes. They love birds, and keep them in lacey cages in gardens, just like the Ottoman Sultans who ordered that stone bird houses be built into the outside walls of their mosques. Turks remain close to the farm and to the earth, relish in the coming of spring and those blooming wild tulips, and appreciate the bounty of the earth, be it rich harvests or honeybees. One of the most famous poems by Aşık Veysel, the greatest folk-poet of modern Turkey, is entitled "Black Earth" and reads as follows: "*My faithful sweetheart is the black earth, for though I wounded her with my hoe and shovel, she smiled and gave me red roses; my only true love is the black earth...*" Galloping still across that black earth in Eastern Turkish highlands are their beloved horses, ever revered as the sacred "Wings of Turks."

As part of their love of nature, they have a particular veneration for water: they never pass up a chance to drink from the numerous public fountains in town or fresh from bubbling springs by the side of the roads. Traditionally, one of the most pious religious acts is to establish a public water fountain. Turks love their water like a Frenchman loves his wine, and they can distinguish various spring waters with the same sophistication as a Bordelais does his vintages. They have their most venerated springs, with Niksar and Ayvaz waters holding a special esteem. They never drive past a roadside spring without stopping to fill up their bottles and canteens, keeping jerry cans and plastic bottles in the trunk expressly for this purpose.

Turks love music: listening to it live or canned, making it, and singing it. They are as diversely talented musically as Americans. There is LOUD and incessant music everywhere in Turkey: on busses, in parks, in restaurants, on street corners, and in shops. They have a musical *horror vacui*. It is often a bit tiring, for you can't have a moment of peace to hear yourself think or listen to the birds chirping in the morning, but in truth, there is no chance of ever feeling gloomy or lonely with all that perky music surrounding you. They enjoy all kinds of music, from folk songs to classic Ottoman pieces to modern pop – and, despite what is said, more people than not admit to the guilty pleasure of *arabesk* music and its syrupy sentiments. The star system functions full force in Turkey, with their musicians and singers treated like minor deities.

I already have spoken to you about the family, but the idea of family in Turkey goes beyond the sense of one household unit. Turks have a communal commitment to their fellow man and view society as a whole as an extended part of their family. Just as they place the family above all else in life, the viewpoint that society must be lived as a harmonious unit is just as important. Our sense of restraint and privacy holds no interest for them. They eat their mezes together; they drink their tea from the same pot. No Turk eats alone, no Turk dies alone, no Turk goes off on a trip alone, no Turk walks down the street alone.

Turks are melodramatic and emotional, with a culture of exaggeration, the dramatic, and the overblown. They are sentimental, huggy and effusive. They have outsized passions, like Texans. Their songs are often dark and gloomy. The obverse of their joyous, humorous side is an often lugubrious nature with the theme of the malcontent exile strongly represented in cinema, literature, and music. The tragic is considered a normal part of life, seen in the old movies that continually replay on television, in their songs, and on the front pages of newspapers, which are filled with stories of passion killings, family dramas, and other such tragic personal events, accompanied by high-color photographs.

Turks are endearingly sweet to each other: constantly touching each other, poking, smiling, saying millions of platitudes, touching hands to hearts, and using your name repeatedly when they speak to you. They can't pass by a child without instinctively touching it, pinching its cheeks, tossing it in the air, or kissing it. No one looks at poetry askance, and the oral tradition is strong, with most Turks able to recite at least one poem of their Yunus Emre or Mevlana, and they can sing the lyrics to all their sentimental favorite songs. Even the Ottoman Sultans wrote poetry in between war campaigns.

Turks are curious. They will look at anything, from vegetable cutter salesmen on ferries, to fistfights, to car crashes, to wedding parties, to people reading books. They do not want to miss anything and will question everything in their surroundings. I used to think it was because I was a foreigner that they seemed so intrigued by my comings and goings, but in fact, they do it with everyone. Once my poet friend started to explain to me about the mystic Burhaneddin, teacher of Mevlana, in front of his tomb in Kayseri, and within five minutes, he had attracted a crowd of a dozen people who gathered around him to attend his "lecture." Once while enjoying the spectacular drive from Boyabat to Sinop, I stopped the car right after the Çengel pass to relish the view from the scenic overlook and to pause to eat a peach. Within two minutes, three cars pulled up and ten Turks got out and surrounded me, chattering away and offering me water and more fruit. If I had stopped, there had to be a reason, and they did not want to miss out on it. I went once to visit a *han* in Ezinepazar, a totally empty village with one barber, a small grocery store, and a baker. Minding my own business, I got out of the jitney and walked over to the *han* and started to take pictures. Once again, just as at the Çengel pass, out of nowhere appeared nine men who happened to be driving by and decided they needed to stop and see what I was doing. Chattering, poking, grabbing my sketch book, peering at my camera, and asking me all sorts of questions, they turned my simple visit to the *han* into a carnival. It didn't end there: after their visit, a machine-gunned soldier came up to me and said that the mayor in the Town Hall building next door (who was observing it all from his window) wanted to invite me to his office for tea, turning what was to be a simple visit to a dusty *han* into a full diplomatic event of over four hours.

Turks are very intrigued by the world around them and receptive to new ideas. They especially want to understand how foreigners think. One winter after a particularly spectacular lunch of Hünkâr Beğendi lamb stew at my beloved Havuzlu restaurant in the Covered Bazaar (Kapalıçarşı) in Istanbul, I decided to boldly request a favor of the head cashier when I was leaving. I asked if it would be possible to buy one of the restaurant's plates. He was quite taken aback by this request, and looking at me askance, said, "*Lady, What are you going to do with these? Just why would you want to buy my plates?*" I realized that I was the first person who asked him for such a thing, and being a curious Turk, he needed to know what it was all about.

Since I sensed that he was a bit wary about the whole transaction, I knew I had to come up with an interesting and reassuring response, or else I was going to walk out empty-handed. "*I collect menus, you see, and plates from my favorite restaurants in the world,*" I explained, "*and in the entire world, yours happens to be one of my all-time favorites,*" I added with a big smile, hoping to clinch the deal. No smile came back from him, so I plunged ahead. "*I frame the menus and hang them in my kitchen to inspire me when I cook. When I look at them, I remember the meal that I enjoyed there, the setting, and the company I shared during that meal. As for the plates, when I eat off of them, I hope that my food will absorb the memory of the food of the excellent cooks that was served upon them, and I seek by this small gesture to honor their craftsmanship and artistry. I use them with the hope that my food will be as delicious as the food that I remember eating off of them. I hope that when my guests use them, they will have some of the same joy that I experienced eating off of them, just as I did here today with your marvellous Hünkâr beğendi.*" I paused to take a deep breath. He continued to blankly stare at me, and finally replied: "*OK, Lady, that's very nice, but I still don't understand what you are going to do with my plates?*"

Turks have no inhibitions. This is perhaps the trait that takes a bit getting used to, for it often appears offensive and invasive to foreigners. They naturally and innocently do whatever they want where you are concerned. They will grab newspapers right out of your hand, poke you, sit right next to you (not near you, right next to you) on park benches, tap your shoulder, come up and ask you the most forward questions (*"You look like you are 45 years old, is that true? Why do you wear such old-fashioned sunglasses?"*): all with no harm meant, just a curiosity about everything around them. It is impossible to sit quietly on a park bench, in a café, or be left alone to enjoy a visit somewhere or to savor a peaceful breakfast without someone coming up to pull out a chair to sit right down with you. They stare directly at you, which is not considered as rude. Being so forward and staring with such impunity in our Western culture would be considered discourteous and aggressively invasive of your space, but for a Turk, it just means that he is being friendly. Do you remember how those women stared at you and poked you when you visited the baths, Lady Mary? That is what I am referring to. Turks are interested in seeing what *you* are interested in. In Kayseri, a museum guard once followed me around like a puppy, from room to room, and stood next to me as I took notes and sketched. He craned his neck to see what I was doing, and when he couldn't get a good enough view, stood within one inch of me and literally breathed down my neck to see. When it just got too much to bear, I slammed my book shut and said, "Enough!" When I saw the hurt look in his face, I realized that he was not being nosy, but showing his interest in what I was doing, since it was taking place in his space.

Turks are patriotic and have the same pride as Americans at displaying their flag. They name their planes after their favorite cities and rivers. They have a strong sense of pride in being Turkish, united by the same language, culture, and destiny. Many of the customs of the Turks have roots in the principles and teachings of Islam, with a curious mixture of the pre-Islamic customs. Some hold tight to the traditional values of their shaman ancestors: some Turks would hang a blue bead in their shops or cars, a very Turkish type of life insurance for some, while for others nothing more than a decorative object. Some even would not pass a sacred tree without tying a votive.

Turks do not like to be contradicted – perhaps this is what the French mean with that mule-headed business. I once asked a bootblack to shine my favorite pair of navy blue kid leather shoes, especially stressing that they were navy blue, not black, and to make sure he did not use black polish. He nodded, pulled out a can and opened it, and I immediately saw that it was black and asked him to stop. He got very angry and said, "*Lady Foreigner! Do you really think that I am unable to distinguish between the two? Of course this is the right color!*" But of course it *was* black, and my gorgeous blue shoes were lost forever, just because of the stubbornness of this Turk who was not going to admit that he did not have navy blue polish in his box.

Turks have a sense of humor, and they don't take themselves too seriously. They can make fun of themselves, can criticize themselves easily, and possess an almost fatalistic acceptance about the imperfections of life. They don't expect things to turn out just right since they know that life itself is not faultless. They are optimistic and know how to laugh heartily. They sit patiently during two-hour power outages; they wait without complaint for hours for a bus to show up.

A Turk will never admit that he does not know the answer to a question, or that he doesn't know what he is doing. If he doesn't comprehend your restaurant order, he will bring you one of everything to make sure you are satisfied. When you hire a personal driver to take you somewhere, he will never admit he doesn't know what you are looking for before setting out. They won't lie; you are right, Lady Mary, but they will cover it up with an elaborate story or subterfuge which often proves quite amusing.

Turks are astute business people and enterprising, quick-witted scrappers. They make things happen and get things accomplished. That is another reason they remind me so much of proactive Americans. They possess a strong sense of individual initiative along with a commitment to social cohesion. They stick together in times of challenge and hardship, are eager for progress, are clever with money, and have tremendous personal courage. They are determined, with the power to wrestle fools. They are survivors.

And lastly, I finish with some odds-and-ends viewpoints. Turks are exuberant, shooting guns off at football games and applauding when airplanes land. Turks have no stigma against beggars, but consider them as rather "alms-takers," helping all fulfill their pillar of faith. They can't swim to save their lives, they don't read books in public, and they are very proud of their sportsmen, especially when they do battle on the playing fields of Europe. Turks have faces that are immediately readable.

The famed hospitality and kindness of Turks will take another letter to discuss. Yet just as I have "my Turkey," I have "my Turks." Such is how I see them, and I hope my vision is neither over simplified or offensive. Did you recognize any of these traits in your tutor Achmed, in your women friends, in your servants, or in any of those 500 Janissaries, Lady Mary?

Undoubtedly the most famous saying of Atatürk, displayed on billboards, on the pedestals of his ubiquitous statues on every village town square, over city hall doors, in the lobby of most public buildings and on mountainsides, is the iconic: "*Ne mutlu Türküm diyene*": How happy I am to say I am a Turk. With the personality traits that I have been able to observe in Turks, he had every right and reason to promote an awareness of this precious and rich natural national resource. This is no false pride. And now the time has come for Turks to shout it out loud for the entire world to hear.

Happy to say I am, sincerely yours,

Kadriye Branning

Diyarbakır, city of watermelons and city walls that can be seen from outer space

Portrait of the Tulipaholic Ahmet III, from a London book published in 1741

The ever-optimistic lottery ticket

A Bursa rose garden

Ottoman stone birdhouse, Amasya Bayezit II Complex

Plastic flower market, Kayseri

Roses to you

İbrahim Kutluay ("Blessed Moon"), star of the 2001
semi-finals of the European Basketball championships

The sacred wings of Turks

An olive oil flower garden in bloom, Manisa

Circumcision room panel, Topkapı Palace

A perfect Tokat rose

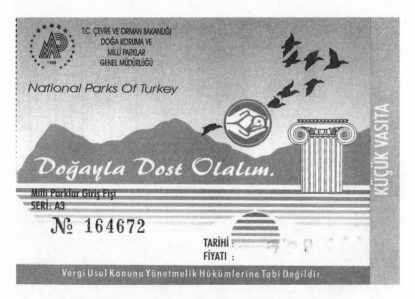

Let us be friends to nature

Roses in your tea

Donation voucher to a sports club

Painted decoration on a jitney bus

Tokat

Konya: "It is forbidden to sit here"

LETTER 13

A noise unto the world

Dear Lady Mary,
In your letters, the descriptions of women are the most sharply-drawn of your portraits. From Ratisbon to Vienna to Adrianople to Paris, you never failed to provide vivid and fascinating portrayals of the European women you met: their hairstyles, fashions, favored topics of conversation, sexual mores, and personalities.

When you arrived in Turkey, you continued to train your incisive eye on Turkish women. Your observations about them have given historians and feminists much important information on the daily life of the period. The encounters with women on your trip across Europe provided a crucial point of comparison for those you met in Turkey. You have left us four outstanding letters describing visits with Turkish women, and in those most memorable letters, you provide insight not only into them, but also to yourself.

In addition to these four letters, there is another one, perhaps the most famous one of the entire *Embassy Letters*, as it was the inspiration for the Orientalist movement in Europe of the late nineteenth century. In this letter you relate your visit to a Turkish bath (*hamam*) in Sofia. Exotica lovers have seized upon that letter to glean all the juicy details about the custom of the Turkish steam baths. The French painter Ingres, with his oils and brushes, along with a hefty dose of imagination, interpreted your precise descriptions of the gestures of the women, their bathing rituals, and the architecture of the rooms to create the iconic orientalist painting "*Le Bain Turc.*" This letter is one of my personal favorites as well because it describes Turkish women so lovingly and honestly. You decided to go incognito to the baths and hired a Turkish coach to drive you there early one morning. Did you honestly think, Lady Mary, that you could slip in unnoticed to the baths with over 200 women in attendance? Now, if it had been me, I think I would have done an about-face, but you held your head high and plunged ahead. Here are your exact words concerning those 400 eyes upon you:

> *"... I was in my travelling habit, which is a riding dress, and certainly appeared very extraordinary to them. Yet there was not one of them that showed the least surprise or impertinent curiosity, but received me with all the obliging civility possible. I know no European court where the ladies would have behaved themselves in so polite a manner to a stranger. I believe, in the whole, there were two hundred women, and yet none of those disdainful smiles or satirical whispers that never fail in our assemblies when anybody appears that is not dressed exactly in fashion. They repeated over and over to me: "Güzelle, pek güzelle", which is nothing but "charming, very charming" ... There were many amongst them as exactly proportioned as ever any goddess was drawn by the pencil of Guido or Titian, and most of their skins shineingly white... perfectly representing the figures of the Graces... the lady that seemed the most considerable amongst them entreated me to sit by her and would fain have undressed me for the bath, and I excused myself with some difficulty. I was charmed with their civility and beauty."*

The other four letters describe in detail your visits to private homes of Turkish women. The first visit was to a fiftyish *"Grand Vizier's lady,"* the wife of Arnand Khalit Pasha. You were invited to dine in her home in Adrianople, and you took along your Greek interpreter for the occasion. You were received and entertained with great civility, served with what seemed to be an excessive amount of dishes by her slaves, and then perfumed by them after dinner. Despite her kindness, you found the woman herself very dull, given as she was to devoting the majority of her time to charity and praying.

It is your second visit that provides one of the most remarkable letters of the entire series. Upon leaving the dull dinner with the Grand Vizier's lady, your Greek interpreter convinced you to visit Fatima, wife of the *Kabya*, or second officer. Now this Fatima proved to be much more vivacious than the pious crone. Fatima received you with ceremony, entertained you with a music and dance concert, and offered you a fistful of embroidered handkerchiefs as a present when you left. Your description of this charmer is legendary:

> *"The fair Fatima (for that is her name) so much her beauty effaced everything I have seen all that has been called lovely wither in England or Germany and must own that I never saw anything so gloriously beautiful, nor can I recollect a face that could have been taken notice of near hers. She stood up to receive me, saluting me after their fashion putting her hand upon her heart with a sweetness full of majesty that no court breeding could ever give. She ordered that cushions to be given me and took care to place me in the corner, which is the place of honor... I was so struck with admiration that I could not for some time speak to her, being wholly taken up in gazing. That surprising harmony of features! That charming result of the whole! That exact proportion of body! That lovely bloom of complexion, unsullied by art! The unutterable enchantment of her smile! But her eyes! Large and black, with all the soft languishment of the blue! Every turn of her face discovering some new charm!... And to that a behaviour so full of grace and sweetness, such easy motions, with an air so majestic, yet free from stiffness of affectation that I am persuaded, could she be suddenly transported upon the most polite throne of Europe nobody would think her other than born and bred to be a queen, though educated in a country we call barbarous. To say all in a word, our most celebrated English beauties would vanish near her... For my part I am not ashamed to own I took more pleasure in looking on the beauteous Fatima than the finest piece of sculpture could have given me."*

When you took leave of her, you state, "*I could not help fancying that I had been some time in Mohammed's paradise, so much was I charmed with what I had seen.*"

The third visit was to Lady Hafise, the favorite of Sultan Mustafa II, deposed by your Sultan Ahmet III, and who died a few weeks later of an apparent poisoning. In this letter you describe her clothing and jewels in great detail, noting that she has an emerald the size of a turkey egg, earrings with gems as large as fat hazelnuts, and the biggest diamond rings you had ever seen. "*This I am very sure of, that no European queen has half the quantity and the Empress's jewels, though very fine, would look very mean near hers.*" She served you dinner, accompanied by luxurious napkins woven with gold thread. After dinner, you took a walk in her garden, and Lady Hafise took you to her bedroom where all her furs were tossed nonchalantly on the bed. You were not fooled and saw right through this subterfuge to flaunt to you the richness of her fur collection.

Your fourth visit was once again to the home of the beauteous Fatima, a year later and this time in Constantinople. The typical diversions included a visit to her quarters and a musical performance by her slaves. Only this time, you could converse with her in Turkish, and because of that, you *"find her wit as engaging as her beauty."* Again, you were totally captivated by this woman, *"handsome as an angel,"* and told her *"what a noise your face would make in Paris!"* to which she replied, *"I can't believe you, if beauty were so much valued in your country as you say they would never have suffered you to leave it."* It is impossible for us to resist this charmer any more than you could.

On other occasions during your stay, you had many opportunities to make other observations about Turkish women, notably concerning their beauty, makeup, fashions and their freedom. You certainly are taken by the beauty of Turkish women. In a letter to your sister Lady Mar on April 1, 1717, you relate: *"I never saw in my life so many fine heads of hair. It must be owned that every beauty is more common here than with us. Tis surprising to see a young woman that is not very handsome. They have naturally the most beautiful complexions in the world and generally large black eyes."*

In addition to commenting on their beauty and fashions, one of the major themes of your observations about Turkish women is their freedom. You insist that veiled women are in truth the freest of all women: *"This perpetual Masquerade gives them entire liberty of following their Inclinations without danger of Discovery,"* and you conclude, *"upon the whole, I look upon the Turkish women as the only free people in the Empire."*

I, too, have had many occasions to observe Turkish women, but I think I have been more fortunate than you, for I have seen women of all walks of life, not just high-born court ladies with diamond earrings the size of hazelnuts, who pass their time in uninterrupted pleasure and are spoiled by husbands who provide for their every whim. There is much more to Turkish women than can be seen in the upper class ladies of the harem. I have met a wide variety of women in Turkey. I have discussed professional issues with women library directors, been treated by women doctors, plucked hazelnuts with a farmer's wife, argued politics with female lawyers, been taught to make kebabs by housewives, shopped with women from Istanbul for gold jewelry and with women from Konya for plastic dishpans, I have read cell phone text messages for an illiterate village woman, and I have sat with country women in their window seats overlooking the street.

It is always said that Turkey is a country of paradoxes, of tugs of wars between many factors. I think this is especially true when it comes to its women. On the one hand, they are at the cusp of professional modernity, with a rate of female doctors and university professors that exceeds those of America and Europe. On the other hand, they are still murdered by their kin in the villages for any sullying of the family honor, events which are vividly reported in full-color on the front pages of newspapers. I have seen women bundled up from head to toe in black veils, and women in tight clothes and low-cut blouses. I have seen women so demure they will not lift their heads and others so brazen and forthright with men that I am taken aback by their wildness. They smoke, drink rakı, and are as sexually-promiscuous as the rest of the Western world... yet they are always somewhere covered, in some way, in the shadow of their relationships to men, be it their fathers, brothers, husbands, or sons.

This paradox has always existed in Turkish culture. In Ottoman times, the sultanate was run by a strong string of queen mothers for over 130 years, the famous "Sultanate of Women" of the 16–17th centuries. Dominant women in power also included the influential French-born Nakshidil, the mother of Mahmut II (1785–1839), who encouraged her son to introduce a wide-range of sweeping, westernizing reforms. Atatürk gave the vote to women before France did (1934 vs. 1944), and he always stated that the world would judge a country by how it treats its women. Of all his political expressions, that one rings truest to me.

I spoke to you about the wide range of physical types of Turks, and it is no different for its women. There are hefty matrons with silk head scarves and long raincoats, pouty-lipped Istanbul bleach blondes; village women with gnarled, knotted faces lined like old wood, with bright smiling eyes peering forth from beyond the headscarf. You see girls in blue jeans and tight tee-shirts walking hand in hand in easy confidence with their mother clad in *tesettür*, the costume of a long, loosely-tailored floor-length raincoat and a floral headscarf.

I have been struck by several predominant traits in Turkish women. The one that strikes me above all others is their gumption, courage, and resourcefulness. These are no-nonsense, hard-working, get-the-job-done type of women. They run farms, businesses, and families. Underneath it all, Turkey is held together today by the modern version of the Sultanate of Women: not the intriguers in the harems you visited, but the female turbines churning the wheels of liberal professions and tilling that black earth. These are practical women who take great pride in their homes and who believe that a beautifully-kept and well-appointed home is an act of love. They have fast and busy hands, whether for tying knots, making *mantı* dumplings, putting away dishes, or embroidering. They are determined, head-strong, and have commonsense.

The concept of the "working women" is not a modern one for Turkish women. For hundreds of years women have worked the lands of Anatolia. They carried arms during the National War. They harvest fields of cotton, wheat and tobacco, tend to farm animals, carry wood and water, sort fruits and onions, look after the house, raise numerous children, and weave carpets of great creativity. Today there are some five million women who work the Turkish land, shearing sheep, laying out fruits and hazelnuts to dry, knitting socks and sweaters, and making cheese and butter. They work under the hot sun in the vegetable gardens and olive groves of the coasts and in the blistering fields of the plains. You see them bouncing along on donkey carts, sitting with their bundles next to them at the market, hoisting huge bales of fodder on their backs, and pitch-forking hay. In the professional fields of labor, I have seen the tornado of a woman that runs the Büyük Postahane Pharmacy in Istanbul in action, tending to all her clients like a triage nurse in an emergency room, barking out orders to her staff, greeting everyone, tending to all with a smile, a touch or a glass of tea.

Turkish women have the same blunt directness as Turkish men, but somehow it is easier to take when a woman asks you your age than when a man does. They observe foreigners with great curiosity, to see what you are made of and if you are respectable. Turkish women are exceedingly friendly. I was once invited to join a wedding henna party in Afyon by the bride, whom I had never met but who saw me sitting by myself. I have been taken in charge by the woman office manager of a hotel in Elbistan, who went beyond her professional duties and did everything she could to become my friend. As you relate in your letter about the hamam visit, "*I know no European court where the ladies would have behaved themselves in so polite a manner to a stranger.*" They are also very caring and respectful to their elders. I note how elegantly and discretely the grown daughter of my Kayseri family brings up coffee to her father's third floor study, served on a golden tray with fine china and napkins, and silently sets it in front of him.

Although I am not as struck by the beauty of Turkish women as you were, I will admit that they are very stylish and feminine, whether they choose the *tesettür* or the miniskirt. They like glitter and gold and embroidered flowers on their scarves, lilac, or pink raincoats and matching small purses. They love dainty shoes and fashionable jewelry. There has been much written lately about the *tesettür* fashions, which are now modeled on runway shows. The idea behind this fashion style is that one may remain covered yet fashionable and that covered clothing can be even more beautiful and elegant than "open" clothes. It is true that after spending time with the stylish girls of Konya, dressed in colorful scarves and coats and discrete jewelry, the women of Istanbul with their uncovered bosoms and legs seem crass in comparison.

The sisterhood of women is a strong one in Turkey. Women stick together, be it in the family sections of restaurants, in their living rooms, in busses, or in the mosque. They do not mingle with men at social events, where women tend to instinctively sit on one side and men to the other. The idea of a cocktail party would not be an easy one to accomplish here. Mothers and daughters walk in pairs, and when one is lucky, you can catch a glimpse of a brace of three generations. Were I ever in trouble on the road, I know I could go up to any Turkish woman and say, "*Please help me,*" and in one second I would be in the haven of her home that night, her gentle hands healing any sickness or problem. This sisterhood transcends all class and social strata. Once while waiting in the Konya bus station for my departure to Beyşehir, I noticed a wide range of physical and class types among the women passengers, although most were dusty villagers with their grain bags, olive oil cans, and boxes wrapped in string. One shalvar-pants (spelled in Turkish as *şalvar*) clad village woman held a screaming baby, and out of nowhere, without a word said, a gold carat-clad cosmopolitan Istanbul lady came up to her, took the baby in her arms, bounced him along, and fished out a candy from her purse to quiet him down.

When I first came to Turkey in 1978, I estimated in my notes at the time that 95% of the women that I saw were covered, falling into two distinct groups: the black veiled chador-style covering and the more modest *tesettür* style. I never saw a woman driving a car alone, a woman waiter or service staff, and few women traveling on busses. Yet now, women are making fast inroads. In 2001, I had my gas pumped by a girl in the Black Sea town of Cide, a first. In 2002, I ate in a *pide* salon in Şavşat, run entirely by women with not one man present, something unheard of before. I see women behind the wheel on roads everywhere now, sitting in restaurants and in business meetings. The age-old view of the place of women in public spaces as a connotation of her virtue is breaking down.

All the women of the world share a common set of values: affirmation of community, hopefulness, belief in the importance of the individual, a concern for personal affection, a generous sharing of self, and generosity. Above all, women will always choose societal values over monetary ones. Women the world over share the same essential components of their lives: work, family, emotional life, spirituality, health, femininity, and hobbies. Turkish women are no different. An Algerian writer once told me that women are the true "men" of this world, and it is up to women to teach men how to truly become men. In that sense, Turkish women will be a powerful factor in the creation of the new Turkey, for they, above all others, understand how things should work for the best for their homes and their children, the true foundation bricks of any successful society. In doing so, they will make a noise that will make Turkey heard unto the world.

Sincerely yours,
Kadriye Branning

Health clinic, Eyüp

Sandıklı

Dancers in Söğüt

Eyüp

Sorting onions in the Issız Han, Apolyant

Erzurum

Portrait of Lady Mary Montagu (private collection)

Making yufka

LETTER 14

A woman alone

Dear Lady Mary,

I wrote to you in the last letter about women, but I feel I need to say a few more things specifically about being a foreign woman in Turkey, especially one who travels alone.

I feel an affinity with you, Lady Mary, for even at centuries distant, our visions of womanhood are very similar. I, like you, am strenuously self-educated. I am interested in the same things you are: visiting mosques and ancient monuments, landscapes, buildings, social life, history, women's dress, religion, marriage and divorce, feminism, and poetry. I want to understand the place and status of women in the world they live in. I, too, have studied the Turkish language and poetry; I have become interested in social life and in Islam and have been brought to question my own religion by looking at another. We both were able to gain insight into various issues because we were outsiders of a certain social standing. I, too, am sad to leave Constantinople, just as you were.

Yet our most common point is that we both know what it is like to be in Turkish society as single women without our husbands. Your husband stayed in a Turkish army camp near Adrianople from September, 1717 to May, 1718, where he was involved in diplomatic negotiations, obliging you to remain alone in Constantinople for some 10 months, practically the entire time you were in Istanbul. I am without my husband because I choose to travel alone.

That a woman would choose to travel alone is a difficult concept for Turks to understand or accept. Since women are taught at a very early age to follow the leadership of men (father, brothers, husband), it is hard to find an unchaperoned woman. Islamic tradition states that no woman should travel for more than three days unless her husband or an appropriate male family member accompanies her. Once in a bus near Kangal, a very modern young lady sat next to me and we started talking. Despite her trendy orange shoes, she was scandalized that I was traveling alone and maintained that is was impossible for me to do so, for that is just not done.

I have spoken to you before about the cohesiveness and collective nature of this society and how the Turks live in a tight community. I think that this makes it difficult for them to understand the difference between being alone and being lonely, and that it is totally possible to be alone and certainly not lonely. What we Westerners view as admirable independence is considered by Turks to be loneliness. Like me, I sense that you knew the difference between the two and had an appreciation and a preference for solitude and privacy combined with an equal appreciation of good company and entertainment.

Despite the sideways glances I get on the road, I persist in traveling alone in Turkey. I have spoken to you earlier about the joys of travel, but traveling alone offers a whole other level of happiness. It allows me to do things I could never do if I were in the company of others. I can visit libraries when I want. It affords me the solitude to write 350 words a day. It allows me to eat what and where I want. Another reason I travel by myself is to garner strength and to show myself that I am self-reliant, courageous, resourceful, and don't need others to take care of me. These trips make me feel strong so that when I return, I can pass on this strength to others. If I can survive the linguistic, social, religious, and cultural challenges of Turkey, then my challenging work and life in a city of vast ethnic diversity become much more manageable.

Another reason I travel alone is that quite simply, I have experiences I would never have if I were travelling with a man or in a group. In Turkey, a woman alone is showered with all kinds of attention and kindness, for Turks just do not want you to feel alone. Meetings, conversations, and offers of roses or glasses of tea just do not happen when you are with a man. The best part of traveling alone is that it is possible to do so, for Turkey is a very safe country. I *never* feel afraid in Turkey. My fate is entrusted to the good care of the 72 million pairs of hands at my service. I am a Lady here, remember, and am always treated with the highest respect and consideration. All the stories you hear about Turks being inconsiderate to women are fallacious. Of course, a woman traveling alone must exert caution, as anywhere. You learn to select your restaurants with care. You must stick with hotel restaurants if there is one, go early, and never drink alcohol, which sends out a message about a potential dubious moral standing. You don't initiate conversations, you don't boldly ask questions, you don't look men in the eyes directly, you don't go around showing too much flesh. In thirty years of travel in Turkey, I have never once been shown any disrespect by a man or felt in any type of difficult situation, something I certainly cannot say when I travel to other countries, even my own.

For you see, those famous Turkish eyes are always upon you, looking out for your safety. You are on their communal radar screen. One of the simplest radar incidents I experienced was also one of the richest, for it resumed the Turkish social traits of cohesiveness, sisterhood, hospitality, and tender acts of kindness. I went into the Kayseri Hatuniye Medrese to visit the tomb in the corner and after coming out, decided to stop for some water at the little café that was set up in the courtyard. I was there for about five minutes, when a woman came up to me and said, *"Hello, excuse me, my friend and I were wondering if you would like to come over and join us at our table, since you are all alone."* She didn't know me but just did not want me to be lonely. Once on a village jitney bus, a woman placed her baby in my lap for the duration of the trip. It was not that she wanted a break from holding him, but rather she gave him to me so I that I would have some company. Another time while eating alone in Eğirdir, a handsome middle age couple passed by my table on the way to theirs, and the man gave me the most gentlemanly bow and said, *"I hope you will enjoy your meal, if you need anything, we will be sitting at the next table."*

A woman alone leaves a mark in people's memories. Last year in Kayseri I treated myself to one of the best İskender kebabs in Turkey, in the İskender Lokantası in the center of town. I had eaten one there over 20 years ago and had never forgotten it. On that day, the head waiter kept circling me, intrigued. He finally came up to me and said, *"You have been here before, right? I remember you. How are you?"* I thought that he either had an astounding memory or that my distinctive looks stood out, but no, it was neither. It was just the fact that a woman alone is such a rare oddity that someone would remember it 20 years later. I have had the exact experience repeated in a restaurant in Konya (15 years for that one) and in Erzurum, where a carpet dealer ran after me down the street, not only remembering me from my visit to his shop twelve years prior, but also the type and price of the rug I purchased.

There is another issue with being alone, one that you felt, too, Lady Mary. A woman alone means a woman without children. You also express in several of your letters your frustration with the obsession of Turks for children and how being childless is a grievous taboo. Turkish women are still defined by the number of children they have. This is the second most frequent question you are asked (the first one being, *"are you married?"*). You discuss in at least six letters the multiple childbearing habits of Turkish women, the importance of bearing children for social status, and the plight of the poor woman who is unmarried and childless. As I have said previously, Turkish families just love children, the flowers of their personal gardens. You lived motherhood in Turkey in a very direct way, Lady Mary. You were pregnant for much of the time you were in Turkey, giving birth to your little Mary on January 19, 1718, noting, *"people looked at me with a great air of contempt until I finally complied with the fashion and I lay in like the others."* A childless woman is still made to feel a little pitied, even today, Lady Mary, but I have every confidence that Turks will come to understand that there are many ways to create a home and hearth: the mother goddess can take many other forms, such as curator for a larger family, the one of society as a whole.

Being alone or childless does not mean you have not chosen to share your life with another person. The question of marriage *alla turca* seems to preoccupy you as well in your letters. These letters establish you as a feminist who sought even in a different culture to understand the complex issues of a woman's place in society and her role as mother and wife. You support the feminist ideals of independence, a life not defined by marriage and children, self-respect, social, political, and economical equality, choices in life, fairness to men, equal opportunities, condemnation of those who support oppression, and an elimination of hierarchy. These are issues that women in the West and in Turkey deal with every day, still seeking the place where they can acquire marketable skills, where the stigma of living alone is removed, where their existence is not defined by their relationship to the home, and where they can be in charge of their choices and future.

On the subject of marriage, Lady Montagu, there is one man who is singularly absent in your letters: your husband. You never mention him in your letters to your friends, give news of his health or of the advancement of his negotiations. Your letters to him are few and far between, and when you do write him, it is in a dry and loveless tone that is startlingly different from the vibrant one you use in the steady stream of impression-packed correspondence with your other friends. Whatever the reason, something had definitely gone wrong in your marriage, and it would appear that he ceased to matter to you. You were a woman truly alone in Turkey.

Upon your return to England, a new era opened in your life, and in this phase, men played an important role. Your writer friends, your son, your business partners, your husband, and your lovers decidedly oriented the direction of your life. But that will be your story to tell, and tell it you did in the many letters you continued to write from abroad where you chose to spend the rest of your life. Yes, you chose to be a woman alone, without your husband or your children, yet never lonely, as your pen and paper became your most generous and loving companions.

Sincerely,
Katharine Branning

LETTER 15

A respect for books is a respect for mankind

Dear Lady Mary,
We both are very fortunate women, for we have chosen occupations that deal with the word. You, with your writing, put words down on paper to create literature. You have used your writing to present many of the ideals you believe in: education for women and health issues, for example. I have dedicated my life to words as well, but in a different way. As a language teacher, I have taught people to learn words and to craft them into communication, and as a librarian, I ensure that these words are collected, preserved, and put into the hands, hearts, and minds of others. We are both very blessed, indeed, to be able to live in the world of words. Did you ever stroll in the rare book market in Istanbul, the Sahaflar? It is an open-air library, filled with the most wonderful treasures a book-lover could hope to discover.

In a letter dated February 12, 1717 to your friend Alexander Pope, you relate your appreciation of Arabic poetry, taught to you by your friend Achmed Effendi of Belgrade through the riches of his library:

> "... he has explained to me many pieces of Arabian poetry which, I observed, are in numbers not unlike ours, generally alternate verse, and of a very musical sound. Their expressions of love are very passionate and lively. I am so much pleased with them, I really believe I should learn to read Arabic, if I was to stay here a few months. He has a very good library of their books of all kinds, and, as he tells me, spends the greatest part of his life there."

In Turkey, some of my most rewarding encounters have been with those who share my profession. Librarians are a very close-knit group in general, linked by commonly-shared ideals, and these ideals are the same whether you are a librarian in Paris, New York, or Amasya. Whenever I travel, I visit libraries to admire their style, and I never fail to see something done differently which I carry home for my own library.

The Turkish word for library, *kütüphane*, translates as "The House of Books." I have had some remarkable meetings with remarkable librarians in some remarkable "Houses of Books" in Turkey. One such meeting was with the librarian in Amasya who delighted in showing me a rare Koran dating from the fifteenth century, the oldest in Turkey, executed by the most famous Ottoman calligraphy master, Şeyh (sheikh) Hamdullah. When I told him that it was the oldest book I had ever held or touched, he taught me the Turkish saying *"Kitaba saygı, insana saygıdır"* (To respect books is to respect mankind). Here again was another example of that overarching Turkish keyword: respect. Rarely have I heard such a simple concept summarize the motivation that made me become a librarian, for librarians do respect humanity at the highest level.

I remember meeting Şirin Tekeli, the founder of the Women's Library in Istanbul, right after it was opened in 1990. Her pride in what they were trying to accomplish was motivating and inspiring. Speaking in flawless French and English, she showed me the 5,000-volume collection housed in an artistically-renovated medrese and explained how the librarians had devised their own classification system in order to make access of these highly-specialized collections more user-friendly. This visit and discussion made me reconsider the traditional venues for the classification of collections and the presentation of information to the public, which has led me on a significant mission in my professional life. I did not, however, adopt for my library the heavy smoking allowed by the staff and readers!

A visit to another Istanbul library was motivating in a different way, for there I met librarians who showed such enthusiasm and belief in their mission that you could not help but be inspired by them. Tucked behind the Mihrimah Sultan Complex in Üsküdar in one of the outbuildings of this complex built in 1543 by Sinan is a tiny box of a public library. Even though it was closed, the librarian invited me in because I was a *"book sister."* She spent the afternoon telling me how libraries like hers are important for the "*gecekondu*" (slum) children, and it is for them that she enthusiastically tackles everything, from restoring the building, cleaning the shelves, purchasing of new furniture, scrubbing the floors, and personally selecting and cataloguing all the books. The library was modest and a tad shabby, but she acted as if she was showing me the Dolmabahçe Palace. From her I again realized that what is truly important in this business is service to readers, not the quantity or quality of the books on the shelves.

Librarians in Turkey have always been ready to open their libraries and their hearts to me when I told them that I, too, was a librarian, the magical password to enter many libraries, archives, and collections. I remember remarkable visits with the librarians as the Üsküdar Şemsi Paşa Public Library of 25,000 volumes, where the head librarian offered me a copy of the Dewey Decimal Classification schedules translated into Turkish to take home with me. Or the tiny public library in Ürgüp, proud with 30,000 volumes and 11 branch libraries that rotate over 10,000 books per year to neighboring villages. This library had a special corner in the children's section, with a bookcase filled with young adult books on Atatürk. A spectacular collection of rare books was to be found in the Library of Bağdadi Necip Pasha in Tire, built in 1397. This Minister of Ammunitions under Mahmut II brought back books from Baghdad in specially-crafted red leather book cases. I have seen other similar rare books in the Kayseri Reşit Efendi Kütüphanesi next to the Ulu Cami. Once again, however, it was the special attention that Turkish librarians pay to their public that impressed me most. At the Public Library in Aksaray, I was invited for a tour of the library of 30,000 volumes, was asked to sit in on a staff meeting, complete with tea and cakes, participated in a lively discussion, and was even treated to a spin in their bookmobile. I have been invited to sign the guest books in the İnegöl Library housed in the medrese of the İshak Pasa complex of 1482 and the Istanbul Köprülü Library, as if I were a special dignitary. Once when visiting the Bayezit University Library in Istanbul, that famous radar of the Turks clicked in, and I was accosted, grabbed, and escorted into the Director's office, with the clerk saying, "*Oh yes, we could tell you were a librarian by the way you were scrutinizing the card catalogue!*" A two hour visit ensued, with a procession of librarians called in to greet me, one of whom took me to show me the rare book collection and a Jalaladdin al-Rumi manuscript dating from 1690. And once a librarian, always a librarian: a rather deaf but dear retired librarian, Hakkı Bey, appeared out of nowhere upon a visit to the Karatay *han* and took it upon himself to be the official guide, since, as he informed me, "*he knew about knowledge*," and of course, knew he had to pass it on.

However, the grandest of all library events I have experienced in Turkey was the 61st International Federation of Librarians Associations (IFLA) annual conference in Istanbul in August of 1995. A fireball of a librarian named Altınay Serenikli (one of those glorious Turkish first names, meaning "*Golden Moon*") organized an IFLA congress the likes of which have not been seen since. The opening ceremonies, held in the Atatürk Cultural Center in Taksim, included speeches by the Mayor of Istanbul, a representative of UNESCO, and the president of IFLA, and for the bouquet final, a presentation by Turkey's first Turkish Culture Minister and my most beloved of teachers, Talat Sait Halman, who whipped the crowd into a frenzy with his amusing speech containing no less than 16 of his famous puns. That evening, a reception fit for a sultan was held for us in a former Ottoman palace, the Çırağan Hotel. Other evening festivities included a concert of folk dancing in the open air theater below the Hilton, complete with a boxed picnic dinner of a cheese sandwich and the most delicious pear I have ever eaten. The next day we were treated to a tour of several Istanbul libraries (the Topkapı Palace manuscript collection, the Reserves of the Archeological museum, and your Ahmet III's library in Topkapı), with a closing concert of classical music at the Taksim Atatürk center. Perhaps this does not sound all that exciting to you, but to me it was glorious. When the diminutive Altınay Hanım came on stage to open that first concert, she opened her arms wide and shouted out a resounding, "*Welcome to my country!*" with a patriotic pride and sense of hospitality that could only have come from a Turk. The crowd went wild.

I even once had a meeting with a friend of libraries long gone: Ibrahim Pasha. I "met" him in my imagination while strolling in the Nevşehir complex he built in 1726, which includes a mosque, a library, and a medrese. Actually, I believe you may have met him in real life, Lady Mary. Ibrahim Pasha was both the son-in-law of your Sultan Ahmet III and his grand vizier. He designed Nevşehir in central Anatolia at the skirts of Cappadocia as a totally "new town." He was an enlightened man, who fostered the westernization of the Ottoman Empire through his contacts with

France, and it was he who stimulated Ahmet III's interest in building – an interest which led to the construction of his Topkapı library and the sumptuous Fruit Room apartments of the Harem. He met, however, with a sad end, as he was executed by the Janissaries. Yet he lives on in this complex, built with an eminence of site and out of the distinctive yellow stone of the Capaddocia region. Oddly enough, it is the medrese of the complex which now serves as the public library, complete with the obligatory statue of Atatürk in the middle; the original library is now used as a soup kitchen. The idea of service to the public is still clearly in evidence.

Yet it was a visit to a small public library in Akşehir that stood out from the others. In the warm, late afternoon hour, a lovely young librarian tucked a basket of wrapped hard candies under her arm and went from reader to reader to offer each and every one of them a smile and a candy to accompany their reading. It was a small gesture as sweet as that candy, a simple one, a respectful one: for as you remember, the way of hospitality, respect, and love is how they do things here in Turkey, even in houses of books.

Sincerely yours in words,
Kadriye Branning

Aksaray Bookmobile

IFLA conference voucher for free bus rides in Istanbul, 1995

Üsküdar Mihrimah Children's Library

Şemsi Paşa Library, Istanbul: "They are waiting for you in the library."

Sahaflar antique book bazaar, Istanbul, 1980

Nevşehir, Ibrahim Paşa Library

İnegöl Public Library in the
medrese of İshak Paşa, 1482

The Library of Sultan Ahmet III
at Topkapı

Amasya Bayezit II Külliyesi
manuscripts card catalog

Manisa Ulu Cami medrese classroom

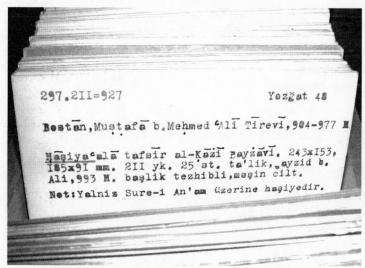

Card catalog of the manuscripts held in the Süleymaniye Library,
Istanbul, the world's largest collection of manuscripts

Üsküdar Mihrimah Children's Library

A WAY OF LIFE

LETTER 16

A platter of baklava from Gaziantep

To Gül Eke Hanımefendi

Dear Lady Mary,
   In those letters describing your visits to harem ladies you not only provided us with rich details about daily life and insights into the character of women, but you also gave us a glimpse of the world-famous Turkish hospitality.

You can rest assured, Lady Mary, that things have not changed much since you were received into those Turkish homes. Turkey may no longer be ruled by sultans, and the clouds seen from your Pera window are now poked with skyscrapers, but that gracious Turkish hospitality is intact and flourishing.

Turkish hospitality is world-famous and justly merits the acclaim it receives. I have long tried to understand why this country is perhaps the most hospitable on earth, and I believe that there are several reasons. The first, perhaps, is due to the nomadic origins of the Turks, which may raise in them a natural empathy for travelers. The Seljuk sultans established a system of caravansarais offering free room and board to traveling merchants for 3 days at the state's expense. The Ottomans continued this tradition by building elaborate programs of soup-kitchens to disburse food to people in need. Like the unspoken bond of sailors at sea, a traveler is never left unattended or in potential danger.

The second reason stems from the Islamic culture. Hospitality is a common characteristic of Muslims around the world. In principle, every

Muslim is called upon to fulfill obligations to others as witness to their service to Allah. It is part and parcel of the Muslim Golden Rule of life, which is to encourage good and shun evil. For Turks, this service to Allah takes the form of a hospitality that beats as naturally as their hearts. This very simple concept is the basis of the communal way of life that all Turks share with each other and their need to guide, lead, and protect each other. The Prophet said, "Eat together and not separately, for the blessing is associated with the company." The old Turkish phrase for an unexpected guest reflects their philosophy: "Tanrı misafiri—a visitor from God." As a result, they offer a hospitality to travelers that asks nothing in return, with families judging themselves by their generosity to guests when they entertain. As the famous world traveler Ibn Battuta wrote in 1330 about his welcome by members of the Ahi religious sect: "*In Anatolia, nowhere in the world will you find young men so eager to welcome strangers, so prompt to serve food and to satisfy the wants of others.*"

Perhaps this last reason is their own very specific Turkish take on the Muslim Golden Rule, summed up in their oft-cited proverb: "*What you give away, you keep.*" Yet whatever reason motivates it, Turkish hospitality is warm and overwhelming in its bounty of gestures, gifts, food, love and kindness, all carried out in gentleness, originality, discretion, and heart-felt sincerity. This compassion puts you immediately at ease. When I read your letters, Lady Mary, I sensed that you felt this gentleness as well, and it is perhaps what inspired your generous tone in the comments you put in your letters. You were not ill at ease there as a foreigner; you were comfortable, and you let cross-cultural confrontations flow over you like water.

When I am in Turkey, I am touched by a hospitality high point at least once daily. It may be a gesture so discrete that you do not even know it is happening, or it can be a complex one that astonishes you with its emotional dimension. Anatolia means "*Land of the Mother Sun,*" and it seems as if each Turk absorbs a part of that Mother Sun and radiates it back to the world. All visitors receive it, but I have been fortunate enough, like you, to experience it in a deeper way than most tourists. Turkish hospitality is extended not just to foreigners or strangers, but becomes a natural way of life among themselves. In speech, they repeatedly use the expression "*Buyurun,*" a catch-all word magnificent in its simplicity, covering a broad range of meanings from "*Please! Here you are! Help yourself! This way please; be my guest; after you!"* It fits every situation, and just their engaging way of saying it, always with a smile and an extended hand gesture, is a little gift in and of itself.

I have already spoken to you about the hospitality that my adopted family extends to me. Yet everyday on the street, hospitality is offered in modest ways, like a cup of coffee served on a golden platter, a door opened automatically, or the most ubiquitous of them all, a glass of tea. Turks will never let you pay for anything or even cover your own way. They take mortal offense when you offer to pay, and you must certainly never offer to pay in front of a man: his masculine honor and his honor as a Turkish host would be extremely insulted.

Turkish hospitality usually centers on food... and tea. You must accept everything offered to you, and they will not let up until you do. In our culture, when you ask someone if he would like something, the one-time yes or no of the guest is taken as the final arbitration. Not here, where the question is asked a minimum of three times, for Turks are convinced you are shy or afraid to say yes the first time around. You described those "fifty dishes" served to you, Lady Mary, and I can attest that an elaborate spread is always presented to a guest, from fresh-picked garden plums, to handmade kebabs, mantı, and içli köfte. I once had an entire two-foot diameter platter of the world-famous Gazientep pistachio baklava sent via a special-delivery courier on a bus from there to Kayseri, some 150 miles away, for my delight at dinner.

The simplest way Turks extend their hospitality is by those tiny tulip glasses of hot, ruby-red tea. With each sip, you have time to savor all the warmth and sweetness of this people. It is a small investment gesture with a large return reward. It slows everything down to a human pace, from checking into a hotel to enjoying the greenery of a public park.

The tea gesture is found everywhere you go, in shops after a purchase, at a quick drop-in visit to a friend's house (etiquette demands the consummation of three glasses), in the drugstore when you go in simply to buy aspirin to ease a headache, the photo shop, and of course, numerous times during the lengthy negotiations to buy a carpet. It becomes an act of protocol for doing business. With each tinkle of the spoon against the side of the glass, a friendship begins and deepens.

The most elaborate show of hospitality is being received as a guest in a Turkish home, an experience something akin to a 3-ring circus with the entire family and neighbors involved in assuring your comfort. They will give you the best bed in the house, orient their entire schedules around you, and act as if they have nothing else in the world to do except take care of you. They are curious to learn about you, such as how you tie your shoes and salt your food, and you must be ready to be scrutinized thoroughly in everything you do. Once I was received in the Izmir home of the parents of a Turkish friend of mine in New York. Nothing was left unattended, with the hostess scurrying about non-stop to fuss over my comfort. As I was eating dinner on the balcony, I leaned against the railing, and when I tried to pull away I realized that I had somehow become stuck to it. I tried to hide my predicament as discretely as possible, and finally at one moment during a change of plates, I was able to yank myself free and saw that the whole side of my dress was covered in white paint. Later that evening, before going to sleep, I tried to open the window to my bedroom to no avail, for it was solidly stuck tight. I tried and tried, and then noticed that my hands were covered in white paint. It was only then that it dawned on me: this yet-to-dry paint was witness to the fact that the family had painted the entire apartment in preparation of my visit, in the time from the phone call two days earlier announcing my arrival until that very morning.

While visiting my Kayseri family, an entire post-dinner party was organized to meet me, with a dozen neighbors being invited over to chat, drink tea, eat fruit and nuts, and enjoy the cool of the evening. All these people came to make me feel welcome, and I felt a bit like a Sultan receiving homage from ambassadors like your husband, Lady Mary. Towards the end of the evening, one of the guests, Muzaffer, took the floor, and everyone became quiet. He started to speak very slowly and simply so I could understand: *"Lady Kadriye, we thank you for coming to visit us. We are happy to have met you. We await you again next year, and only this time, we want you to bring along your husband. We hope that your trip will go smoothly and safely. May God bless you."* With that, everyone stood up, kissed me, and left. No ambassador to the Sultan Ahmed's court was ever more gracious or elegant.

Turks still act as if you are in their home even when you are outside of it. Once in a restaurant in Afyon, an entire party of about 20 people came in for a family celebration, and seeing me there, invited me to join their group for the evening. One is extended the same type of honored guest hospitality in offices and places of business. A place of business is nothing more than an extended home, and when you enter it, the same rules of artful living apply. I spoke to you about how I had once been commandeered on a *han* visit into the office of the mayor of Ezinepazar. When I arrived at that concrete municipal building overlooking the square, I was duly escorted by his assistant up the stairs to his second-floor office, past framed color photocopied portraits of all the Ottoman sultans and the famous Seljuk ones as well. We paused for a moment in front of a glassed-in display case, the "*Şehit Köşesi*" war memorial. It displayed the black and white photographs of the local soldier boys lost in the recent clashes with the PKK terrorists, a huge golden bust of Atatürk, and big vase of red plastic flowers: a simplicity as poignant as the Vietnam Veterans monument in Washington, D.C. Arriving in his office, I found a place of business that certainly did not resemble the ones we know in the West. This one had a desk more impressive in size than any French minister's, complete with blotter, pen holder, telephone set, the mayor's name and title on a big gold plaque, a spread of the daily newspapers, and a set of three Turkish flags in a little stand. There was more: two couches and six armchairs, cut crystal ashtrays, a huge color flat screen television, bookshelves, computer, a dining table with eight chairs, a three-dimensional portrait of Atatürk as well as framed pictures of mountain scenes on the wall, vases of flowers, and three cages of chirping yellow canaries. I was received with greater pomp than you were on your harem visits, Lady Mary, I can assure you. The mayor started an animated conversation that lasted over three hours. He madly rustled around to find papers on his desk and bookshelves, wildly pulling out things from his drawers and files. He called in his assistant and dumped a stack of this material (crop reports, local statistics, and articles on the *han*) in his hands and asked him to make photocopies for me. A huge wall air conditioner was turned on with a flourish from the remote control on his desk. Tea, soda water, and coca cola appeared, all together, for me, and the mayor was served a Turkish coffee. We viewed a DVD of the local public circumcision festival that had taken place a few weeks earlier on the square in front of the *han*, and he then asked his assistant to burn me a copy to take home. I then spotted on the bookcase a specially-commissioned modern Iznik plate with his portrait and the *han* in the background. I emboldened myself to ask where I could purchase one of these treasures, and as quick as a flash, the beleaguered assistant was called in to wrap it up for me to take home. In my workday, I can barely find time to squeeze in 10 minutes for unexpected visitors, and here he had taken over 3 hours with me, sending me off full of liquids, documentation, and gifts.

Travel affords Turks boundless ways to show creativity in their hospitality. As a foreigner (and a lady), every effort is made to arrange the whole busload of passengers so that I can be assigned the coveted seat #1, right behind the driver. When you check into a hotel, there is always bowing and a posse of bellboys to seize your luggage. I have been taken in charge personally by the skipper of a boat for a guided tour of Van's Akdamar Island, and in Amasya, a man told me that I was waiting in the wrong place for the jitney to Ezinepazar (how did he know where I was going?) and grabbed me by the hand to escort me a half a mile away to the correct place. An owner of a terrace restaurant in Antalya, now unfortunately long gone, sent over ice cream and crème de menthe as an apology for the rowdy people sitting at the next table. The female entertainers that sing in restaurants always make it a point to go around and greet every table, pausing a while at my table to say hello, learn my name, and make me feel like a special guest to the performance. In small village pilaf lunch spots, you are often given food you did not order just because they are so excited to have a foreign visitor in their modest establishment. In Beyşehir, the cabdriver I hired to take me to the ruins of Kubadabad stopped every five minutes to pluck me different kinds of fruit from the rich groves surrounding the lake: apples, pears, peaches, plums, cherries, and mulberries. Later that evening, he invited me to the lakeside park to watch the sunset over the lake and drink tea with his family.

Some of the greatest displays of hospitality come from the Turks who are just plain proud to show off their historically rich country to foreigners. It is one way of saying *"how happy I am to be a Turk."* It is the man in Edirne who has moved his workshop to the back of the 1609 Emekçioğlu Ahmet Paşa Kervansaray and took me on a personal guided tour of the *han*. It is the bent-over old man with a cane in the Seljuk cemetery of Gevaş, who hobbled around with me to make sure I saw the tomb of Halime Hatun, a *"Karakoyunlu Hanımefendi,"* or honored lady of the Black

Sheep Turks. It took place in Niksar on a visit to the Ulu Cami, whose imam then escorted me up to the citadel as my own personal guide, spending the entire afternoon with me. He told me he did it because no foreigners come in to visit his mosque, and for that reason, he considered that I was somehow sent from God and needed to be entrusted to him.

It is the two-hour private guided tour by the director of the Gevher Medrese in Kayseri, who made me sign the guest book. It is the old men sitting comfortably on the square of the dusty village of Hortu in front of the tiny monument honoring the birthplace of the folktale hero Nasreddin Hoca, but who move so that I may take a photograph of it. It is the men in the grocery market across from the Seljuk mosque in Birgi who pull out the largest iron key I have ever seen to open its door for me so that I could see its original carved wooden shutters and pulpit. In Sivas one late afternoon, I took a cab to visit the Tomb of Şeyh Hasan, and afterwards the cabdriver discretely asked if he could take me somewhere. "*I know a place that I think you will like a lot,*" he timidly offered. Usually one should be wary of such propositions, but since this is Turkey, I had no fear. He then proceeded to take me out the see the Eğirli Köprü, the distinctive one-lane L-shaped "bent" bridge, still solidly standing over the Kızılırmak River despite the major earthquakes of 1939 and 1942 that destroyed virtually everything else in the area. The photograph I took of the bridge in that sunset moment, summing up the kindness which allowed me to discover one of the finest Seljuk bridges in Turkey, sits on my desk today.

One of my greatest fears, Lady Mary, is that Turkish hospitality will disappear. I worry that the onslaught of foreigners now pouring into Turkey will erode the infinite patience of the Turkish people and erase their feeling that these often-disrespectful people are a divine gift from God. Yet when I think of how this hospitality shown to visitors has endured so strongly since Ibn Battuta's words in 1330 and your experiences in 1718, I suppose my fears are ungrounded. All I need to do is to remember freshly-painted rooms and platters of baklava sent from Gaziantep to put my fears at rest. Yes, yes, and forever yes, I would love another glass of tea.

Sincerely yours,
Kadriye Branning

The platter of Gaziantep baklava sent in my honor

Neighbors over for tea, Kayseri

Eğirli Köprü, Sivas

Gevas, Halime Hatun Tomb

LETTER 17

Cushions and cakes

Dear Lady Mary,

In each of my travel journals, I keep a special section entitled *"Heart-breakers/Show-stoppers."* On these pages I note all the extraordinary things that happen to me during the trip that literally take my breath away. These are not only the architectural, artistic, or natural wonders that I marvel at during my trips, but the human gestures and encounters that are just as impressive as those historic and geographical sites. For you see, the Turks just do not content themselves with being the most hospitable people in the world: they have to go above and beyond this already noteworthy sense of charity by offering you some astonishing and incredible acts of human kindness.

Most of these acts are in fitting with their sense of politeness and natural human elegance. They can be very simple gestures, such as the offering of a glass of tea, an outstretched hand, a smiling warm *"buyurun,"* or a splash of cologne to the very elaborate, such as a poem dedicated to you or that platter of baklava from Gaziantep. But what takes you by surprise each time is that they always come unexpectedly and are given with genuine, spontaneous kindness. They are conferred with a friendliness so easy, open, and natural that they seem like a way of life, and I have come to believe that they are the most indicative symbols of the genuine humanity of the Turkish people. These people seem like angels from above on earth: always looking out for you and helping to make your day more beautiful and meaningful.

How can I explain these gestures to you, Lady Mary? The ones I have experienced are mostly related to adventures on the road, and since you were rarely left alone to encounter Turks on your own, I believe you truly missed out on discovering some of the richest treasures of this country. Maybe the incidents I will relate do not seem exceptional to you, but in the tense, urban environment in which I live, things do not have time to unfold like they do in Turkey, and everyone builds wary walls of privacy around them. The heart-stopping deeds I have experienced in these many years of travel have been either demonstrations of outright respect, gracious compliments paid, humble gestures tendered, or the offering of considerable gifts.

As I have mentioned before, the Turks are an exceedingly polite people, always offering a "*Buyurun,*" a tea, or a kind word to every person they encounter during their day. Even the way they sign off from their letters resumes their whole attention to politeness: no boring "Sincerely yours" salutation from these people, but one that says "*Saygı ve sevgi*": with respect and love. You always precede a request for something by saying "*İzin ver,*" meaning, "If you give me the permission to do this..." I have learned that the quickest way to dispel any unfortunate incident attacking my personal safety or integrity has been to hiss or bellow out a strong "*Ayıp!*" meaning "Shame on you!" which so insults a Turk's self-image that the troublemaker will disperse immediately. Only twice in 30 years of travel have I been spoken to abruptly or with disrespect, and those two times were out of anger at the unfortunate actions of my political leaders, not at me as a person.

I have often been told that one of the reasons that Turks are so kind to me personally is that I make an effort to respect them, by dressing appropriately, behaving in accordance with their decorum, and above all, by speaking their language. Perhaps this is true, but they respect all foreign visitors. They do not put on a show just for foreigners but are genuinely polite and reverential to each other. Village simpletons and beggars are especially treated with respect. On my first trip to Turkey I was walking in a quiet neighborhood and a blind man approached me, holding out a dog-eared faded postcard to me. At first I did not understand the encounter, but then I realized that he was "selling" me viewing rights to the little kitty on the postcard in exchange for a coin. He was not a beggar in this fashion, you see, he was offering me a service. A man standing nearby came up to him and said, "*Amca* ("My uncle," a term of endearing respect for older people), *you must leave her alone, she is a foreigner and will not be able to understand,*" and with that, came over, took him by the elbow to steer him away from me, and at the same time discretely slipped a coin in his hand. Amca's honor was respected, I was not made to feel uncomfortable, and the man knew that he had taught me a lesson about the Turkish way of alms-asking and giving. Another incident in Konya showed the same sense of compassion. I had gone into a pharmacy to get some medicine, and when I came out, I immediately sat down in a tea garden next door to rest and take the pills. The head waiter, being a sharp-eyed Turk and having noted that I had come out of the pharmacy and was now unwrapping pills, understood that I was not feeling well. Before I could order a tea, a beggar woman came up and sat down at my table and tried to get money out of me. The waiter immediately interceded, and said to her, *"Please my aunty, leave her alone, she is not feeling well"* and took her by the arm, sat her at another table, and gave her a cup of water. By treating her with respect, not dismissing her or shooing her away, he saved the honor and dignity of the three of us. When it came time to pay for my tea, he said that that it was his pleasure to offer it to me as an apology for my having been inconvenienced at his place of business. Another experience with a village simpleton happened in Eğirdir. I was enjoying a quiet Sunday morning stroll around the town admiring its outstanding Seljuk monuments when I became increasingly aware that a man was following me, observing me, and dogging my every move, but nothing more than that. It was also on this morning that I decided to take a big leap into the modern age and have the photos on my digital camera transferred to a data disk for the first time. The camera was brand new, and I was totally unfamiliar with the process and very nervous about trusting a photo shop in such a small town with such an important responsibility. On that camera were the photos of an entire summer of research, and to lose them in the transfer process would have been a catastrophe. The shop owner immediately sensed my anxiety over the operation and did everything he could to reassure me. He brought out the young head-scarved girl technician from the back to show me that even a girl like me was capable of doing this. As she took my precious chip to the back room (patting my hand in the process), he assuaged my apprehension by offering me a chair and tea, showing me a photo album of the region and offering me a set of photos of this beautiful lake area as a souvenir. Just as I was starting to feel at ease, into the shop burst the man who had been following me all morning, and glaring at me, sat down in the chair next to me and started to blabber incoherently. It was then that I realized that my tagger was a simpleton. Right on his tails a second man entered the shop, who spoke to the shopkeeper and told him that he had been keeping his eye on my "friend" all morning, since he noticed that he was following me. Even I was unaware that there was yet *another* pair of eyes following me all that time, benevolent ones this time, so discretely was he taking responsibility for my safety. The shopkeeper sized up the situation immediately, led the man outside, sat him down under the plane tree across from the shop, and brought him a tea. My guardian angel then proceeded to go out to him and quietly tell him it would be best to leave this foreign *hanımefendi* alone. He stayed with me until I got my chip back from the smiling young lady, and beautifully-burned CD in hand, I exited the shop knowing that I was no longer in any sort of danger – and that the simpleton had no idea that he had done anything wrong.

Encounters with authorities have also proven to be dignified and respectful, even when I was clearly guilty of the offense. Once on the road in eastern Anatolia, I was driving with a friend who had picked up the nasty Turkish habit of passing at the crest of a hill. It always made me very ill at ease (especially since I was sitting in the passenger seat), but back-seat driving was never appreciated. One afternoon she pulled this maneuver, and unluckily for her, a police car was waiting in prey just for such offenders on the other side of the hill. The officer duly pulled her over and came strolling towards us, ominous with his gun and severe sunglasses. He came up to the window, scrutinized the interior of the car, gruffly asked for her license and registration, and scanned it over with great seriousness. I could tell my trembling friend was scared to death, but I was actually secretly pleased that she was finally going to get reprimanded for this dangerous practice... although I was wondering how I was going to break the news to her sainted mother in San Francisco that she had been hauled off into a Turkish prison. He handed the papers back to her, leaned over close to her face and very slowly and very sternly enunciated: "*DO NOT ever do that again. Do you understand me? Do not EVER do that again.*" And with that he turned and waved us on. That severe, yet dignified, remonstrance served everyone in the situation with respect. And she never did do it again.

Even when I was once caught innocently photographing military grounds, everyone, from the soldiers with their machine guns in the back seat of the car to the gendarmes in the station, showed me nothing but respect, with a dash of good-natured amusement thrown in.

The odd thing is that Turks do not like it when you try to play their own game with them and have a hard time accepting acts of kindness from others. One year my friend and I decided that we wanted to bring a gift to the manager of the hotel in Antalya as a thank you for the many kindnesses he had shown us over the years. Before leaving New York, we carefully selected a pen set as a gift, and upon our arrival, discretely left it at the front desk with a card. Five minutes later there was a knock at the door with the concierge returning our package to us. We were quite hurt and could not understand why it had been returned to us. We went to dinner, and when we came back, we found our room transformed with fresh towels, turned down beds, perfume bottles in the bathroom, fresh terrycloth bathrobes laid out on the bed, flowers in vases, a giant fruit basket and a thank you card... in return for our gift, which had been refused! He was uncomfortable perhaps with our display of respect given *alla turca*, but appreciating our thought all the same, he reciprocated in typical Turkish fashion.

Flowery, sweet, overt, and totally ingenuous compliments are another way that Turks shine in their show of kindness. Never shy about expressing themselves, Turks can often be very forward with their emotions. Such frank tenderness is rarely evoked so freely in our Western culture. Lady Mary, you relate a very touching compliment paid to you by your friend Fatima: "*I proceeded to tell her [Fatima] what a noise such a face as hers would make in London or Paris. 'I can't believe you', replied she agreeably; 'if beauty was so much valued in your country as you say, they would never have suffered you to leave it.'*"

Some of these compliments are real heart-stoppers indeed. The ones that accompanied roses or the ones paid by eager suitors were of course always flattering (including that horse business that one time). Oddly enough, it is the ones paid by women that have been the most pleasurable for me, just like the one you received from your Fatima. Once I was in a grocery store in Kayseri, ambling about selecting items and just observing the array of goods for sale, which is always an interesting pastime for me on my travels. I became aware that I was being followed, and when I glanced over my shoulder, I saw that it was by a young woman employee of the store. In New York, it is very common to be followed in small grocery and drug stores like this, but it always signifies that the security guard suspects you of potential shop-lifting activity. However, this young lady seemed different, and she kept getting closer and closer to me with each aisle turned. Finally she drew near me and gave me the biggest smile, took me by the hand, and led me over to the fruit display, where she encouraged me to look at her peaches, "*So fresh!*" she said, and then she guided me over to shelf after shelf, enthusiastically showing me goods like a child shows a guest his favorite toys. She turned to me and blurted out, "*I like you! You have such beautiful eyes! I like you! Please come back again and we can become friends!*" Yes, we could have become friends, like you and your Fatima, for a woman that joyful was irresistible, as was the little twelve-year old Sevda in a restaurant in Akçaabat. Helping her father out one evening when he was short-staffed, she waited on our table with all the professionalism of a seasoned *maitre d'* in a four-star restaurant. She showed me the very same behavior as that young woman in the grocery store in Kayseri: she just wouldn't leave my side for a second. She ran along side of me when I went to the restroom, turning on the water, handing me a towel, holding open the door, and then at the table, constantly hovered to put the salt shaker in front of me, to pour my water, and to fold my napkin with each change of course. When I asked my Turkish friend why she was so attentive, he laughed and said, "*She likes you! She told me that she thinks you are very pretty and she likes your dimples, which are as big as hers.*" And sure enough, when it came time to leave, she came up me, waved goodbye, and cried out to me for all the restaurant to hear as I reached the door: "*I like you very much!*"

As I said earlier, Lady Mary, Turkey is a country of small gestures, some of which are the biggest of the heart-stoppers. My favorite Turkish small gesture is what I call "*the magic hand*": in every circumstance, if a Turk can stick his hand out to help, he will. Those flying hands just can't keep to themselves. Like the wave of a fairy wand, Turkish magic hands proactively sense what needs to be done and reach out to do it. I arrived late one night at the bus station of Tokat to find the place in sheer pandemonium, for it was a soldier's holiday. All the young boys were coming home on leave, and their large families were there to greet them. I got off the bus and sat my suitcase down for a second to put away something in my purse, and when I looked down, it had disappeared! Seized with panic, I looked around, and saw a short, burly Turk running away with it tucked under his arm. I took off after him, and in the distance, I saw him set it down right at the head of the taxi stand. He did not know me, but he knew that I had gotten off that bus alone without a family to greet me and would need a taxi, and instinctively that invisible magic hand extended and grabbed. After he set it down, he ran back to help the group of people he was with, without a word to me or giving me the chance to say thank you. One time in Kayseri I was waiting to board the bus with my heavy suitcase, standing alongside a shalvar-clad peasant woman holding a baby in her arms. When the door to the bus hissed open, in a split second of synchronicity she tossed the little toddler under her arm and onto her hip, grabbed the handle to my suitcase with her free hand, and started to lift it up the steps. Without one ounce of premeditation or thought, she had that hand out and in a lightning moment gave me the boost that made my challenge of getting up the steps an easy one.

I have mentioned before how it seems that there is a Turk behind every tree, observing everything. Too countless to enumerate would be the imperceptible eyes and hands that have watched over me like a guardian angel, such as that man in Eğirdir. They are always on the lookout for you, to make sure you get on the correct bus, go in the right door, and pick the best peach. These gestures usually do not cost a penny and are within the reach of everyone to do. In their simplicity they appear more generous than the lavish presentation of fifty dishes you were given, Lady Mary. I have told you about the gardens of roses that have been offered to me over the years, but there is so much more. When you fall, they pick you up and gently put you on a stool. When you pass out from heat, they do the same and bring you a glass of water to boot. They will give you bus tickets. They offer you rides into town in their farm carts when you are standing by the side of the road waiting for a jitney. They will offer you a seat and a glass of water when you go into a pharmacy simply to buy some aspirin. They will close their doors of business to escort you places. Taxi drivers will return things you leave in their cabs to your hotel. They offer you fruit and, of course, glasses of tea at every chance they can. It comes from Ahmet the hotel clerk in Tokat who signs off his fax to you with a smiley face and a "*God bless you.*"

Once when I was visiting the oasis town of Karaman, I wanted to visit the Şeyh Alaettin Karabaş Veli İmaret but could not find it. Hot and frustrated yet determined to see it, I popped into a barber shop and asked if anyone could point me in the right direction. The barber, who was in the midst of giving a client a shave and a haircut, started conferring with the man in his chair, and said to me, "*No problem!*" and proceeded to leave his customer sitting all lathered up in his chair and walked me over to the complex, which was no short distance! In Kayseri early one Sunday morning, I went to visit the ruins of the Keykubadiyye Palace on the grounds of the PanSu Sugar and Water Factory. Due to the status of my guide, the historian Muhsin İlyas Subaşı (as well as his impressive persuasive powers), we were able to convince the guard on duty to allow us in, but he agreed to do so only under the condition that he accompany us for security reasons. We set off down the road when all of a sudden, he bellowed "*Stop!*" and my heart sank, thinking that he was having second thoughts about taking the responsibility for letting us visit. But no, he rushed into a building and came running back to the car with his arms full of bottles of cold water and soda for us to take along. It turned out that he had no idea that he was guarding not just a factory, but the very site of the palace of Alaaddin Keykubad, the greatest of Seljuk sultans. He will remember forever the inspiring history lesson he received that day from this famous Kayseri historian, as much as I will remember his gift of those bottles of water.

Another example of a small gesture came from a construction worker at the Bimarhane in Amasya who took me into the closed renovation worksite and showed me around because he sensed that I was curious and interested in what he was doing. A small gesture took place in Safranbolu in a gorgeous lokum shop dating from 1942, with its stunning original cut glass and carved wood décor intact. Its owner, who was standing in the doorway, saw me on the street and sensed that I was feeling faint. He came out, took me by the arm, and ushered me into his shop where he placed a chair under me to sit down. One small gesture took place in Tokat, in a fruit shop, where once again I was feeling faint from the heat and was given a peach crate to sit down on. A young boy came in at the very same moment to deliver the *pide* (oven-baked cheese bread) lunch ordered by the owner, who proceeded to place the warm packet on my lap with a stern, *"Here, you must eat this in order to feel better!"* No amount of protesting on my part could change his mind or even convince him to at least share a part of his lunch with me.

It is not only pide and tea and roses that have been showered upon me, but all kinds of fresh fruit. In Amasya, I once came out of the pool where I had just completed my 40-minute lap swim, and there next to my chair on a little table had mysteriously appeared a peeled and cut peach on a plate with a fresh soft drink, entirely unrequested. While visiting the Um-ur Bey Mosque in Bursa, I was so absorbed admiring its unusual 1454-foundation charter posted next to the door on two separate marble plaques that I did not notice that a teenage boy had come up and was standing next to me. Slowly he extended his cupped hands to me. Inside of them was a mound of what looked like precious pearls: in reality, fresh white mulber-ries that he had picked for me from the tree in the mosque courtyard. It was the first time in my life I had ever eaten this succulent, honey-like fruit. In Konya, the guard at the Karatay Medrese plucked fresh apricots for me from the tree in the garden. It was another incident involving fruit that al-lowed me once again to enjoy a moment of remarkable small thoughtful-ness. I had been invited to visit the mystical Şeyh Turesan Dervish convent on the top of a remote mountain on the road between Kayseri and Ürgüp. Before heading there in his jeep, my host Şuayip Türker stopped at a gro-cery store to buy fresh fruit to take to the gatekeeper and his family. When I offered to participate, I was of course refused and was even made to feel that I had seriously offended him. When we got to the convent and un-loaded the numerous bags of watermelons, peaches, apricots, and grapes from the jeep, Şuayip put them all in my arms. When the gatekeeper and his children came rushing out to greet us, Şuayip pushed me gently on the back and said, *"Go, don't be shy, you go offer them the fruit!"* It was his way of helping me establish contact and start a friendship with these peo-ple, as if it had been my idea in the first place to bring to them fruit and purchase it with my own money.

The most touching of the small gestures are the ones that are offered you by poor people, who have nothing else to offer you but their kindness. Their gestures elevate them to a position of greater dignity than any sultan. Once in Tokat I sat on the low wall outside the Hatuniye Cami waiting for the prayer service to end before I could go in and visit the mosque. A hunchbacked shoeshine man lumbered over to me and brought me a burlap bag to sit on. The bag was dustier than the place I was sitting on, but that was not the point. He gave me something, and even in his poverty, he was able to offer a meaningful gift. It would appear that the people of Tokat love to give cushions. Another time while waiting outside for the prayers to end at the Garipler Mosque before entering, an elderly woman who lived in the house next door and saw me sitting there from her window, came out carrying a bright kilim cushion for me to sit on while I waited. Have you ever done anything so simple and genuinely thoughtful, Lady Mary? I don't think I have. On two different occasions, visits to one of my favorite mosques in Turkey, the Murat Hüdavendigâr Mosque on the top of the Çekirge Hill in Bursa, offered me unforgettable experiences of kindness from modest souls. In this complex of quiet spirituality, Sultan Murad I, one of the most famous of Ottoman sultans, lies buried in a tomb across the street from the impressive mosque he built. There is a small tea garden surrounding his tomb, and I always stop there to enjoy the trees and flowers, to listen to the rustling breezes at this high spot over the city, to study the noble mosque across the street, and to contemplate the life of this tragic sultan, murdered on the battlefield of Kosovo by an enraged Serb. Once when I was sitting there, a destitute old man shuffled over to me and extended a very grimy hand holding one of the famous plump Bursa peaches for me. When I left and went to pay for my tea, the waiter said that he had taken care of it as well. He was as poor as his hands were dirty, that man, and yet he was able to offer a fresh peach and a tea as if it were an invitation to a banquet. Another time after a visit to the mosque at the end of a long day, I was too tired to walk down the hill and decided to take a taxicab to my hotel. Before I got in, the driver walked me to the rear of his cab, where he opened the trunk. Inside of it were some ten loaves of freshly-baked bread, still warm from the bakery where he had just purchased them to take home to his family for their evening meal. Their aroma was mouth-watering, as if the trunk were a mini-bakery oven of its own. He reached in, grabbed one of the hot loaves, and stuffing it into my hands, said, "*Here! This will be for your dinner!*" He, like that man in the tea garden, gave what he could, which made the gift all the more unsparing and charitable.

Cab drivers often give more than just a ride to your destination, as I have shown you. On the road to the airport in Tokat to take my return flight to Istanbul, I chatted with the cabdriver and told him how much I loved his city above all others in Turkey. He asked me why, and with each reason, he nodded his head and smiled. Soon we stopped along the road and he got out of the cab and disappeared. Just as I began to wonder what he was doing and if I was going to miss my flight, he came running back, opened the door and thrust in my lap a plastic bag filled with over 3 kilos of ripe peaches. "*These are for you; here is a little something to remember Tokat by, so that you will not become lonely for us when you are in the big city of Istanbul.*" Even in his modest state, he could offer me a rich present. Needless to say, they were the sweetest peaches I ever ate.

Yet the sweetest of all the small gestures I have received came from a group of teenage girls in Sivas. I paused to rest one afternoon in a lovely tea garden in the main Konak Square in the middle of town. As I sipped my glass of tea, I noticed that there was a party of six teenaged girls at the next table, drinking tea, chatting, laughing, and unwrapping a home-baked loaf cake. Perhaps it was someone's birthday, perhaps they were celebrating the end of the school year, or perhaps they were just enjoying their friendship. I was so plunged in my thoughts and in my reading that I did not see that one of them had come over to my table. In her hands was the home-made loaf cake that I had seen on their table, now cut up into slices. She extended the plate to me, and said, "*Here, we would like to share with you a piece of our cake. I hope you enjoy it, I made it all by myself.*" I was touched to be offered the honor of the first piece, and even more so because, in an ironic twist of circumstance, it just happened to be *my* very own birthday that day. It was almost as if she had known that fact. Of all the festive and festooned creamy cakes I have enjoyed in celebration of my birthday, none has tasted sweeter than that plain loaf cake, received from the hand and the smile of a total stranger.

Turks can have big and boisterous personalities along with those sweet and tender kernels inside of them and are capable of offering dramatic gestures as well as those humble ones. For example, one year when flying from New York to Istanbul, I removed my contact lenses at the beginning of the flight. As never happens, and much to my dismay, it went sailing through the air, and I had no idea where it landed. I hunted and hunted around my seat, but as you can imagine, in the close and crowded area of an airplane, it was a hopeless venture. When we landed and everyone trampled out, I decided to have one last look in the area around my seat. Soon, four air hostesses joined in on my hunt with me, determined that they would find it. Even though they were tired after the 12 hour flight and were probably more eager than I to get off that hot plane, they were not about to give up, and cheerfully clambered about on their hands and knees like little children playing treasure hunt. All of a sudden I heard one of them cry out: "*Buldum!*" (I found it!). How that young woman could have found something so small and how that lens had not gotten trampled is still a great mystery to me. But she believed she could find it, and being a Turk of the persistent and stubborn ilk, she managed an impossible miracle.

A big gesture can also be a discrete one. Once in a bookstore in Kayseri, the owner said he wanted to offer me a gift, and placed a book in my hands. Not just any book, it was a red-leather bound volume, with gold lettering and page endings. I looked at the cover and saw that it was a deluxe edition of a new English-language translation of the Koran. Each chapter, preceded by a page of explanatory notes, was beautifully translated, with a facsimile of the original Arabic in a little sidebar. As a librarian I was impressed by its magnificent quality, and as a guest, I was touched that this man sought to potentially open a very big door to my life by this gift.

Unfortunate incidents can often be repaired by big gestures of kindness. I took the bus once from Eğirdir to Konya, and for the first time in 30 years of travel I was put in the rear of the bus, in the very last row... and seated next to a man. It was very startling and, I must admit, put me rather ill-at-ease because it seemed so out of place. Yet I thought how silly I was being. I sit in the subway every morning next to men, so what could be the issue here? I did not pay much attention to the man sitting next to me, other than the fact that he was middle-aged and had ham-hands. It was only when I started to hear him muttering things to himself and making strange noises that I saw that he was behaving in an inappropriate manner. Even though this has happened to me in other situations on the subway in New York City and Paris, that it should happen to me here, in Turkey, on the very first occasion I found myself sitting next to a man on public transportation, was extremely upsetting to me. I grabbed my bag, abruptly stood up and ran forward to the driver and the bus valet and demanded that I change seats immediately. Although I did not explain the reason why, they must have sensed something. The next morning I awoke with a start from a sound sleep at 5 a.m., bolted straight up in my bed and cried out: *"My camera! Where is it?!"* How I could have sensed that it was not in my bag and how that intuition hit me at that specific moment during my sleep is something I cannot fathom. I tore the room apart, but of course, as the unconscious wisdom of my dream had told me, it was not there. The only thing I could think of was that in all the confusion of the incident on the bus the afternoon before it had fallen out of my bag. I grabbed my ticket stub, tore down to the bus station, and went to the office of the bus company and explained my story. They made some calls and about 5 minutes later the clerk said, *"Sit down, my Lady, someone will bring it, yes, something was found."* A glass of tea appeared. I dared not hope that it was my camera, filled with a summer of research photos, which if lost would have meant an entire trip in vain with all the time and money spent for naught. About 15 minutes later, six young men appeared, including the valet of the bus trip the day before. They had my camera in their hands. I started to cry out of frustration that I could have been so careless to lose something this valuable, hurt at the memory of the incident on the bus, and especially at the sudden realization that it was the morning of the fifth anniversary of a very sad September day for New Yorkers. I couldn't stop crying, now from relief and, embarrassed, muttered some incoherent thank yous and then headed away. I then realized how rude that was. I wiped my tears and went back to the man at the counter and said that I wanted to leave them all a little token of my appreciation, to which he replied, *"Oh no, Lady, it is for us to thank you for giving us this opportunity to be of help."* All had been made right by his smile.

As I have said before, Turks have a built-in radar system that allows them to be aware of everything in their radius. Nothing, and I mean nothing, gets by them. One Christmas, I decided to take my husband to Istanbul. When I wrote to the Arena Hotel, I asked if they would reserve an especially nice room for us as this trip was my gift for an important milestone birthday of my husband. When we arrived, indeed they had reserved for us the finest room in the hotel, looking out onto the most sublime of all of Sinan's mosques, the Sokollu Mehmet Paşa. On the late afternoon of New Year's Eve, my husband's birthday, we returned to the hotel chilled but happy after a long ferry ride up the Bosphorus. After a few minutes, there was a knock at the door, and I opened it to find a waiter with a tray, plates, napkins, and the most lavishly-decorated cake, complete with candles and accompanied by a card from the hotel staff wishing my husband a happy birthday. They had obviously noted his birth date from his passport when he checked in, and remembering my initial request, set it upon themselves to create their very own gesture for his birthday. Although this birthday cake was much more elaborately be-decked than my simple one in Sivas, for my husband, the emotion was the same: never had he experienced a sweeter birthday treat.

And it is just not in Turkey where the Turks perform these gestures of kindness. It is in their blood wherever they are, and they take it with them like a suitcase wherever they migrate. When I was living in Paris, I would often eat in a small Turkish restaurant and became friendly with the waiters there. One evening I told them I was moving to a new apart-ment the next day and how excited I was to be changing to a different and better neighborhood. *"Where do you live now, and where will you be moving to?"* the head waiter Metin asked. I told him without think-ing. I should have known better. The next morning, at 8 a.m., as I was starting to move my things out to my little car, a white mini van pulled up in front of my apartment building, and out tumbled six burly Turks, not one of them speaking a word of French. *"Metin sent us to help you move today, to make sure everything goes well."* I was dumbstruck. They scurried up those steps as fast as squirrels up a tree, and those swift hands and strong backs piled everything into the van in no time, drove it to my new address, and carried it all up again – only this time, up 6 long and narrow flights to my new apartment, located under the eaves of a Paris mansard roof. They accomplished all this under two hours and then dis-appeared in a flash, not giving me the time to offer them water, lunch, a tip, or my even thanks. They did it because Metin knew that a woman alone needed assistance, and he asked for their help. They did it because they were generous of their time and muscles. I never was so happy in any home in my entire life as I was in that 6th floor walk-up in Paris, and I am convinced it was because of the auspicious start to my life there, of-fered by the incredible act of kindness of those Turks.

And so you see, Lady Mary, this is what I mean by heart-stoppers and show-stoppers. These gestures of incredible kindness, both small and large, are some of the most valuable gifts I have ever received in my life. I would not trade one of them, not one slice of that plain cake, not one moment of repose on a dusty cushion, not one hoist from a hand extended, for anything in the world. My life has been made so incredibly rich because of them, and with wealth this abounding, who needs Lady Hafise's diamond earrings the size of hazelnuts?

Sincerely yours,
Kadriye Branning

Birthday cake offered to Stephen E. Gottlieb from the Arena
Hotel, Istanbul, December 31, 2005.

LETTER 18

Displays of greatest magnificence

D ear Lady Mary,
You were born in one of the finest homes in England, the great
Thoresby Hall located in the lush Nottinghamshire countryside.
This Palladian house, with its 275 rooms, sits on an estate of hundreds of
acres, complete with a deer park, a 65-acre lake, and a quarter-mile canal
that runs through formal gardens and feeds numerous fountains. You were
thus well-positioned to make the comparison between your palatial ancestral home and the Grand Signor's home in which you stayed in Edirne. As
usual, no element escaped your observant eyes, and you provide a very detailed description of its architecture and furnishings:

> "*Every house, great and small, is divided into two distinct parts, which
> only join together by a narrow passage. The first house has a large court
> before it, and open galleries all round it, which is to me a thing very
> agreeable. This gallery leads to all the chambers which are commonly
> large, and with two rows of windows, the first being of painted glass...
> This is the house belonging to the lord, and the adjoining one is called
> the harem, that is, the ladies' apartment... more gay and splendid, both
> in painting and furniture. The second row of windows are very low, with
> grates like those of convents... They use no hangings, the rooms being all
> wainscoted with cedar set off with silver nails or painted with flowers,
> which open in many places with folding doors and serve for cabinets, I
> think more conveniently than ours. Between the windows are little arches
> to set pots of perfume or baskets of flowers. But what pleases me best is
> the fashion of having marble fountains in the lower part of the room,
> which throws up several spouts of water giving, at the same time, an*

*agreeable coolness and a pleasant dashing sound... each house has a
bagnio, which consists in two or three little rooms..."*

Your description is very similar to the restored Ottoman homes that I
have visited in Turkey. Many outstanding examples of these houses have now
been turned into museums, in towns such as Kütahya, Birgi, Sivas, Tokat,
and Diyarbakır. These house museums have allowed me to imagine what life
must have been like in them, in the same way you were curious as to how
people lived in that Grand Signor's home in Edirne. I have learned from these
well-restored beauties how walls were lime-washed white and how the floors
were covered with meadows of bright kilims. I noted the great detail paid to
the gaily painted scenes on walls and wooden ceilings and how the built-in
cupboards (*yüklük*) stored the fabrics of life, such as napkins and towels as
well as the copper pots and vases such as you saw in Edirne. During the day,
the bedding linens, and blankets of the entire family would also be stored in
these cupboards, freeing up the floor space to create an airy and accommodating space for living, known as the *sofa*, for all the communal activities of
the family: receiving guests, eating, bouncing babies, prayer, and handiwork:
just as it is still done in village homes to this day.

What especially captured your fancy in Turkish homes were their furnishings, especially the *sedir*, the traditional low benches that are set along
the window wall, as well as the projecting alcoves on the upper floors:

> *"The rooms are all spread with Persian carpets and raised at one end of
> them about two feet. This is the sofa, and is laid with a richer sort of car-
> pet, and all round it a sort of couch raised half a foot, covered with rich
> silk... Round this are placed, standing against the wall, two rows of cush-
> ions, the first very large and the next little ones, and here the Turks dis-
> play their greatest magnificence... These seats are so convenient and easy
> that I believe I shall never endure chairs as long as I live."*

Indeed, to tuck your legs under you on the low bench of a *sedir* amidst
the joyous burst of color of the kilim cushions, surrounded by chattering
friends drinking tea or to snuggle in the cocoon of a window alcove to
watch the streetscape below are two of the small and perfect samples of
pleasurable life to be experienced in Turkey.

Those restored Ottoman mansions are indeed very impressive, but my
favorite homes in Turkey are the more simple and modest ones, the ones
where I have had the honor of being a guest. Turkish homes are havens of

peace, foyers of family joy, and the bricks of the whole society. The interiors of Turkish houses are always light and airy, comfortable and friendly. They can be furnished with the lavish baroque-style overstuffed furniture that modern urban Turks seem to favor, or they can be outfitted with simple, kilim-covered *sedir* low banquettes. No matter what the taste in furniture, the common bond in both modern and traditional homes will be the presence of magnificent carpets. The Turks never seem to wander far from their nomadic origins, and these carpets, whether they are machine-made or hand-woven, will always be spectacular examples. Furthermore, in every home, no matter its station, there will be flowers: in a plastic bouquet on a side table, in window boxes, outside the entry door planted in olive oil cans, on curtains, on rugs, in pictures, on teapots, or in those little alcove arches you mentioned, Lady Mary. Inside of homes, flowers become the symbol of life and God's goodness, His joyful gift of surprising color and sweet smell, nourished by the rains of His heaven, and blossoming like the family that takes root in the blessed soil of the Turkish home.

Above all, every home, from castle to village cabin, will be spotlessly clean. In contrast to the muddy streets outside and as an antithesis to their chaos, Turkish homes are immaculate and pristine. You are perfectly right, Lady Mary, when you state, *"'Tis true, they are not at all solicitous to beautify the outsides of their houses..."* It never fails to amaze me that no matter how plain and decrepit the outside of the building appears, no matter how mucky, noisy, or aggressive is the street running in front of it, once you step into a Turkish home, there is a sense of peace in a place where order and spotless cleanliness reigns. No one may enter a Turkish home without first removing his street shoes so that none of the grime of that grubby street can penetrate this sanctum of purity. You noted this as well Lady Mary: *"The houses of the great Turkish ladies are kept clean with as much nicety as those in Holland."*

But there are two homes I have visited in Turkey which stand out in my mind. I have already spoken to you about what it is like to be taken into a Turkish home and be adopted by a family. And every time you enter a Turkish home, no matter how short the visit, it is as if you are being adopted in some way by the family. Such was the case in the village of Yörük Köyü near Safranbolu, a village of breathtaking beauty and a living museum stage-set of fine eighteenth-century Ottoman wooden homes. I spent the afternoon peeling hazelnuts in the courtyard of one of these huge homes in the company of the head of the household. Later on, he invited us inside for tea. This immense traditional Ottoman home, built to house four extended families, had been since transformed for more Republican tastes: there was a "*tuvalet ala franga*" (western-style toilet) and a deep freezer chest sat with pride in the middle of the *sofa* space. The owner's very aged mother observed all from her perch in the alcove window seat, sitting to catch the cool breezes, contemplating the beauty of the surrounding countryside, and following the conversations amongst us. Right before sunset, I accompanied the daughter of the family to the nearby pasture to drive the cows home to store them in the courtyard of the house, the *hayat*. This word *hayat* means "life," and it comprises a ground-floor paved yard, ventilated by wooden lattices. Keeping livestock and baskets of peeled hazelnuts close to the "life" of the home, the people sleeping above it, seemed all too familiar and normal for this Midwesterner.

The second home that particularly impressed me consisted of one room. It belonged to the custodian of the Şeyh Turesan Dervish lodge outside of Kayseri, which was built for the confraternity of this holy man active in the area in the thirteenth century. The dervish lodge is a mystic place set on a dramatic windswept mountaintop, overlooking the vast and dusty plain where the soldiers of Tancred stormed forth to the Holy Land on the First Crusade in 1097. It is perhaps the beauty of the countryside, the isolated quietude, the onus of history and the legend of the dervish himself that all joined to confer to this spot a rare spirituality. After visiting the dervish lodge, I was invited into the caretaker's home for tea. As his wife bustled about to prepare it, I observed the single room which constituted the home. It was very large, decorated simply with turquoise carpeting the color of Seljuk tiles, whitewashed walls, and kilim cushions propped against the walls. There were no pictures to clutter the walls, no blaring radio or television, and no freestanding furniture except for the potbellied heating stove in the middle of the room. There was a silence so total that I could hear the echoed memory of the Crusader's sighs carried from the plain below in the rustling of the wind in the trees, the clank of their armor in the chatter of birds, and the resonance of their beating drums in the faint buzzing of the bees from the nearby hives. There was not one piece of lint on that carpet, not one shadow of a stain on it or on the walls. All emphasis in this room was put on the people who animated it and on the conversations shared.

It is certain that I was the first foreigner ever to step foot in that room, and I was treated no less royally than the victorious Seljuk Sultan Kılıç Arslan himself. The mistress of the house came in with her tray laden with tea and fresh fruit and knelt with grace and solemnity to place it on the floor in front of us. She shyly smiled at me and poured it with the same innate and natural elegance of any well-bred Thoresby lady, I can assure you. In this way you can see, Lady Mary, how a one-room Turkish home can be as rich as a castle of 275 rooms or the palace of a Grand Signor, and how it is in their homes that Turks can display their greatest magnificence.

Sincerely yours,
Kadriye Branning

Home of the keeper of the
Şeyh Turesan Zaviye

Dining on a sedir, Pandeli's
Restaurant, Istanbul

Ottoman home interior, Safranbolu

Old wooden house, Üsküdar

*Communication in the days
before pocket phones*

A lone holdout, Beşiktaş

Ottoman home interior, Safranbolu

Süleymaniye neighborhood, Istanbul

A home above a Seljuk tomb, Tokat

Old wooden houses, Üsküdar

LETTER 19

A right notion of life

D ear Lady Mary,
Exciting and momentous events always seem to be happening in
Turkey, no matter what the period of history, but little did you
realize that you were lucky enough to live there in one of its most famous
eras. This period is named after that bright, dagger-petalled flower that
grows wild in the forests of Turkey and which has hence become its unoffi-
cial symbol: the tulip.

Indeed, the "Tulip Era" of Ahmet III is considered one of the most
important phases of artistic creation of the entire Ottoman Empire. It was
perhaps not as spectacular as the eras fostered by the great court-sponsored
art workshops of Sultans Süleyman the Magnificent, Selim II, and Murat
III, but then again, few ages of the world's artistic heritage could compare
with those blockbuster years. Ahmet's period was noteworthy more for its
frivolity than for its ground-breaking cultural advances. "Tulip Time" was a
fun time. After more than four centuries of war, conquest, and defeat, the
Ottomans suddenly decided to take a break and enjoy a period of pure pleasure, and the "Tulip Era" of Ahmet III thus became a time of peace, lavish
entertainment, and literary creativity. This period started the month you
left Turkey, stimulated by the signing of the Treaty of Passarowitz in July,
1718, which concluded the war with Austria whose end your husband tried
so hard, albeit unsuccessfully, to negotiate.

It would appear that the tulip reigned more powerfully than the sultan
during this period of about 12 years. This turban-headed flower became
the symbol of the sensuality of the creative arts and a notion of carefree,
joyful life raised to a level of art. There were music festivals, great parades

in the Hippodrome, dances, outdoor excursions, pleasure gardens, and trips down the blissful Bosphorus. Not only were tulips planted in every garden all over the city, but they also sprang to life on embroideries, ceramics, and miniatures.

Besides the appearance of tulips in gardens and artwork, the Tulip Age pioneered new direction and dimensions to the Ottoman society. It was the period in which relations with Europe intensified. Impetus was conferred to science and intellectual exploration with the creation of libraries, the commissioning of translations, and the arrival of the first printing press for the publication of books into Turkish. Ibrahim Pasha, Ahmed III's son-in-law and grand vizier, became a very influential person in the Empire, for he sent a diplomatic and cultural mission to France to observe their modes of civilization, art, education, engineering, and technology. This mission led to a vibrant exchange of goods between Europe and the Ottoman Empire, such as fashions, porcelain, and clocks as well as the introduction of novel ideas, just as is happening once again in today's Turkey.

Ahmet III was a big builder as well, accenting the city with his magnificent fountain outside the entrance to the Topkapı Palace in 1728. What a shame you left before it was built and were never able to see it, Lady Mary! I think of you every time I pass in front of it. He also built the spectacular fountain on the quay at Üsküdar. Ibrahim Pasha, named grand vizier the month after you left, used his power to build two fountains at the mosques in Şehzadebaşı and Ortaköy. Once again, all were unfortunately built after your departure. You were, however, witness to the building boom of Bosphorus waterside wooden palaces, known as *yalı*, which began at this time. You wrote to the Abbé Conti that "*Nothing can be pleasanter than the canal, and the Turks are so well-acquainted with its beauties, all their pleasure seats are built on its banks... there are near one another some hundreds of magnificent palaces.*" Soon after you left, in 1721, Ahmet III built his famous pleasure palace, the Sa'dabad, or "Abode of Felicity" in the Kağıthane meadows near Eyüp. The river stream was diverted to fill the marble canals, copied from the engravings of Versailles brought back to him from that cultural mission to France.

The spirit of this entire era was captured in the famous paintings by the court artist Levni of the circumcision celebrations of Ahmet's sons and in the verses of the poet Nedim: "*Let us have fun, let us all dance and play, for it is tulip time!*" But alas, this period of insouciance and indulgence, of too many parties and prancing and not enough bread and salt, led to an uprising by the common people, and your sultan Ahmet III was toppled, bringing the Tulip Age to an abrupt end in 1730.

Even though you did not witness the heyday of the Tulip Era, you certainly did observe first-hand how much the Turks instinctively incorporate a hefty dose of pleasure into their lives. For I can tell you that it was not just in your day that Turks *"had fun, danced and played"*: they do it everyday and in every way. Turks live for what I call the four F's: family, friends, food, and fine settings, in any combination or arrangement. They have perfected the skill of having a good time to a high art: they even have a word for this semi-official national sport of achieving a state of bliss: *Keyif.* Despite all of the problems and difficulties they face in their daily lives and a fascination with the tragic, Turks manage to maintain an outlook of constant cheer and high spirits. This is a culture where a positive attitude triumphs over suffering and negativity. It is hard not to have a good time when you are in the midst of Turks, whether it be drinking tea, barbecuing lamb chops, flirting, sniffing roses, listening to a saz player, or dancing in a seaside discotheque or at a village wedding. You smile more when you are with a Turk. You laugh more. You have downright fun. As you state to the Abbé Conti:

> *"Thus, you see, sir, these people are not as unpolish'd as we represent them. Tis true their magnificence is of a different taste from ours, and perhaps of a better. I am almost of the opinion that they have a right notion of life; while they consume it in music, gardens, wine and delicate eating, we are tormenting our brains with some scheme of politics or studying some science to which we can never attain, or if we do, cannot persuade people to set that value upon it we do our selves... I allow you to laugh at me for the sensual declaration that I had rather be a rich Effendi with all his ignorance, than Sir Isaac Newton with all his knowledge."*

This right notion of life starts with the mundane everyday tasks of life, which are somehow elevated to a degree above the routine. Whether it is a simple kindness, a word, or a gesture of sweetness, no aspect of life is considered too humdrum to deny enhancement. Street life and market places offer a full array of merriment and surprises at every turn, all destined to tempt your senses. They can take form, for example, in the extravagant displays of foodstuffs in the market places, where a simple vegetable vendor becomes a visual performance artist deploying a great sensitivity to shapes and colors as he stacks his goods, pulling a rabbit out of his hat at the end of his performance by cutting up a juicy-fleshed fruit and putting it on top of his elaborately-constructed pyramid. Jewelry dealers pay just as much attention to their wares, stringing along rows and rows of bangle bracelets of different tones of golds, all radiating their heat under the bright lights like dancing sunflowers in the Anatolian sun. In the make-shift shops and stands in the bazaar or on the street, the same attention is shown to the display of merchandise, no matter how plain the product. A mere layout of screwdrivers becomes a Jackson Pollack explosion of shape and color. The wide and weird array of merchandise becomes a circus sideshow, with hats, gloves, fans, vegetable peelers, underwear, lighters, old picture postcards of flowers, locks, nail polish, imitation perfumes, pink plastic pans, kettles, bright yellow and pink blocks of soap, underwear, fake designer shoes and handbags, brooms, and dustpans, all laid out with meticulous attention and joining together in a riotous parade of colors. Not to be forgotten in all of this are the street urchins or down-and-outters who sell their individual kleenex packs, pairs of socks, or single cigarettes with the flourish and flair of a Parisian department store clerk.

Deeds above the mundane include such attentive gestures as the bootblack who whisks out a white cloth like a magician on stage to cover your socks to protect them from the polish. It can be the scaffolding of colored towels drying outside barber shops, fluttering in the breeze like dress burgees on a ship. It is seen in the consideration paid to the wrapping of packages in paper or string, no matter how inexpensive the goods, from feminine needs to alcohol to diapers, just to ensure a bit of discretion between you and the eyes on the street. It is the sweet lemon cologne sprinkled in your hands when you arrive in an office or when you leave a restaurant.

Their manner of doing business is courteous and dignified: the simple pleasure of buying something becomes an adventure, a way to get to know people, to share, and to learn. When you enter into negotiations to purchase an item, glasses of tea appear, signaling that not only will business be done, but a relationship will be formed. Shops are never locked, and if the shopkeeper does go out to grab a bite to eat, he puts a chair in the entryway to signal that he is gone, and no one would think of breaching the threshold until it is removed. And although it becomes oppressive at times, the omnipresent music blasting from shops is a way of adding optimistic vitality to the streetscape. Hotel life is much the same, with no area too small to miss an opportunity to make a fuss or to shower attention. Touches of sweetness are everywhere: the bows and scrapes accorded as if you were a United Nations diplomat passing, doors held open with a smile and a wink, sliced carrot coins placed atop the feta cheese slices that peer up at you like little smiley faces to greet your morning with cheer, and the plastic rose tucked into the lapel of your terry bathrobe to make you feel like you have a secret admirer.

Another refinement that appears on the street is the art of prominence of site. The Turks site their homes, mosques, and monuments with exacting science and have an instinctive sense about how to best position their monuments for dramatic and strategic effect. In the solitude of the mosques of Murad I or Yıldırım Bayezit atop their aeries in Bursa, the wind in the trees plays an eternal hymn to the tragic destiny of these two sultans. Unforgettable as well are the Ottoman homes scrambling up the hill at Safranbolu, like chessboard pieces set in harmony so as to preserve the view of their neighbors.

One of the most joyous refinements of the Turks, in my eyes, is their love of eating outside. It can be a fancy restaurant rooftop terrace, a tea garden in a park in the center of town, an impromptu picnic near a fountain or a fast-running stream, an alfresco supper on an apartment porch or a stop alongside the road under a huge tree to eat a peach: these people know that fresh air enhances the flavor of food like a fine wine. I grew up with much of the same love of eating outside, with my father organizing picnics in the middle of winter snowfalls, cookout breakfasts in parks, excursions with saltshaker in hand to tomato fields in bloom, and festive picnics with the family in forest glens. For this reason, I always associate eating outside with spontaneity, joy, and fraternity. And so, when I discovered this people, who so enjoy eating food *al fresco*, I felt right at home. Turks have a love of summer picnics in orchards, in gardens, in national parks, in their beloved high meadows (*yayla*), under trees, and in any spot of natural beauty. Their repasts can be very leisurely and simple with fresh fruit, honey and bread, or the more elaborate barbecue of grilled meat. An amusing custom is the "eat it as you cook it yourself" that is found in many restaurants and roadside stops, where a portable grill is brought to your table, leaving you in charge of grilling your meat or fish just to your taste. As much as they love eating outdoors, Turks do not favor sidewalk cafés, as they find the city street to be too unclean.

In a letter to Alexander Pope from Edirne you speak of this love of gardens of "*tall cypress trees filled with turtledoves*":

> "*The whole ground is laid out in gardens, and the banks of rivers set with rows of fruit trees, under which all the most considerable Turks divert themselves every evening, not with walking, that is not one of their pleasures, but a set party of them choose out a green spot where the shade is very thick and there they spread a carpet on which they sit drinking their coffee...*"

And in no better place does the consummation of "*music, gardens, wine and delicate eating*" you mention take place than in the *yaylas*, the summer mountain plateaus that are veritable national shrines to the Turks. These highland pastures are the Elysian fields of the collective subconscious of the Turks, who design their carpets to resemble the many colors of their flower-bespangled meadows. The tradition of transhumance is in the blood of these descendants of the Central Asian Turkomen, who came to Anatolia starting in the eleventh century. Their survival depended on the constant search for fresh pastures for their goats and sheep according to the season of the year. Although this traditional way of life is no longer practiced for the majority of Turks, it still lives on in their souls. With every spring, the hearts of Turks turn to the cool beauty of these mountain pastures, and they head to the hills to enjoy relaxation and community with nature. Their gushing streams, white afternoon mists, and bleating sheep become some of the famous heroes that shine in their folk ballads. Turkish children run free in the grass, climb trees and rocks, and families gather at night in the small huts that are constructed as summertime shelters. The foods they eat here are as fresh as the air of the warm days and cool nights: butter, cheese, milk, bread, and yogurt. Whether the *yaylas* are located in the Black Sea region, in the Toros or Kaçkar mountains, or on the skirt of Mt. Erciyes is not important. What is important is to feel free, to share food with family, to live nature in harmony with the seasons, to live a sense of adventure and, above all, to be liberated from time.

Although you did not get to enjoy a visit to a *yayla*, you did savor the intoxication of Turkish weather and nature:

> "*The climate is delightful in the extremist degree. I am now sitting, this present 4th of January, with the windows open, enjoying the warm shine of the sun... and my chamber is set out with carnations, roses and jonquils from my garden.*"

It would be so enjoyable to sit down with you, Lady Mary, on a spread carpet in the waterfront garden of one of those "*hundreds of magnificent palaces*" or on a *yayla*, to partake of some "*chosen conversation with one esteemed,*" to recite aloud some of those verses your tutor Achmed taught you, and to eat fresh peaches and drink tea together. We could laugh and enjoy high-spirited merriment just like the Turks do every moment of their day. We would put Sir Isaac Newton and his laws of motion aside, and we would "*have fun, dance and play*" just like Nedim. We could become friends in the way that friendship often so sweetly and gently unfolds in such instances in Turkey. That is refinement, indeed, and the right notion of life.

Sincerely,
Kadriye Branning

Terrace set for dinner under the plane trees, Beyşehir

"Kendin pişir kendin ye": as you grill,
so shall you eat, Fethiye

Fire-fighting tools
at the ready, Edirne

Drugstore wrapping paper, Bursa

Potatoes, Beşiktaş Market

Eggplants for sale, Hatuniye Market, Konya

A nature morte of peppers, tomatoes and spring water bottles, Tatvan

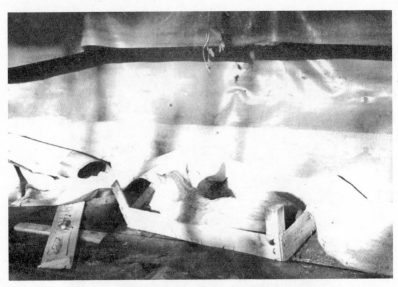

Kitty Keyif: a market day snooze

Tools for sale, Istanbul

Tools for sale, Istanbul

Klee-colored wares, Kadırga

Afşin

*Summer squash for sale,
Hatuniye Market, Konya*

Street scene, Konya

Kitty Keyif, Sahaflar Bazaar, Istanbul

Fountain of Sultan Ahmet III, 1728

LETTER 20

I was hungry

Dear Lady Mary,
There is perhaps only one area where I differ with you in your appreciation of Turkish culture. In the letter describing your dinner with the Grand Vizier's Lady, you lament:

> *"She entertained me with all kind of civility, till dinner came in, which was served, one dish at a time, to a vast number... I am a good judge of their eating, having lived three weeks in the house of an effendi at Belgrade, who gave us very magnificent dinners, dressed by his own cooks which the first week pleased me extremely but, I own I then began to grow weary of it and desired our own cook might add a dish or two after our manner..."*

Oh, Lady Mary, bring those vast number of dishes unto me, should you not want them! Contrary to you, I never weary of the wide variety of foods available in Turkey. I will admit, though, that I have heard others express this same sentiment as you do concerning the alleged monotony of Turkish fare. Once in Antalya I met an Atlanta peach of a lady, a Southern belle from the tips of her frosted locks to the tips of her manicured nails. In her accent thick as sweet tea, she bemoaned, *"Tomaters, tomaters, tomaters! I am just sick of 'em! They eat 'em at breakfast, they eat 'em at lunch, they eat 'em at dinner; everything you get here has tomaters in it! I just can't wait to get home to get me some good ole gravy and grits!"* I was not going to try to convince her that, quite frankly, my idea of paradise is a place where you *can* eat tomatoes from morning to night, so I let it pass. Despite them tomaters (or because of them), I consider Turkish cookery to be a veritable cuisine and one of the most elevated of the refinements of the country. In this letter I do not want to convince you otherwise about your unenthusiastic reception of Turkish food. I do not want to go on and on about the savors of the table in Turkey or describe the taste of every dish: that I will leave to fanatical food writers. I just want to share with you some of my personal joys with the dishes I have appreciated along the way.

Turkish food is like the Turks themselves: direct, uncomplicated, straightforward, savory, and bountiful. Just as Turks have faces that are immediately readable, so it is with their cuisine. There are no hidden agendas, secret ingredients, *tour de mains,* or elaborate reduced sauces in this food. It is bold and direct, and you know exactly what has gone into its making. Yet simple does not mean boring, for these dishes are some of the tastiest I have ever enjoyed – and I consider myself well-versed in the joys of the cuisine reputed to be the finest in the world, that of France, to be able to make such a comparison.

Now it *is* true that you must enjoy lamb, and lots of it, to appreciate this cuisine, for that is the coin of the realm: pork is forbidden and beef is not common in every region. Yet failing that, farm-fresh chicken and a sea-fresh fish from the three different seas that surround Turkey – the Black, the Aegean, and the Mediterranean – await you at every turn.

Even though Turkey is a country of heavy meat eaters, life can be a paradise for those who do not eat meat, and this is where I find the greatest joy in the Turkish table. I know of no other country that is so accommodating to those who choose not to eat meat. The cornucopia of fruits and vegetables is unparalleled, even in France. The tradition of cooking vegetables in olive oil and serving them up as starter dishes can transport any vegetarian from earth to heaven. It is humorously said that a Turkish man can divorce his wife should she serve him eggplant in the same way twice in one month – such is the imaginative variety of their vegetable styles.

Personally, it is perhaps because I enjoy modest, uncomplicated fare that I find so much to appreciate here. I eat simply: the humble dish of rice pilaf with chickpeas and a dollop of full-fat yogurt on the side, served with loving relish even in the most unpretentious truck stops, is one of my most favorite meals on earth. Ayran, the yogurt drink that is the beverage of choice with most meals, reminds me of the pitchers of buttermilk I drank as a child at our Midwestern dinner table. And what would be my second favorite meal in Turkey? A perfect, fuzzy peach, round as a baseball. You have never tasted what was intended to be a peach in nature until you have had one in Turkey. Flawlessly ripe, of flesh both soft and firm at the same time, bursting with sugar that smarts the tongue, and juices that squirt to cover every taste bud of your mouth.

In contrast to very simple fare, one can also find the remnants of the sophisticated cuisine of the kitchens of the Topkapı Palace, as refined as the Sultan for whom it was prepared. Notable food historians are documenting these dishes and their preparation so that they will not be lost, and it is certain that the less-complicated versions of these dishes that have filtered down to the Turkish kitchens of today provide the same level of enjoyment to the ten million households in Republican Turkey as they did to the courts during your time in Ottoman Turkey.

Everything is fresh in this country of Turkey, picked so that you can still feel the warmth of the tree in the apricots and the bricks of the oven in the crust of the bread. Their food is as varied as the countryside and its people, with a wide range of pride-filled regional dishes available in every corner. This is a food of affirmative flavors, from pungent honey, pongy chive-flecked cheese, potent *pastırma* (air-dried cured beef), and tart and tangy ayran.

I have already spoken to you about the joys of the Turkish breakfast table, but Turks are perhaps at their finest around the dinner table, borne witness by their custom of *mezes*, the myriad of assorted little dishes that start off the meal. Like a small snapshot of the country, they are varied and tempting tidbits that always leave you wanting more. I enjoy the way Turks eat their *mezes* communally, with the whole table sharing from the same platter. Several *meze* dishes, sometimes up to a dozen, are placed on the table, and everyone dips in together, creating a sense of community that is instinctive and nurturing.

Turks are big eaters, and they devour food with great gusto. They highly salt their food: without tasting or thinking, some Turks will give an automatic ten shakes of the salt shaker to any dish when it is put in front of him.

Turks have a patriotic fervor. It comes out not only at the sight of their fluttering crescent flag but also at their table. I once had a Turkish friend who had never traveled out of the country, and I spent much time describing to him the richness and delights of France where I was living at the time, many of which are of course concentrated on their table. I used to dream about the meal I would cook for him, were he ever to visit me in Paris. One day I started to describe for him what pleasure it would be for me to cook for him his first French meal, and I then proceeded to describe how I would compose the menu. *"Oh, for you something special... to start, a soufflé de fromage, followed by a terrine de saumon aux épinards, and for the main course, an émincé de volaille au sauce roquefort, followed by a salad of delicate lettuces, a cheese platter, and for the grand finale dessert, a mousse au chocolat: voilà!"* I was drooling, literally, at the prospect of my menu and for the joy of cooking for him, one of the greatest signs of love I know. He got an alarmed look on his face and cried out: *"Stop this nonsense! I don't want to eat these foods! I only want Turkish foods! They are the best foods and all those other dishes just can't compare in any way!"* Such was my painful lesson that certain Turks have little curiosity about the foods of other cultures and consider their table sacred, and that... well, a man with no desire to have me cook a French meal for him was certainly not to be pursued. So it would appear that a *poulet à la crème* cannot win out over a kebab, and in this case, a love story ended over Turkish food.

It is said that the greatest natural resource of Turkey is its capacity to feed itself and that it does not need to rely on any food imports, a reserve that in the end may prove more vital than petrochemicals or coal. More than that, food allows the Turks a persuasive way to show off their famed hospitality. You described, Lady Mary, the service of dinner during your visit to Lady Hafise: *"She gave me a dinner of fifty dishes of meat, which, after their fashion, was placed on the table but one at a time...."* Even today, those dishes just keep coming out, one at a time. They are not served in portions like in Europe, but in a prolonged, drawn-out service which fosters a growing sense of community with each successive plate. When I was first received in the family home I spoke to you about in a previous letter, I believe I was treated in no less a regal fashion than Lady Hafise showed to you. In the cool of a garden pergola, I was served home-made *mantı* (baby meat dumplings, a speciality of Kayseri) and fresh-baked bread, followed by a crisp-chopped tomato and cucumber salad, along with white beans in sauce. Next appeared the main course of paper-thin lamb chops grilled with green peppers and served with a rice pilaf, accompanied by a chaser of orange soda. The desert course followed, comprised of a chocolate pudding with crushed hazelnuts and pistachios sprinkled on top. Yet it did not stop there. The table was cleared away and tea was "cooked": a huge samovar appeared along with some ten dishes of different kinds of nuts, dried fruits, and apricots. Neighbors then dropped by, and along with them, appeared huge trays of fresh fruit: melon, watermelon, grapes, a pear, and an apple on each plate for every person! Perhaps not the fifty dishes of your Lady Hafise, but I can assure you, it did not seem to be one less.

Service in restaurants is always very refined, with a sleight-of-hand magic show of switching plates and cutlery with each course change. Your napkin is always folded if you get up during the meal, chairs pulled out, crumbs dusted away, and water poured for you. They do have one custom which takes some getting used to, but once again, it is done out of concern for you. As it is considered an affront to leave an empty plate in front of someone, so you will often experience your plate being whisked away while you are finishing your last bit with fork still lifted mid-air. You often get served your many dishes all topsy-turvy, not in the order you asked, often with substitutions – and of course, sometimes dishes that you did not request, for, as I have said before, the waiter always knows what is best for you, despite what you voice as choice. When they open a bottle of wine, the cork is put immediately back in place, or even better yet, they will insert in the bottleneck a napkin folded in an elaborate fan shape. All of this does not allow the wine to breathe, and despite trying to convince them of the necessity of this, they will firmly tell you that leaving a bottle open will only invite the flies to take a sip.

France claims to have some 600 cheeses, which is fairly accurate. But not to be left behind, the Turks can claim bragging rights with the wide variety of their *köftes* (dishes made with ground meat) and *kebabs* (dishes mostly made with lamb meat). The Turks were born to skewer, stew, and grill. There are some 291 different kinds on record, of an astounding variety: meat grilled, stewed, fried, braised, roasted... or even just raw. Many köftes and kebabs are named after the region in which they are made, once again registering the pride of place felt by the Turks (İzmirli, Akçaabat, İnegöl, Tekirdağ, Harput, Tokat, Adana, Beyti). Others are named after the way they are cooked, or after their inventor (Salçalı, İçli, Mangal, Odun, Testi, Döner, and Satır from Trakya, İskender, Beyti, Cağ from Erzurum, Tandır, Ali Nazik kebab from Van), or their special ingredients (sardines:

Hamsi), or what they resemble: "Itsy Bitsy" (CızBız), "Chubby lady thighs" (Kadın Budu), or "Bird-heads" (Kuşbaşı kebab).

Finally, I have yet to resolve a linguistic issue with the Turkish language, one that involves food. Why, oh why, when expressing "I am hungry," is it always said in the past tense?

Whenever I am feeling a little tired, sad, blue, or out-of-sorts when I am home in New York, I know exactly what I must do to remedy the situation. I get out some lamb, an eggplant, an onion, and a few of those tomaters, and I get to work. The therapeutic powers of a kebab for me are legendary. As I peel that purple eggplant, I imagine I feel the hot sun of the Anatolian plains in their skins; when I fry up those chunks of lamb and chopped onions in butter until they smell wonderful, my spirits start to lift along with the heady vapors. For you see, Lady Mary, when I cook a Turkish meal, I think of the copious bounty of food to be found on the tables of Turkey, and especially of the abundance of love to be found sitting around them. I am not, never was, or ever will be, hungry in any way in Turkey.

Sincerely,
Kadriye Branning

Bakery, Kars   *Dried fruits, Samatya market, Ankara*

Istanbul bread stamp   *Diyarbakır melons*

Winter vegetables in the Ortaköy market

The famous etli ekmek of Konya

A pide lunch stop, Yeniköy

The most celebrated of the famous
Bursa İskender Kebabs

Winter vegetables in the Ortaköy market

Preserved fruits, Hacı Abdullah restaurant, Istanbul

Lamb chops, Kavak village

Fish market, Ankara

Roasted chick pea merchant, Corum

Melon men at the Beşiktaş Market

Melike Hatun produce market, Konya

Paça saloon, Afşin

BOĞAZİÇİ

Döner, Kebap ve Pide Salonu

Tel : 213 60 90
Yeni Çarşı Şadırvan Karşısı No : 29   NİĞDE

Simit peddlar, Eminönü

GÜZELYURT RESTAURANT
ERZURUM - TURKEY
TEL : 9(011)11514
FAX : 9(011)19222

Bill, Amasya Şehir Klübü

LETTER 21

The "TT"

Dear Lady Mary,

In your letters you are constantly underlining how you find the taste of the Turks to be so refined, albeit different from ours. This taste, which permeates every aspect of their lifestyle, revolves around those famous "four F's" of family, friends, food, and fine settings, and leaves none of us untouched. You certainly are right when you state that *"these people are not so unpolished as we represent them, this true their magnificence is of a different taste from ours..."* Yet there is one little particularity of Turkish culture that seems to escape the realm of this exacting refinement. It is what I call the *"Turkish Touch,"* otherwise known as the "TT."

Now there is another famous "touch" I am familiar with, called the "French Touch": it is the commitment to stylishness and excellence that the French people confer to all their products and creations from fashion to cuisine, and it has even come to mean their distinctive, graceful style of rugby playing. But the concept of the "Touch" in Turkey is something entirely different.

The "TT," as I see it, is a particular Turkish way of applying, intentionally or not, a slight imperfection to everything they do. Something is always slightly off, not meshing together as it should, or... sometimes downright wrong. Nothing major, however; you can rest assured that everything still works just fine, but there is always just a little quirk, an eccentricity, a foible, an oddity, or a mix-up, much like that idiosyncratic line or startling word in a poem that grabs your attention and makes you think a little differently about what the poet is really trying to say.

Most Turks tell me that this is not done intentionally, but yet it is on some level, for they appear to be uncomfortable when everything seems too faultless. Life is not perfect, so neither should be our surroundings. Only Allah is perfect, so we must never lose track of that, and in consequence, we must remain humble and not get too big for our boots. This is how I understand the way the TT works. It is a little prayer to the majesty of Allah.

I come from a culture that strives to be perfect in everything it does, from medical care, fashion, customer service, putting men on the moon, or making test tube babies. It is thus very easy for me to spot these TTs, as they stand out like sore thumbs when seen through my Western, exacting viewpoint. Yet I learned very quickly not to condemn them or to look down on them. I know that they have nothing to do with a lack of skill, attention, or care to the final product: any culture that can produce an architect like Sinan and other such master artisans knows the right stuff from the wrong. It is just that one must remain humble, human, and honest. We all make mistakes, remember? Well, here they are, everyday in every way, stage front for all to see to remind you of that. Such is life on our planet, in our neighborhoods, in our homes, and in our hearts.

The most classic and time-honored example of a TT can be seen in Turkish rugs, where weavers intentionally insert a very small mistake into their pattern: a jolt of conflicting color, a broken border, a little cluster of mistied knots. It is the minute reminder that we are in the material world, not in the spiritual realm of shadows and dreams.

The most blatant TTs are the incorrect and often very humorous mistranslations on signs, menus, and even in scholarly books. One would be horrified to eat some of the things that appear on menus. For example, I cite to you the English translation of the first sentence in one of the most impressive art history books I have read in any language (I will not give you the title, as to not offend the author or editor): *"The culture of the ancestors of Turks has coused the architecture to be continuous and with pains."* Now a mish-mash like that certainly dares you to carry on for the next 350 pages. After an extensive and expensive ten-year renovation of the Bayezid Pasha mosque in Amasya, the inscription panel in English is filled with egregious mistakes. Or how about this gem lifted from the official Turkish government tourist brochure from the town of Kahramanmaraş, describing the delicacy of their famous ice cream: *"Sahlep gets the milke*

harden and process of beated the ice creem provide it to become solid."
Sounds delicious.

Some of the most outlandish bloopers ironically appear in some of the most famous and fanciest of places, from the Topkapı Palace to the Hilton Hotel. In view of my past translation experience, I once asked a Turkish culture official if I could propose my services as an editor or proofreader for their state brochures and publications. You are spending an immense amount of money on these marketing products, designed to attract foreigners to your country, I argued, so it would be beneficial to have them in stylish and correct English. He just stared at me, dumbfounded, and replied, "*But you just don't understand! We Turks do not want things perfect! That is not our way!*" I tried to explain to him that his target audience did not perhaps share this viewpoint, but I could see that I had upset him and did not push it any further. Yes, Turks do not appear to want things to go perfectly, for it puts them ill at ease, just as my impertinence had done to him.

The construction world offers a glittering showcase for the TT to shine in all its splendor. The orientation of every light switch plate in Turkey is a perfect example. They are rarely plumb, and always manage to be screwed in place offset by about 10-22°. TTs can be found in the joining of tiles, which wind up either crooked or sometimes even upside down (yes, I have even seen decorative tiles with clusters of grapes hanging upwards). It is in the cracks that appear overnight in a freshly-laid marble floor or a plastered wall. It is the death-defying ski-jump incline of handicapped access ramps. It is the frightening skeleton scaffolding systems used during construction or renovation projects. It is the toilet that does not flush when you want it to, and then roars off on its own in the middle of the night, waking you up and flooding the floors and your shoes.

It is table legs never of the same length. It is the painted faux marble mihrab in lavender, baby blue, and pink in the historic Hacı Özbek Mosque in İznik or the blinding fluorescent tubes running around the one in the İplik Cami in Konya like airport landing lights. It is busses scheduled to leave at a certain hour and no one caring if two hours go by without any sign of any movement, except for the ordering of endless rounds of tea. It is Turkish Air flights of yore cancelled with no warning, with absolutely no one flustered that they just missed their connecting flight to Paris.

It is tee-shirts that shrink after one washing, with, before that, their dye that rubs off of you, turning you into a Turkish Tuareg. It is leather that smells downright feral and cheesy plastic shoes that are so rigid that they crack after one wearing. It is the mangy cur wandering around the glamorous new *Site Kulesi* shopping mall in Konya; it is the cat that moseys in and weaves around the legs of the diners in the toniest of restaurants; it is the plastic bucket placed on the grand staircase under the world's largest chandelier in the Dolmabahçe Palace to collect the dripping rain from the leaky ceiling above; it is the cow strolling into the pool area of a 5-star hotel to munch the tender greenery in the flower pots, with no one caring to chase him away from their *chaise-longue*.

Indeed, travel and hotel life are rich in TTs. It would appear normal to have TTs pop up in the tiny, modest hotels of the provinces, but surprises are often in store for you in the 5-star [*sic*] luxury establishments. TTs are found in the 5-star hotels in Anatolia where the receptionist does not speak a foreign language and where there is only one TV channel. They can be seen in hotels where all the elevators are out of order at the same time (again, with no one seeming to mind and no complaints heard), in suites furnished with luxurious Turkish towels and sheets with gaping holes. And watch out for those dangerous wrinkles in the dining room carpet that down at least one soul per day. A TT is the handwritten room number scotch-taped to the door key, a huge nail hammered in the wall to hang up the hairdryer in the locker room of an exclusive hotel spa, an elevator sign that indicates 3 when it arrives at floor 2, unrequested wake up calls at 5 a.m., dull knives and hot room refrigerators, and a mangy, crooked Christmas tree decorated with fake snow in the lobby... in July.

TTs abound on the streetscape, such as the low electric wires that run from building to building and graze your head (Kars having a particularly distinguishing record on this one), ATM machines placed so high up on the wall that even a 6-footer like myself has to stand on a stool (courteously provided, of course) to reach them, the neon blinking palm tree in city parks during snowstorms, and flower gardens planted in recycled empty olive oil cans in front of national museums.

A particular favorite TT group of mine are the fantasy maps that are handed out at local tourist offices. Lovingly hand-drawn, they are absurdly illegible and oftentimes downright backwards, making your discovery of the city an Alice in Wonderland experience. When I was once handed one of these murky maps in a tourist office in Bursa, I emboldened myself to ask the clerk if he perhaps had a better one to tuck into my bag to help me find my way on the street? The clerk's face brightened, and he disappeared in a scurry of excitement. He came back a few minutes later, struggling to carry a heavy 5x7 foot framed cadastral map that he had removed from the wall in the Director's office. Plopping it in front of me with a weighty thud, he said, "*Could this possibly be of help?*"

But a TT can be a tender and sweet attention, too. It is the plastic flowers with dainty resin dew drops glued on them in the vases of *pide* joints trying to pass for the Sultan's table, spoons and forks lovingly wrapped up in paper napkins tied in a bow, posters of the Swiss Alps in restaurants in the middle of dusty plains, watermelons carved to look like graceful swans, and in the blue flowered bathroom tiles decorating the inside of the Siirt Ulu Cami.

Or a TT can be incongruous and astonishing, such as the muezzin's call heard at 4:09 one morning in Kars, giving way to a mesmerizing atonal fugue that haunts me to this day, or the majestic marble sidewalks lining the streets of the dusty farm town of Afyon.

I have learned that these imperfections give breathing life to the objects and to the world around us, and I have come to share a fondness for them, just like the Turks do. They have taught me to be less fussy, finicky, and critical. When I see a TT, I often smile, as they can sometimes be quite comical. Yet they always warm my heart because behind them I feel the hand of a very human person, in this case, a Turk who knows his place in the cosmic order of things. And they teach me not to take myself so seriously, for you know what? No one is perfect... except for our Almighty in heaven.

Sincerely,

Kadriye Branning

Pide restaurant, Silvan

Poolside in a luxury hotel

Dolmabahçe Palace   Restoration work, Konya

Kastamonu   Kastamonu

Clear the way

Handicapped ramp

Merry Christmas in July

Kars

BEYAZIT PAŞA CAMİİ

Künç Köprünün kuzeydoğusundadır Çelebi Mehmet Devrinde Amasya Valisi Beyazıt Paşa tarafından 1414 yılında yaptırılmıştır.

Ters T plan şemasına sahip Zaviyeli camilerdendir Son cemaat mahallindeki kemer erdeki şlemeler ve geometrik süslemeler ilgi çekmektedir.

BEYAZIT PAŞA MOSQE

it is placed northeast of the Künç bridge. At the reign of the Çelebi Mehmet it had made in 1414 by the Amasya governer.

It has one of the mosque that reverse T shape corner. The archs, which are placed last ommunity, draw attension because of the geometric adonns and handworks.

Adonns and handworks

LETTER 22

A carpet of 70,000,000 knots

Dear Lady Mary,

How I would love to take an afternoon boat ride up the Bosphorus together with you for a picnic excursion! We could get out at one point along its banks, spread out a Turkish carpet to sit on, and enjoy tea, pastries, sweet watermelon, the view, and lively conversation. Actually, we really don't need a boat or the Bosphorus to create a setting of delight: anywhere you spread out a Turkish carpet becomes a mini-meadow of pleasure.

In your letters, you provide us with many details concerning the daily life of the times, such as fashions, furniture, jewels, food, customs, dance, and music. This attention to detail has placed you as one of the leading recorders of the material culture of eighteenth-century Turkish court life. Your sensitivity to fashion was particularly acute: you describe the tunics worn by the Sultan on his way to the mosque, the harem chief's elaborate costume, the trappings of the retinue of guards, and of course, all the gowns worn by the court ladies you visited. Although you are not what we would call today an ethnographer in the purest sense, you certainly did pave the way for them by realizing that no detail of daily life is too small to pass unwarranted. You looked carefully, you listened, you noted. Your eye to minute details illuminated a broader picture.

You made fewer comments about architecture and the arts than you did about fashions. Perhaps because I am an artist myself, these are the things that I notice first whenever I walk down the street, enter a room, or travel. However, when you did provide details about art objects, your eye was as sharp as ever. Relating your dinner with Lady Hafise, you described the napkins of thin gauze embroidered with gold flowers: "*... It was with the utmost regret that I made use of these costly napkins, as finely wrought as the finest handkerchiefs that ever came out of this country.*" You went on to describe the china bowls with solid gold covers, gold knives with hafts set in diamonds, and a golden wash basin and embroidered towels. In one of your final letters, you describe the Bosphorus *yalı*s and their decoration of:

> "*white pavements, roofs gilt and walls covered with japan china, wainscots of mother of pearl fastened with emeralds like nails, and the whole adorned with a profusion of marble, porcelain dishes of frit of all sorts, colored plaster, jars of flowers, windows sashed with the finest of crystalline glass and the most exquisite painting of fruits and flowers.*"

Architecture, too, is the subject of one of your most vivid letters, the one in which you describe your visit to the Selimiye mosque in Edirne, built for Sultan Selim II by the famous architect Sinan in 1569. You were right to say that this "*building is very well worth the curiosity of a traveller,*" as it is indeed considered Sinan's masterpiece. Dressed in Turkish clothes in order to discretely gain entry, you illustrate it in such detail that subsequent depictions by modern architectural historians are put to shame. Not one feature escapes your attention in this long letter, from the courtyard, the domes, the portico with its antique verdigris marble pillars, the high proportions made possible by the single dome, the marble balustrades, the Persian carpets, the "*great pulpit of carved wood gilt,*" the sultan's private gallery for worship, the thick white candlesticks, and the "*four high towers*" (minarets) outside (which you had the curiosity to climb!). Many today would agree with your opinion that: "*It is the noblest building I ever saw.*" I especially enjoyed your delight at its decoration: "*The walls seemed to me inlaid with such very lively colours in small flowers, I could not imagine what stones had been made use of, but, going nearer, I saw they were crusted with japan china which has a very beautiful effect.*" I am charmed by the fact that you mistook the thick, raised glazes on İznik tiles for stones, and am impressed that you could discern the Asian influence in them.

Your portrayals of the Selimiye and the *yalı* are so specific and vivid that I see them as clearly as if I were standing there myself and are more evocative than any photograph. That said, the fact that you make little mention of carpets surprises me. Was it because Turkish carpets were already so familiar to you that you felt they needed no describing? The great hall carpets of the sixteenth century, those gigantic room-size pieces woven in the court workshops of Sultans Süleyman I, Selim II, and Murat III, had long made their way to England to grace the finest manors of the land. Certainly there must have been one at your ancestral home of Thoresby Hall. Although those workshop carpets are magnificent, I confess that I prefer the smaller rugs, like the one we would take with us to sit on for our Bosphorus tea party: the carpets made by one pair of hands, those of a woman weaver alone in front of her loom.

Turks produce some of the finest carpets in the world, and rare is the visitor who returns from a trip to Turkey without one tucked in his suitcase. Yet for a Turk, a carpet is more than a pretty thing to put on the floor: it is a piece of art.

When we refer to "art" in the Western world, we think of the baskets of fruit, naked ladies, and landscapes that hang on the walls of museums or the paintings which are fervently collected for millions on a raging art market. We think of snooty, high-brow art collectors, intellectuals of the aesthete, or artist pop stars like Picasso or Matisse. The average Westerner also carries with him the connotations of art as urban, religious, abstract, intellectual, male-dominated, upper-class, and generally pertaining to the medium of oil on canvas.

However, perceptions are different in Turkey. Turks have a concept of art meaning something done with a high level of craftsmanship and careful attention paid to detail. The emphasis on technical proficiency and discipline is as important as inspiration and intuition. Art is for every man, the common man, the villager as well as the urban dweller. Turks are a practical people, so their arts are practical too. They work with the materials that surround them in their world: walnut from the northern forests, marble from the quarries near Afyon, handspun wool from live sheep, vegetable and herb dyes, and solid clays. There is no room for frippery in the art objects of Turkey: use is the ruling factor, and the object must be above all practical rather than merely decorative. Turks produce three-dimensional objects, articles made by hard-working hands with tools and needles, in front of fires and looms. Handicrafts form the basis of their art and include such media as calligraphy, mother-of-pearl, *ebru* (marbled paper), weaving, leather-working to form coats and saddles, *oya* (edging embroidery), felt-making, knitting, quilting, ceramics, coppersmithing, basket making, and woodworking. Turks make houses of wood and rock filled with panels of tiles, they weave garments and home furnishings, they turn out glass beads to wear or to decorate their animal trappings, and they carve wooden spoons to eat their delicious stews and soups. Decorative elements are chosen either from the natural world, most often their beloved flowers and birds, or from the more intellectual and mathematical symbolism of geometry.

Turks have strong feelings about their country, their families, their faith... and their crafts. They believe that mastery and skill are the central components of art. They cherish the religious and historical importance of the decorative ornamentation they use. Turks also try to connect a sense of sacredness to their art by making it as beautiful and as perfect as humanly possible, for being skillful is praise to God. They are bold and frank in their work. Much like their food, their art is direct and no-nonsense – formed by their heritage, religion, and regional cultures, a heritage so important that they are pleased to reproduce it over and over again. The objective of the Turkish artist is actually quite straightforward: the artist wishes to create a useful object of beauty, using the utmost level of skill with a desire to execute an object that will reflect his love of God and his family and that will be of service to his fellow man. It is as simple as that.

Why did the Turks choose carpets, the French food and fashion, the Americans music, the Italians cinema, and the British gardens in which to express their cultural identity? Who can say, but art is an expression of man's existence and it unfolds differently to each culture: it is an expression of the material culture of the era in which it was created, a reflection of a specific time, place, and culture as well as the vision of its creator. You can discover much about Turkey by looking at the objects they make. In those frustrating moments when I think I will never understand their spoken language, the language that is articulated to me by their artifacts, notably carpets, is completely comprehensible and brings me closer to these people.

I admire their art which combines a respect for tradition at the same time it seeks to change and grow. The Turkish way of seamlessly combining the old and new in their daily lives has always made me feel comfortable when I am there. Roman ruins mix with Seljuk medreses and Byzantine walls and Ottoman fountains, gardens and roses bloom alongside concrete walls, highways hurl past ancient bridges and aqueducts. It is a mix where the bustle of streets belies the calm of the interiors of homes, and places of commerce and religious shrines lie cheek-to-jowl. There is room here for separate artistic voices to be heard and respected, just like you hear at prayer time, where the difference of a split second at the start of each muezzin's call and the variation of pitch in each song combine to create a different riff on the same line, echoing the varied cries of the gulls you hear chattering over the Eminönü sky.

This respect of the old and the new also applies to their handicrafts. Crafts comprise "their" art: the beaux-arts schools of sculpture and painting we know in the West have not traditionally played a major role in their artistic expression. They hold in great esteem people who turn wood, plait baskets, and knot wool. There is no separation between art and craft here, because craft *is* art. This confidence in their role as artists in the full sense of the term is one of the strongest pulls that Turkey exerts on me personally as a craft artist myself.

The power struggle of art vs. craft has raged in the West for the past 30 years and is only now starting to subside. "Art" has traditionally been defined as objects conceived exclusively for aesthetic contemplation, whereas "craft" is considered an object primarily defined by its utilitarian function. Art historians and scholars have long debated these differences and have managed to find a comfortable ground: the many art museums dedicated to traditional arts founded in the West in the last 20 years attest to this. Yet traces of segregation remain. As a glass artist, I must use my hands to speak strongly and competently, and when I gaze upon an object made by a Turkish artist, I can feel his strong hands there too. That is why, perhaps, I was drawn to Turkey: it is a land full of competent craftsmen artists. Turkish artisans know that the excellence of art lies in the fusion of use and beauty. If an object is made with talent, skill, dedication, and love, it becomes "art." Period.

When I make a glass vase or goblet, I have the chance to express creativity, hard work, and skill. The Turks think this way too. Their objects are wrought with intention and love, and that is what differentiates them from mass-products. An eye balances it, and a hand touches it. It contains that spark of individual will and spirit, and yes, in some cases, a very distinct TT. Turks believe that art should accompany the everyday gestures of pouring water, toting vegetables, and stirring pots; in doing so, their art ennobles these acts of everyday daily life and fills them with dignity, beauty, and grace.

In the end, "object" artists share the same quest as fine artists. We explore creativity, we invest ourselves in our art by developing our skills, we are curious, we push beyond the status quo to dare and to dream, we try to learn from our work, we believe that the process is more important than the product, and we try to understand the "deep art" within us and heed our internal third eye. I see the shadow of all of these quests when I look at a Turkish rug or a wooden spoon. In each eye-catching flower on an Iznik plate, I feel the love of nature and its colorful confusion that is shared by all Turks. With each upward stroke of calligraphy, I feel a heart lifting to Allah. In each knot, I see the face of a Turkish woman and feel her warmth and joy for life.

Oh yes, those knots! Of all the Turkish arts, I am especially attracted to those colorful carpets. Like those golden stones I spoke to you about earlier, their knots speak to me as powerfully as words. As I said to you at the beginning of this letter, Lady Mary, I have a special affection for small village and nomadic rugs, the ones we would take with us to sit on along the Bosphorus for our picnic. I am not talking here about the great hall carpets of the sixteenth century, which are a totally different production than village rugs. Those were a male, court-sponsored production, highly influenced by the Persian aesthetic with weavers working from elaborate cartoons drawn by court artists. No, I am talking about what I call the "*magic carpets*": rugs produced in small villages or by nomadic tribes. The majority of the finest examples that still survive were woven from 1850 to about 1925 using natural vegetable dyes. They still shine as vividly as the day they were woven, and their colors and patterns inspire the carpets being woven today. Then and still today, all kinds of magic hands participated in their production: the hands of the men and women who raised and tended the sheep, sheared their coats, carded the wool, spindle-drop spun it into fiber, collected the herbs to make the dyes, dyed the wool, made the looms, and knotted the carpets from visual and hand memory. These utilitarian rugs were made for religious, household, or agrarian use or to tuck in dowry chests or to sell at market. Villagers carried these rugs on their backs; they ate on them and slept on and under them. They served as doors, carried salt and food, cradled babies, covered work animals, decorated tent walls, or even constituted in and of themselves the foldable walls of tent homes. Magic carpets can be knotted rugs or plain-weave kilims and embroideries, and they can take a wide range of forms according to their use. A rug is a living part of the Turkish home as much as the people who reside there.

I find these rugs instantly appealing. I am not a "carpetologist," and I do not look at them as an art historian. Rather, I look at them as an artist, and I react to these rugs on a purely visual and sensual level. When I encounter a rug, I am not down on the floor counting knots any more than I would analyze the pigment on the canvas when I look at a painting by Cezanne. These pieces of so-called mundane medium and ordinary patterns are often compelling work, surprising in their intent and symbolism, with their weavers creating pieces that are as beautiful, spiritually moving, and as intellectually nourishing as any so-called major artwork.

I have been inspired by Turkish carpets to incorporate the same design principles I find so appealing in them into my glass art. These rugs are highly-colored, with shade schemes that use pastels, primaries, and a blending of all the tones of the rainbow. Often, one hot, flashy color is chosen to stand out boldly. They are unapologetic, punchy and spontaneous, and intrepid in design and color. They are not afraid to dare with symmetry-breaking patterns and chaotic colors to the point of insolence. Their power, color, and clarity can astound you; yet in other instances, they emanate a quiet peace from the delicate soft signature in the joining of their design and color elements. Their wool is dense but pliable, which gives these rugs a sculptural aspect. I somehow feel that they are alive, perhaps because in some way the wool in them always does remain alive. Alive too, perhaps, because I can still smell the traces of nature in their mellow natural dyes, made from the plants, minerals, and animal matter of the natural world around us. Village rugs sparkle, vibrate, and sing like the flowers, sunshine, birds, animals, stars, rainbows, and fields of green that you see depicted in them. These rugs are not shy about being imperfect; in fact, they often seek to incorporate a knotting "TT" to show that they remain humble. Those apparent little imperfections of craft are the small marks of humanity in the finished piece. All these unassuming rugs ask is to be loved just as they are. For all these reasons and many other intangible ones, these rugs just make me plain happy and joyful.

My fascination with carpets stems not only from an artistic viewpoint, but also because they speak to me as a woman. It is undeniable that I am drawn to these village and nomadic rugs because they represent a woman's art. Rugs and textiles have always been predominantly the art of the feminine, blossoming far from the domination of a male viewpoint.

Rugs are self-portraits of Turkish women. It is their personal statement with private meanings, yet at the same time, they are a very public announcement towards the world. They help the weaver feel connected to her surroundings, much like the letters you write to your friends, Lady Mary. She plays with knots, just as you and I play with ideas and words. A carpet is as individual as the woman who makes it, and when I look at one, I always think of the woman behind it, for each rug has a touch as individual as the hair of her child or the skin of her husband. Is she short or tall? How many children does she have? Does she love her husband or does she argue with him? Is she pretty? What does her laughter sound like? Does she dream about the same things I do? What are her passions and her lusts? I try to guess her age by the level of her craftsmanship. Although they are unsigned and anonymous, they are very private and intimate windows onto her soul. I feel a bond with them as I can read a part of myself in these rugs along with her. Her touch and her love are there, in the same way as she gives it to the arms of her husband or to the children in her lap. I imagine I see redheads in the bright square carpets of the Western part of Turkey, brown-haired women in the muted yellow central Anatolian prayer rugs, and dark-haired ladies in the dusky saddle bags of the East.

I work in molten glass, a challenging and demanding material to master. For this reason, I can appreciate the same production challenges that confront the weaver, for knotting is a difficult art form as well. Sometimes I almost feel like I am sitting beside her at the loom. I can sense the varying strength and tension of her hand with each change of day in the squish and squash of her knots. I feel her frustrations when she got into trouble with her pattern not coming out right or when she lost track of her touchstone imaginary red focus dot 2/3 up the loom. I apprehend the same fear and hope that the piece will come out right in the end, for it takes courage to make beautiful objects, Lady Mary.

I see in these carpets the expression of a woman's viewpoint of the world, and I find there the same components of my life as a modern, Western woman: work, family, emotional life, society, and spirituality. These rugs have an inner life and story, released through the arrangement of color, the script of pattern and other "storytelling" symbols of totemic and magic significance. I find this search for expression of the hidden female world quite courageous. I wish I could meet the women behind these rugs because they possess qualities that I strive for in my life: they appear to be sharp, clever, skillful, generous, creative, patient, orderly, and industrious multitaskers. These are women I admire and would wish to have as friends.

Turks believe that our destiny is written on our foreheads, that God determines our fate preeternally and that our own will does not control the world; this, however, does not mean that there is no human free will. I believe that in these rugs, the weaver can exert freedom. She can determine how her hand, eye, and mind will come together to translate her spirit. She can choose her colors for a reason: the red of apples, her blood, her heat, the sunset? Or the blue for the sky she sees when she is happy? She chooses her border to say something via its symbols. Did she end it abruptly to express a pain? She chooses the patterns she will repeat, either an age-old design or one she invents on the fly. We can only guess these motivations. Each woman's story, her hand, and her very heart are poured into these pieces. It is as if she is saying: "*Today, on this loom, I am in control, and my decisions are mine and mine alone. My children do not belong to me, nor does my husband. But these are my knots, and this rug is my chance to connect with every other woman, by tradition, by my heritage, and by my future. It allows me to express my inner self, my hopes and aspirations, my skill, and above all, my love.*"

Those knots hold much more than twisted yarn for her; they hold her dreams as well as her reaction to life's joys, sorrows, and confusions, and the rug becomes an intense personal statement possible for all to see. I wish that it could be possible for all the women of the world to find such a creative outlet for self-expression.

Beyond their artistic beauty and the female connection that bond me to these rugs, I admire most of all how they symbolize the vibrancy and distinctiveness of the geographical regions of Turkey. Turkey is a country with a varied landscape, which is translated into these rugs. There are olive groves and cotton fields in the stout, square rugs of the Western Aegean, fields of yellow sunflowers in the prayer rugs of Central Anatolia, and the wild power of mountainscapes in the Kurdish rugs of the East. I especially appreciate the sociological link between these kaleidoscopic carpets and the country and people of Turkey that I have come to know and love over the past 30 years. Rug weaving is as old as mankind, and the country of Turkey is comprised of rich layers of cultures going back 10,000 years. I see these rugs as an unbroken mirror of the astounding historical and cultural heritage that has formed this land and its people. I especially see in the mirror of these village rugs the reflection of so many of the qualities that I admire in the Turkish people: simplicity, directness, warmth, caring, industriousness, diligence, generosity, sincerity, concern for the societal well-being of their fellow man, and a conviction that life should be shared as a family in the smallest and largest sense of the term. Yes, Turkey is a colorful carpet of a country, knotted with 70,000,000 souls.

Sincerely,
Katharine Branning

Staircase to Pandeli's restaurant, Istanbul

Interior of the Cem Sultan Tomb, Bursa

İplikçi Mosque carpets, Konya

Entry to the Museum of Ethnography, Kayseri

Kilim horse trappings and decorated farm wagon, Erzurum

Carpets fit for a Sultan's prayers, Alaeddin Mosque, Niğde

LETTER 23

I found Him in my heart

Dear Lady Mary,

When I travel to Turkey, I usually stop over for a few days in Istanbul before heading out to "my Turkey" of central and eastern Anatolia. These few days allow me to adjust my rhythm from the frenzy of New York to the calmer pace of Turkey, and to ease into the joys of being there: I attune my ears to the sweet flow of Turkish, I taste my first spoonful of yogurt, I hear my first "*YOK!*" and "*VAR!*"; I see my first sunny smiling faces, I experience my first act of kindness, I observe a new TT, and I experience my first call to prayer. These few days prepare me to more fully absorb and respond to the differences between my Western, urban society and Anatolia.

In a similar fashion, Lady Mary, your trip across Europe served as an important preparation for your encounter with Turkey, as it provided you with your first true exposure to cultural differences. The customs in Europe certainly did not resemble those of your Anglican England, especially as concerns religion. The letters you wrote from Europe are filled with descriptions of the fussy and ornate appointments of the Catholic churches you saw there. In contrast to the simplicity of your Protestant faith, all of this appeared to you as silly idolatry. I identified with much of what you described, for I experienced a similar reaction when I went to live in Catholic France, where the elaborate Gothic cathedrals were far removed from the plain wooden pews and unadorned altars of my Methodist church at home.

After witnessing all that "popery" along the way, everything changed when you arrived in Belgrade and stayed in the home of your tutor, the effendi Achmed. He offered you your initial exposure to the Islamic faith, which you identified as a religion more in tune with the simplicity of Protestant worship. As Protestants, we both arrived in Turkey with minds more open to this religion, with its lack of appointments, images, and finery attached to liturgy. In your pursuit of intercultural understanding, you spoke regularly with Achmed during the three weeks you stayed there:

> "*An intimate daily conversation with the effendi Achmed Bey gave me opportunity of knowing their religion and morals in a more particular manner than perhaps any Christian ever did. I explain'd to him the difference between the Religion of England and Rome, and he was pleas'd to hear there were Christians that did not worship images or adore the Virgin Mary. The ridicule of transubstantiation appeared very strong to him. He assur'd me that if I understood Arabic I should be very well pleas'd with reading the Alcoran,... 'tis the purest morality delivered in the very best Language. I have since heard impartial Christians speak of it in the same manner... "*

Your visit to the Selimiye Cami in Edirne confirmed your ease with the simplicity of Islam. You state:

> "*In my opinion it is a great addition to its beauty that it is not divided into pews and encumbered with forms and benches like our churches, nor the pillars disfigured by little tawdry images and pictures that give the Roman Catholic churches the air of toyshops.*"

You talked much about religion in your letters. You spoke of the Jewish population in Edirne and how they made themselves indispensable to the sultan's business. You tried in your letters to correct many of the negative, Western perceptions of Turkey and its religion. You refuted the Western view of the irrationality of Islam; you went even so far as to question Europe as the birthplace of Reason and the impossibility of only one authoritative translation of God's word and will. Although you spoke critically about the Catholic faith of Europe in your letters, you tread gentler waters when it came to Islam. You managed to "*keep distance from doctrines and differences, and see only the societal aspects of them.*" I have tried to do the same in my encounters with the Islamic faith.

And what a marvelous, eye and mind-opening guide this Achmed proved to be for you! After you arrived in Adrianople, you wrote to your friend the Abbé Conti on April 1, 1717 and shared your impressions of Islam:

"'Tis certain we have but very imperfect relations of the manners and religion of these people, this part of the world being seldom visited but by merchants, who mind little but their own affairs, or travellers who make too short a stay to be able to report anything exactly of their own knowledge."

As a woman of keen intelligence, sensitivity, and curiosity, it is not surprising that you sought to investigate the customs of Turkey. Most importantly, you were lucky to be more than a *"traveller who makes a short stay."* Millions of tourists visit Turkey each year, the majority coming from non-Muslim countries. They enjoy the natural beauty of the countryside, visit historic sites of numerous levels of civilizations, and relax on beaches and in discothèques. Most will pay a visit to one mosque, organized by their tour group. Invariably, the visit is to Sultanahmet, the famous "Blue Mosque" on the Hippodrome in Istanbul. Before that visit, however, those tourists will have already noticed skylines poked with distinctive, pencil-shaped minarets, headscarved women, and the omnipresent call to prayer. The call to prayer is projected throughout the city via loud speakers five times a day, often awakening those disco-tired tourists at dawn. These frequent calls are often the only hint these visitors receive that Turkey is a country that lives its faith in a very public way. You, however, Lady Mary, took the time to develop an understanding of the Islamic faith as it is truly lived and felt by the Turks.

Turkey is a country where you encounter piety of great depth, translated into a faith that is lived every day in conspicuous manners. Again, most tourists are not in Turkey to discover or understand the rites, customs, or traditions of this living faith of Islam, and they often come with a maligned view. It takes more than an admiration of those blue tiles to grasp this faith; it involves understanding what goes on in those mosques, the reason people bow and bend in worship on those colorful carpets and how the lessons learned there are carried over into life outside their walls. I, too, marvel at the domes of Sinan and those Iznik tiles, and I particularly admire the skyline of the seven hills of Istanbul, each crowned with a royal mosque. Yet to visit Turkey without trying to understand what all of this represents would be akin to ignoring the significance of the stained glass windows of Chartres or the observance of Lent in Rome. It is important to understand why everyone clicks prayer beads, why coffins lay bare in mosque courtyards, and why there are so many greetings and expressions in the Turkish language related to Islam. It is essential to comprehend how spirituality is lived in both houses of worship and in private homes, and what the exact message Sinan was trying to convey with spacious domes, lavish tiles, and open spaces of worship without seats.

Like you, Lady Mary, traveling in Turkey has allowed me to question my own Christian beliefs and has led me on a search for a common ground of spirituality with Islam – and there certainly is one. We all search for a sense of meaning and purpose in our lives, and finding that truth can take many paths, religion being one of them. Everyone on earth – the atheist, the pious, or the agnostic – possesses some form of spiritual impulse. Everyone seeks the answers to the same questions relative to the reason of our human existence, what is important in life and the afterlife, the role of love, service, and moral law. Most of us are taught to seek these meanings in the traditions, spokespersons, sacred texts, saints, clergy, and prophets of established religions. Yet the truth is more layered than one religion can provide answers for, so the more a human being learns from traditions other than those of his own upbringing or culture, the more he will be able to carve his own meaning and truth. These meanings can indeed be found in religion, but also in art, philosophy, nature, in work, in private and intimate self-dialog, in science, or in service to others. There is not one path, one voice, one text. The world is too big for that.

My encounters with Turkey have taught me how big that world is and have encouraged a respectful confrontation with my own ideas that have often surprised, moved, angered but ultimately refreshed my insights. In the Turkey of today, as in my own country, we are questioning the role of religion and morality in everything. Not just in the holy spaces of worship or in dealing with the major issues of life and the hereafter, but in the everyday issues of marriage, family, community, ethics, scientific quandaries, sexual normalcy, political morality, and governance. Instead of proposing strict answers to the dilemmas these issues raise, the more we contemplate them through the wisdom of varied religions, the better chance we have of sharing them, confronting them, and finding a workable solution that respects all thoughts.

Some of the most difficult spiritual issues I struggle with every day are the questions of evil, the heartbreak of death and tragic events, the frailty of freedom, suffering, and the relevance of organized religions. I am not ashamed to say that I doubt, that I struggle, and that I get angry, for all of this helps me keep these questions in the forefront of my existence and explore them as much as I can. Moments of crisis help build my spirituality, aid me to decide if life should be lived with or without a god, but they also give me the courage to try to repair what I see wrong around me.

Despite these struggles and moments of doubt, I am also not ashamed to say that there are miracles that I just cannot rationally explain and inexplicable moments of perfect joy and love that I cannot believe are just happenstance. There are flashes of mystery when I feel as if the finger of God is touching me and which I cannot explain away through the measurable phenomena of science. The meeting of a sister soul, falling in love, living a moment of natural beauty, a miraculous medical recovery, an escape from an accident or tragedy, for example, are things which give me the courage to explore the more difficult dilemmas of fear and evil. The sense of order and intelligence that I perceive in these moments shapes the chaos of daily life and provides an unexplainable magic which leads me to believe that there is an essence to our life that must be called God or spiritual faith.

Despite my faith, the horror and senselessness in our contemporary world is often difficult for me to bear and accept. However, my encounter with Islam has given me encouragement, as it has made me revisit what I believe is important in my own religious practice and in the true richness of my Christian tradition. I revisit forms of religious observance in a different light and seek other forms of meditation on these complex issues. To understand these personal issues, as well as the portrait of living Islam in Turkey and the current societal challenges it poses in Turkey, I have met and spoken with a sophisticated urban mystic, a university professor of comparative religions in Kayseri, poor women in villages, devout military officers struggling to reconcile the love of Atatürk with the love of Allah, sema students in Konya, virulent leftist atheists in Istanbul, old Greek women in Pera, Alevi musicians in Elbistan, and people from all walks of life. The portrait of the many different expressions of faith in Turkey has not been an easy one for me to grasp, for it is one of many colors, shapes, and subjects. As easy as it is to admire the "*japanned china*" of those Iznik tiles you saw in the Selimiye Mosque in Edirne, Lady Mary, it is as hard to grasp the true meanings of all the expressions of faith in Turkey.

As complex as Islamic life in today's Turkey appears to be, one thing is certain for me. I have always felt comfortable in Turkey because this is a land where the history of Christianity is to be found on every street corner.

Anatolia, the land of modern Turkey, has been witness to many layers of civilizations for the past 10,000 years. Numerous empires have left their traces here: Urartians, Hittites, Lyceans and Lydians, Armenians, Greeks, Romans and Byzantines, Seljuks and Ottomans, and the Republic of Turkey of today. Although the politics, languages, customs, and religions of these civilizations were different, they shared universal values, the vestiges of which have filtered through to blend into the culture of today. These are universal, "humanistic" values: the emotions and feelings that go to the heart of human experience and which unite all individuals on the earth, no matter in what place or in what time. Of all these humanist values, it is perhaps the one of charity that is the most beloved of the Turks. From Yunus Emre to Mevlana to the present day, the same song has been chanted: this is a tolerant place, a place where people have a right to find their spirituality on the path they choose.

As a Christian, I have found immense richness in this country, combining the traces of history and faith in natural ease to constitute an almost personal Holy Land. My "*Türkiyem*" is a land of faith. Istanbul was the new Rome, a city where Constantine stopped the persecution of Christians. The Nicean Creed that I recited over and over in church as a child was written in Iznik, the city that made all those tiles for Sinan's mosques, the "*japanned china*" you so admired in the Selimiye, Lady Mary. When the great flood waters receded, it is believed that Noah's ark came to perch on the top of Mount Ararat in Eastern Turkey, where the Urartians had established their kingdom. The Old Testament tells us that Abraham was born in the city of Ur, near the Euphrates River, a city later to become known as Edessa, seat of the first major Crusader state established during the First Crusade of Baldwin II in 1096. Today the city is known by the Turks as "Glorious Urfa": Şanlıurfa. Glorious indeed it is, for a more impressive interfaith holy site than this one would be hard to find outside of Jerusalem. In nearby Harran, Abraham's two sons, Isaac and Ishmael, were born. Isaac met his wife Rachel while drawing water at a well in Harran, and their marriage charted the destiny of the world. Isaac and Rachel's descendants included Moses, King David, and Jesus. His brother Ishmael's descendants included Muhammad, founder of the Islamic faith. To walk the streets of this town is a veritable pilgrimage to the essence of the world's three mono-theistic religions and all that they symbolize for humanity. The hot dust of this town is filled with the memory of the prophets of all these faiths, and you walk very humbly through the narrow backstreets and bazaars of this town on stones polished by the centuries of Biblical footsteps.

As a Protestant Christian, it is of course the footsteps that Paul left in Turkey that are particularly meaningful to me. Paul was originally born in Turkey, in the town of Tarsus, now near the modern city of Mersin in the Çurukova Plain. To find him, I made a special pilgrimage to Antakya, the Antioch-on-Orontes of Antiquity, to visit this town that served as the base for his first missionary activities. It was this place where the movement of the followers of Jesus began using a name, Christians, to identify them-selves. Paul was called here by Barnabus, a follower of Jesus, to work along-side of Peter, Mark, and John to communicate his insight into Christ's teachings. I wanted to discover first-hand this famed Antioch, the city that inspired the naming of the dynamic and famous university near my child-hood home in Ohio; this celebrated Antioch whose name rang out from the pulpit in the scripture readings of Paul's letters heard in church services while I was growing up; this historical city sung in praise in French history classes when it was seized by the Crusader Bohemond to become his king-dom: yes, this mythical place, where the footsteps of Christianity were first taken. As I walked along the streets of this now backwater town, it was hard to imagine that this city was once one of the largest in the entire Ro-man Empire, the very rival of Alexandria, filled with handsome public buildings, sports arenas, aqueducts, and private villas decorated with luxuri-ous mosaics. I tried to visualize the profile of the city at that time, a cross-roads of trade and the seat of not only luxury, but of earthquakes and de-pravity; a city so powerful that it beckoned Paul to set up his first mission here for seven years starting in 47 AD. As I walked on the beach of Çevlik, the nearby village which serves as Antioch's port, on its strand now forgot-ten, polluted, and dirty, far from those glory days of Antiquity, I tried to imagine the depth of faith that inspired Paul to push off his little boat from here to set out across the Mediterranean for Antalya on his first preaching mission. As I stared out westwards over the water, I tried to envision the fiber of this man who was possessed with a passion to preach the news of the love of God as embodied in Jesus. I realized then that I was witnessing the very spot that forever changed the destiny of the world as we know it: the Christian Church was born right here in the gritty sand where I stood. I heard Paul's voice echoing in the lapping waves: *"There is neither Jew or Greek, there is neither slave nor free man, there is neither male nor female: for you are all one in Christ Jesus."* I later followed his footsteps in Antalya, where he got off that boat to spread the word of love, traveling from there on foot and by cart over the hot and dusty roads of Anatolia. I visited Kastamonu, considered by many to be the site of the community that inspired Paul to write one of his most significant of letters, the Epistle to the Galatians. This letter was provoked by his anger at the members of the church there that he himself had founded and who had since wandered from the original teachings of Jesus. I tried to imagine him pounding his fist on his table in such anger to write *"You foolish Galatians!"* a remonstrance that I grew up hearing in Sunday sermons and which became the symbol for the consequences of not adhering to the true path of love. I remember, too, reading in the New Testament Book of Acts of the episode where Paul preached in a synagogue in Konya. Now, when I ramble in the curving backstreets of this holy capital city of the Seljuks, I try to imagine where that synagogue could have been, and I hear in my ears the echo of Paul's voice mingling with those of Alaeddin Keykubad and Rumi.

I have visited all of the sites of the famed Seven Churches of the Apocalypse, some in ruins, some built over, described by John in the Book of Revelations. Jesus apparently told John to *"Write in a book what thou seest, and send it unto the seven churches which are in Asia; unto Ephesus, and unto Smyrna, and unto Pergamum, and unto Thyatira, and unto Sardis, and unto Philadelphia, and unto Laodicea"* (Revelations 1:11). These were more communities of Christians than churches, yet they were the cradle that spread the Christian faith to the rest of the world. They are located in Turkish cities that have lost trace today of their importance as Christian sites: in Izmir (Smyrna), Bergama (Pergamum), Akhisar (Thyateria), Sardis, Alaşehir (Philadelphia), and Eskihisar (Laodicea). The most poignant one is in the former Greek colony of Ephesus. It was here, in the shadow of one of the most important libraries built in Roman times, that John brought Mary, mother of Jesus, to live at the end of her life. The emotional impact of all these sites is the same: I am walking the verses of the Bible.

I have visited abandoned Byzantine churches hidden in the thick, white mists of the lush Black Sea Mountains, such as Barhal and İşhan near Artvin as well as the impressive cliff-side wall of the Sumelia Monastery. I was particularly touched to see the thirteenth-century Hagia Sophia Church in Trabzon, whose elaborate stone portals were most certainly carved by Seljuk artisans. I have wandered through the cemetery of abandoned Armenian churches in the fields at Ani, now with only flocks of birds to recite the Scripture. I have overlooked the plains where Crusaders stormed across Turkey in their misguided attempt to save the Holy Land and Jerusalem from the dreaded Turk.

Next to all of these Christian sites of course stand the monuments from other eras and faiths: Hittite altars, Roman temples, synagogues, Seljuk and Ottoman mosques. The religious richness in Turkey is unlike any country in the world. I have visited the ruins of the Roman-era synagogue of Sardis and read Hebrew inscriptions in its mosaic floors. The major mosques of the Ottoman Empire, those great monuments of Sinan, stand testament to Allah in Istanbul, yet it is not in this city of man's desiring that I feel my faith or the faith of others. Rather, it is in the heart of *"Türkiyem,"* my Turkey, that Turkey of the Central Plateau, where the witnesses of many faiths can still be heard raising their voices in praise across the crossroads of those golden plains. In this jumble of monuments I have found the universal truths of all the faiths represented in this Holy Land of Turkey. And so you can see, Lady Mary, how Turkey has not only deepened my own Christian heritage, but has also opened the doors to understanding the faiths of others. I am sure that most Turks do not realize the emotional impact that their country has on Christians.

What I have seen in Turkey underneath that *"japanned china,"* what I read in the Koran, and what I have discussed with countless Turks has confirmed what I already expected: my faith and the faith of Islam are built on the same principles, found over and over again in the sacred texts of Islam and Christianity. The ground that lies at the core of the three major religions of Christianity, Judaism, and Islam, is one and the same: love God and love your neighbor. It is as straightforward as this.

Every Muslim recites the opening chapter of the Koran, the *Al-Fatihah*, ("The Opening"), a majestic praise to God, at least forty times daily in his canonical prayers. Over and over again it reminds Muslims of the pow-

er of God and His attributes of goodness and mercy today and in the afterlife and of his power to forgive our sins.

> *In the Name of Allah, the Compassionate, the All-Merciful.*
> *Praise be to Allah, the Lord of the worlds.*
> *The Compassionate, the All-Merciful.*
> *Master of the Day of Judgment.*
> *You alone do we worship, and to You alone do we pray for help.*
> *Guide us to the Straight Path.*
> *The way of those to whom You have favored with Thy Grace,*
> *not those who deserve anger nor those who go astray. (Al-Fatihah, 1:1-7)*

This ritual repetition drills in the message that one must be devoted to
God with all one's heart, soul, mind, emotion, and will. When I read the
Al-Fatihah or hear it recited in mosques during prayer times, I hear the
echoes of the Bible in my ears, both the solemn Old Testament book of
Deuteronomy, "*You shall love the Lord your God with all your heart, and
with all your soul, and with all your strength*" and the words of Jesus in
Matthew 22 and Mark 12, where he gives the "greatest of commandments": "*You shall love the Lord your God with all your heart, with all
your soul, and with all your mind. This is the first and greatest command-
ment. And the second is like it: 'You shall love your neighbor as yourself.'
On these two commandments hang all the Law and the Prophets.*" This is
what I as a Christian have been taught: to love God fully with my heart
and soul and to be fully devoted to Him. How different is this than what
the Muslim feels when he recites the *al-Fatihah*?

In that passage in Matthew, Jesus clearly stated that the second of the
great commandments was to "*love thy neighbor as thyself.*" In Islam as well,
there are countless injunctions about the necessity and importance of love and
mercy for the neighbor, which in Islam forms the second basis of their faith,
just as it is in Christianity. For a Muslim, showing love to people around you
is a living part of faith in God, and without showing this love to your neighbor, there can be no true love for God. The *Hadith*, or sayings of the Prophet, attribute these words to Him: "*None of you has faith until you love for
your brother what you love for yourself.*" In Turkey, this love of the neighbor is taken very seriously, and does not exist only in the realm of prayer. It
forms the basis of all life, with Turks believing that without giving to others
through generosity and self-sacrifice that which we ourselves love, we do not

truly love God. This charity can take the form of one of those abundant small gestures of goodness that I talked about in a previous letter, those often unseen gestures that make Turkish hospitality so powerful are indeed little prayers come to life. There are also bigger almsgiving gestures more ritual in nature, such as animal sacrifices on the days of Kurban Bayramı (Eid al-Adha) or monetary donations to neighbors in need or charitable foundations. Charity is the strongest social glue in Turkey, an implicit understanding of how Islam should be lived. It is the most potent manifestation of the Islamic golden rule; that is, to encourage the good and discourage what is evil. Although Christianity and Islam share the same golden rule principle, in Turkey it is much more evident in daily life, and there, no one doubts that service to people is service to God and that the power of personal example is the strongest of the diverse roads to Him.

I admire this social aspect of Islam and the importance Turks place on charity and alms-giving to the benefit of the community. Islam views the individual as the worker bee in the hive of humanity, with all thoughts directed to doing what is best for society as a whole. Despite the fact that Islam and Christianity are two very different religions in the way they are practiced and lived, the common ground of their two major commandments cannot be any more similar. So why should it be so difficult to walk down the path of humanity hand in hand towards investigating this commonality instead of trying to isolate the differences and warring upon them? There is one God, only one God, and we are to love Him and our neighbor, whether you are a Methodist in Ohio or a Sunni in Konya. This love is what is truly essential to our faiths, no matter how it is practiced, in pews or on rugs, with steeple bells or with muezzin cries.

In Turkey, there is a very individual take on the Islamic faith, one that is in tune with the modern technological world, democracy, and the rights of women as well as one that carries the traces of their shaman forefathers. One ecounters many practices that are outside of the five-pillared official practice of Islam, such as the folk practices of wearing or carrying blue evil eye beads, fortune telling, astrology, conjuring of spirits and petitioning dead saints at their tombs, belief in shamanistic figures and sorcerers, interpretation of dreams, sacrificing of roosters and chickens at holy places to ensure marriage or children, visiting large trees for ceremonies to bring luck, and the particularly paradoxical habit of considering it evil to admire children too much. I have always been intrigued by the pieces of cloth tied on trees and bushes for votive wishes and how Turks will make pilgrimages to Christian holy sites with the same enthusiasm as they would an Islamic one. In their eyes, if a site is imbued with spirituality, what does it matter whether it is Christian or Muslim? It is holy, period, and that is good enough. When you look at these seemingly eccentric and unconventional popular practices, they are not any stranger than some of the orthodox rites encountered in established Christian ceremony, such as communion wine and Easter eggs.

There are many things that I admire and respect in the Islamic faith as I have come to know it in Turkey, just like you did, Lady Mary, when you wrote that letter to the Abbé Conti. First and foremost, I suppose like you, I admire the simplicity of Islam, with its freedom from ritual, blatant iconography, pomp, and ceremony. I especially agree with you Lady Mary, on the inspiration gained by the impressive architectural spaces created by vast single domes that are uncluttered by pews. When I visited the Byzantine rock churches of the Göreme Valley of Cappadocia and gazed upon the mysterious and elaborate iconography of saints, snakes, and scary stories painted in comic book style on their walls, it all felt somehow very juvenile after having heard the majestic muezzin's call from the solid grey granite Seljuk mosques in nearby Kayseri the day before. Moving for me as well was standing in front of the 500 year old plane tree in the City of the Dead in Bursa and contemplating the plain and touching open-domed türbe grave of Sultan Murat II the Mystic, built *"so that the rain of heaven might wash my face like any pauper's."* Simple, as well, is that *shahada* profession of faith, the first of the 5 pillars of the faith. This profession is a personal dialogue with your belief, not an elaborate sanctified ceremony. The confession becomes the foremost prayer to God, and the simplicity and privacy of this dialogue is one of the most appealing aspects of the faith.

Another important thing I admire in Islam is its tolerance towards other religions, and that many of the world's prophets – Jesus, Moses, Abraham, David, Solomon, Adam, Jonah, Noah, Isaac, and Jacob among others, are considered in the Koran as such. I read in the Koran that *"the Messiah Jesus son of Mary is a Messenger of God and His Word which he conveyed to Mary and a Spirit from Him."* (Al-Nisa', 4:171).

I also admire the strong sense of morality that Turks feel, assured of knowing what is right from wrong, taught to them by the Koran. It especially condemns and curses all racism and terrorism. The Koran states: *"Killing a human being is tantamount to killing the whole of humanity."* I value, too, the commonality that Christianity shares with Islam. The mosque, like the church, is a place for ritual and a place of safety, peace, and refuge. The Christian sense of service to others, stewardship of God's gifts, acceptance of God's message and will, and forgiveness of sins to you and to society are important in Islam as well.

Although I would find it difficult in my busy daily life to go to a mosque five times a day to pray, I do appreciate the moment of reflection that is inspired in me when I hear the muezzin's call to prayer on the streets of cities great and villages small. In that moment I stop all to regroup my thoughts relative to the day that I am living and rejoice that I am alive at that precise moment of time. By stopping in my steps, I, too, participate in the unspoken code of behavior the call to prayer triggers. Activity in the street subsides for two short minutes, people pause, conversations are hushed, horns cease their honking, hawkers calm their cries, radios are turned down, and the sidewalks become silent. An unspoken blessing falls upon the neighborhood and its people. I, too, stop and listen to its beauty and take time to say my own personal prayer. The call reminds me that I must put my soul to the service of others, just like a Muslim does. When I hear it I think of the transgressions I may have committed that day to others. It stimulates me to ask myself, *"OK, did you speak any harsh words, hold any evil thoughts, could you have been nicer to someone?"* I have three highly successful photographer friends in Konya who spent a full day showing me the sights. At the end of the day, we visited the nearby village of Sille, where they paused during the visit to enter a mosque for the late afternoon prayer. Afterwards over tea, I asked what the ritual of prayer meant to them, why they took so much time in their very busy professional days to do it, and how they managed to carve the time to fit it in. They patiently explained to me that it was not a question of "fitting it in," and that those few minutes gave to them a sense of constant physical and emotional refreshment that helped them to confront the challenges of their busy days. One of them, Feyzi Şimşek, turned to me and said, *"If not only Muslims, but if everyone in the world could share these same moments of peace each day, perhaps there would be fewer problems in the world."* The simplicity of his statement was obvious, and for one moment in the clarity of the late afternoon setting sun, I shared his optimism.

Islam is one more bridge for me to cross between Turkey and my country. I believe that my role as a translator and promoter of dialog between faiths is an important one, for if I as a Christian can speak about Islam to my family and friends, to help them understand its beauty and originality, then I will have done a service to all. I wish in some small way to enhance my countrymen's spirituality in the same fashion that mine has been widened and deepened through exploration of values common with Islam. It would perhaps make for a place of peace, the ultimate goal of all religions.

Turkey, its people, its way of life, and its version of Islam have taught me so many things. I have seen that encountering religious pluralism and varieties of religious practice can strengthen you. I have discovered that the love of nature is an important part of our souls and plants splendor in our hearts. I have seen how the family can be the center of all community and love, and how this family cell creates a sacred, trustworthy space set apart from the daily bustle of life. I have realized the power an individual can play for those around him and how one touch of love can radiate hours of harmony. I have discovered how people can be ambassadors of goodness and how their gestures of kindness can be an instrument towards making the world a more harmonious place. I have learned from the lessons of love taught by Rumi and the Sufis that the unexplained realms of faith are indeed real and should be honored. Their mystic approach to devotion has shown me that to be spiritual is to love everyone and everything, with a goal to make gentle this life on earth. They have taught me that what is given from the heart recycles back into your heart. All these lessons, filtered through my own religion, traditions and viewpoints, have convinced me that love is simply behavior geared to the good of the other, and that God is this spark of life and love within each of us, in all the beauty of nature, and in the miracles of our daily life. Most importantly for me, I have come to believe that God represents the conviction that light, beauty, and good will prevail. God is hope.

Perhaps the greatest lesson is that the future must be confronted with this hope, and not despair. I choose to believe that Muslims are a peaceful nation, and that Islam is not set out to destroy those not on their side. How could a faith this tolerant of Jesus in its Holy Scripture be set out with evil intent for Christianity? The naysayers will say I am naïve, but I must believe in this: it forms my hope. This conviction can no longer be the food of gentle interfaith dialog sessions, publications by religious leaders, or joint ecumenical services. The relationship between the religious communities of Islam, Christianity, and Judaism is now the most important factor in contributing to meaningful peace around the world, for quite simply, if these groups are not at peace, the world cannot be at peace. In our globalized world full of villainous and powerful weaponry, religion cannot be used as a pawn in the power game between self-aggrandizing governments or foolish fanatics. In America, we live in a land like no other on earth: where Jews, Christians, Buddhists, Sikhs, Hindus, Muslims, and atheists all share the same thanksgivings and right to worship. It is up to America to show the world that a peaceful coalition is possible at home and then abroad. And it is up to Turkey to show the world how peaceful Islam can be, a religion to be admired and emulated rather than one full of evil intents. The common future of all the neighbors of the earth is in play and rests in the hands of us all. As Jesus said: "*Blessed are the peacemakers.*"

Your letters, Lady Mary, each and every one of them, were little peacemakers, and I hope that they, and other pens, will continue to inspire the will of fraternity. In closing I will leave you with the words of the most eloquent of the peacemakers, Rumi. The poignant wisdom of this great Sufi of Turkey captures perfectly a spirituality that should guide us all in our efforts in this direction:

> "*I tried to find Him on the Christian cross, but He was not there; I went to the Temple of the Hindus and to the old pagodas, but I could not find a trace of Him anywhere.*
>
> *I searched on the mountain and in the valleys but neither in the heights nor in the depth was I able to find Him. I went to the Kaaba in Mecca, but He was not there either.*
>
> *I questioned the scholars and philosophers but He was beyond their understanding.*
>
> *I then looked into my heart and it was there where He dwelled that I saw Him; He was nowhere else to be found.*"

Sincerely,

Kadriye Branning

The Süleymaniye Mosque, Sultan of the Istanbul skyline

Hatuniye Mosque, Kayseri

Page from a Seljuk-era Koran, 1278   *Nest of storks, Green Mosque, Iznik*

Preparation of tables of sweets for Şeker Bayram, Istanbul

Ahi Evren Dervish Zaviye, Kayseri

Noah's mountain: Ararat

Door to the Şeyh Turesan Zaviye

Votive ribbons tied on the site of the Ashab-ı Kehf Complex,
built on the site of a former Byzantine church

Votive ribbons on 500-year-old mulberry tree, Hacı Bektaş Zaviye

| TAKVİM | HİCRİ : 9 REBİÜLAHIR 1416 |
| | RUMİ : 22 AĞUSTOS 1411 |

Vakit:	İmsak	Güneş	Öğle	İkindi	Akşam	Yatsı
Vasati:	4.56	6.26	13.08	16.47	19.39	21.04

Prayer times as announced in the daily newspapers

Postage stamp depicting the Tomb of Rumi, Konya

Tile panel on the minaret of the Great Mosque of Siirt

Selimiye Mosque, Edirne, photo from 1985

SECTION 5

HORIZONS

LETTER 24

A pox off your home

Dear Lady Mary,
I often like to play a game with myself when I am standing in long lines at the post office, on endless car rides, while waiting for delayed planes in airports, or sometimes even when I am just drifting off to sleep. I like to think of all of my blessings, all of the rich and wonderful things in my life. I make lists of all that I cherish about the various parts of my life: the people and animals I love, nature, my glassblowing, my work, and.... my country. As concerns my country, I like to make lists of all the odd, magical, stupendous, and even silly things it has given to the world, such as Bob Dylan, jazz, modern medicine, democracy, religious freedom, William Faulkner, and hamburgers. I also play this game with France.... and with Turkey.

Indeed, perhaps Turkey did not give the world the Reformation, the Enlightenment, or the Industrial Revolution. Yet it has throughout history, in ways both small and large, been a player on the world's stage.

On a personal level, Turkey has given me much. I hope you can see that in these letters I am writing you, Lady Mary. Oh, not only an appreciation for art and architecture and talking stones and a sense of another culture and an opportunity to cross physical and metaphysical bridges, but also the warmth of very human relationships, a faith in humanity, a lesson in determination, and a belief in the goodness of my fellow man and in humanity as a whole.

All vigorous cultures borrow and share amongst each other. Turkey has shared with the world its realm of comfort and luxury, with such furnishings as the divan, the kiosk, and the sofa; the concept of cleanliness, with thick Turkish towels, the steam bath, the massage culture; and the fashions of the kaftan, the turban, fine brocades and velvets, the cassock, and Orientalism and the odalisque. It has shared the delights of its table, and we now cannot imagine life without coffee and yogurt, or pastrami, halvah, shish kebabs, lokum, or caviar. I wonder if every Frenchman realizes each morning as he sips his café au lait with his croissant that his breakfast was brought to him by the Turks. Our vocabulary has been enriched with administrative terms such as pasha, lackey, bashi-bazouk, and sanjak. Turkish caravans brought the luxurious treasures of the Far East to the salons of the fine homes of Europe. Turkish culture offered the canon of world literature the heartbreakingly arresting verses of Rumi and Yunus Emre. It shared the lessons of its powerful creators like Sinan and Atatürk. Turkey gave us the game of bridge, the "Turkey Carpet," and the most magnificent of flowers, the tulip.

Yet perhaps the most important legacy that Turkey has given the world was one that you made possible, Lady Mary. Yes, it was due to you that the Ottomans could leave a lasting mark on the world: oddly enough, by *not* leaving marks.

Turkey gave the world the soft cheeks of children to kiss.

You know what I am speaking about. When you were 26 years old, enchanting the salons and courts of London with your beauty and wit, you were dealt a devastating blow that would have buckled other women in your entourage. But not you, Lady Mary. Right before Christmas, 1715, you were struck with smallpox. The sickness itself lasted some 20 short days. Its horrid scarring and pockmarks, however, lasted your lifetime. Your skin became deeply pitted and you lost your eyebrows and eyelashes. You do not mention it in any of your letters, but I cannot imagine the effect it must have had on your self-image, how it must have strained your marital relations even further, and even how it must have made you the pity of the London social circles. You had already seen your own brother die from the disease. Although you tried to hide your face with face paint, it must have taken an extreme amount of courage to confront your life as if your famed former beauty had nothing to do with who you were or what people saw in you. Four months later your husband received news of his appointment as Ambassador to the

Ottoman court, and by July, a mere seven months after this life-changing event, you were on your way to Turkey.

There is absolutely no pang of self-pity or jealous of others in your rapturous letters describing the stunning beauty of the women you met in Turkey. Yet I cannot help but feel you were particularly sensitive to it because your very own beauty had been lost, and that these women seemed all the more lovely in view of your own disfigurement. What courage it must have taken for you to enter that steam bath in front of 200 half-naked women, to expose your scars in front of all of those beauties with "*skins shineingly white.*" What fortitude it must have taken for you to walk in front of dignitaries and the Sultan's court, thinking that all were whispering behind your back, pitying this poor English lady with such horrid skin. No wonder you repeat so often in your letters references to those "*skins shineingly white*" of Turkish women. Your own English porcelain rose skin was once as milky as theirs, but the dreaded bane of smallpox removed this vanity from you.

In the beginning of your stay in Turkey, when you were in Adrianople, you witnessed something that must have been an astounding event for you, a victim of this dreaded curse. In an age when there was little understanding between Christian Europe and the Muslim Middle East, you were remarkable for your objectivity in encountering this new culture and what must have seemed like its odd customs: and this one must have seemed very odd, indeed. You wrote in a long letter on April 1, 1717 to your friend Sarah Chiswell:

> "*A propos of distempers, I am going to tell you a thing that I am sure will make you wish yourself here. The smallpox, so fatal and general amongst us, is here entirely harmless by the invention of engrafting (which is the term they give it). There is a set of old women who make it their business to perform the operation. Every autumn, in the month of September, when the great threat is abated, people send to one another to know if any of the family has a mind to have the smallpox. They make parties for this purpose, and when they are met (commonly fifteen of sixteen together) the old woman comes with a nutshell full of the matter of the best sort of smallpox and asks what veins you please to have open. She immediately rips open that you offer to her with a large needle (which give you no more pain than a common scratch) and puts into the vein as much venom as can lie upon the head of her needle, and after*

binds up the little wound with a hollow bit of shell, and in this manner opens four or five veins...The children or young patients play together all the rest of the day and are in perfect health till the eighth. Then the fever begins to seize'em and they keep their beds two days, very seldom three. They have very rarely above twenty or thirty in their faces, which never mark, and in eight days' time they are all as well as before their illness."

This "engrafting" that you witnessed was nothing less than an inoculation – with dead smallpox virus – against smallpox. Witnessing this event proved as life-changing for you as the original encounter with the disease and gave you a chance to show your true mettle. For instead of running away from this procedure which could have seemed heathen, your natural curiosity led you further, and you decided to inoculate your very own son in Turkey.

"... Every year thousands undergo this operation, and the French ambassador says pleasantly that they take the smallpox here by way of diversion as they take the waters in other countries. There is no example of anyone that has died of it, and you may believe I am very well satisfied on the safety of the experiment since I intend to try it on my dear little son."

With the help of a doctor from the British Embassy, you had the courage to perform the procedure on your 5-year-old son. In a letter to your husband in March 1718, you state, *"the boy was engrafted last Tuesday and is at this time singing and playing and very impatient for his supper. I pray God my next letter may give as good an account of him."*

We forget today what horror this disease wrought in the world. In your eighteenth century alone, over 60 million people died of it. Your own Queen Mary II, under whose reign you were born, contracted it, and it killed 5 other European monarchs in that century. It destroyed the Incan Empire of Peru and the Aztecs of Mexico in the sixteenth century. It killed 90% of the Native American Indian population in the eighteenth century. The worst was reserved for young children less than 5 years of age: 8 out of 10 of them would die of it, and of those who survived, a full third would become blind. It scarred Stalin and Henry VIII, Queen Elizabeth I and Abraham Lincoln. In the twentieth century, over 300 million people continued to perish from this blight. Stocks of the smallpox virus still sit in secret labs in Russia, England, and the United States, ready to be used as biological warfare, a weapon which will prove more deadly than any nuclear bomb or missile head.

Yet, despite the raging devastation of the disease, a preventive treatment had been known for centuries. Known as inoculation, it was thought to have been practiced in India as early as 1000 BC, to be picked up later by the Chinese. The Indians rubbed smallpox pus into the skin lesions, and the Chinese had patients sniff ground smallpox scabs. In both cases, the patient would develop a mild case of the disease and would fully recover. It is also believed that the inoculation process was known to Arab doctors in the sixth century. Knowledge of these types of inoculation processes spread to Ottoman Turkey where the practice became widespread, and that was exactly what you witnessed in Adrianople. The Turks used walnuts as the culture, injecting the nutmeat with smallpox pus and letting it ferment in the warm protection of the shell.

You finished your letter to Sarah Chiswell as follows:

> *"...I am patriot enough to try to bring this useful invention into fashion in England, and I should not fail to write to some of our doctors very particularly about it if I knew any one of 'em that I thought had virtue enough to destroy such a considerable branch of their revenue for the good of mankind, but that distemper is too beneficial to them not to expose to all their resentment the hardy wright that should undertake to put an end to it. Perhaps if I live to return, I may, however, have courage to war with 'em."*

And war with 'em you did. After returning from Turkey to England, you launched a fervent campaign to promote the practice, and crossing this bridge proved quite rocky. You were not perhaps the first person to relay information on inoculation to England (an Italian physician in Constantinople had submitted a report four years prior to your return), but it was you that they listened to. You had your daughter inoculated in public by the very same embassy physician that had treated your son in Constantinople. It is believed that your little Mary was the first person in England ever to be inoculated. You brought the method to the attention of the London College of Physicians, where some surgeons were courageous enough to conduct successful trial experiments. Your example and personal urgings led the royal family, aristocrats, and prominent politicians to inoculate their children, ushering in a period of popularity for the practice among the upper classes in England. Alas, the enthusiasm for it was short-lived.

Despite the initial successes in the years of 1721–23, the religious opposition soon mounted against the practice of inoculation. The public debate on the issue was ferocious and extreme. Many so-called "men of God" believed that this procedure was against the will of God, who used smallpox as punishment for Satan's work and to naturally control the populations of the poor. This foolishness tainted the medical profession as well, which began to resent that the successful procedure had not been discovered by their own ilk, but by "shamans" in non-Western countries, and that, to boot, this procedure was being promoted by... a woman. That woman being you, Lady Mary. They tricked the results of test cases, published papers denouncing it, and sought to prove that the procedure had a higher death rate than once thought and was responsible for the spread of other diseases, such as syphilis. The trend for inoculation died out, and you yourself began to regret that you had introduced this Turkish custom to your homeland, as it brought much persecution and disgrace to you and your family. Yet you persevered, not cringing from this very public controversy, by anonymously publishing a scathing pamphlet denouncing the "*knavery and ignorance of physicians*" and placing the blame directly on them, not on the virus.

If only people had listened to you! Much heartbreak would have been spared you if they had. Your very own sister, Lady Gower, declined your invitation to have her son inoculated at the same time as little Mary. He died two years later of smallpox. The most ironic of tragedies happened when your friend Sarah Chiswell, recipient of that enthusiastic, vigorous letter describing the engrafting events of Adrianople, died herself of the disease in 1726.

Following the swirl of venom and controversy stirred up by you in England, the next chapter of your story picks up in my country. Your efforts were recognized in the "New" England, with several prominent doctors lending support to the movement, despite a swirl of controversy there as well. A slave from Barbados arrived in Boston in 1721 and explained how he had been inoculated in his native Sudan by the same scratch technique of Adrianople. This confirmed the original results your efforts launched in England, and American doctors began to use the technique.

After a successful outcome of an epidemic in Boston in 1722, where the inoculated survived untouched, the practice became well-accepted. George Washington ordered that inoculation be performed on all Revolutionary War soldiers who had not already had the disease. In this way, your efforts even participated indirectly in the victory of our war of Independence from your King George III.

Your story then crossed back over the Atlantic to England. A very bright young man named Edward Jenner started to put all of the pieces together. As a boy, he observed that dairy workers who contracted the animal version of the disease, cowpox, never caught smallpox. After becoming a doctor, he never forgot this intuition, and after further research, he presented his observations in a paper to his local medical society. His theory became widespread in the Western world by 1800. He was courageous enough to inoculate his own son like you did, Lady Mary, but this time, not with smallpox, but with cowpox virus. His experiments and research led the way for the cowpox vaccine to be used as an immunization for smallpox in humans. A vaccination for smallpox had been found.

You did not live to witness this success. Yet it was your daring to introduce the procedure and your tenacity to see it through that has saved millions of lives since, all over the world.

Would it have been possible for Jenner to do what he had done 79 years later if you had not paved the way first? If you had not had the courage, fortified by your own personal horror with this disease, to confront all the naysayers and lead the way, I am certain that he and the other true men of science would not have been able to press on to find a way to a complete sweep of the disease. Your role was as important as any man of science and as powerful as any vaccine, for you had the broadminded bravery to take on the medical community and public opinion, often as virulent as the pox you were trying to combat.

After successful vaccination campaigns throughout the nineteenth and twentieth centuries, the World Health Organization certified the eradication of smallpox in 1977. To this day, smallpox is the only human infectious disease to have been completely eliminated from the planet. That is your legacy to the world, Lady Mary, all stemming from the careful observation of a procedure in a small room in Ottoman Adrianople and your conviction in its worth and your courage to cross a bridge with it. Never more shall the curse "*A pox on your house!*" be heard in the land, except in plays by Shakespeare. Never more will mothers have to bear seeing their children die or being scarred by this plight. Now and for ever more, the mothers of the world will be able to kiss the soft-petaled unscarred cheeks of their children, all because of a gift brought from a remarkable country, by you, a most extraordinary and courageous woman.

With my most respectful reverence,
Katharine Branning

The wretched Flavia, on her couch reclined.
Thus breath'd the anguish of a wounded mind,
A glass revers'e in her right hand she bore,
For now she shunn'd the face she sought before.
How am I chang'd ! alas! How am I grown
A frightful spectre to myself unknown!
Where's my complexion? Where my radiant bloom,
That promis'd happiness for years to come?
Then with what pleasure I this face survey'd!
To look once more, my visits oft delay'd!
Charmed with the view, a fresher red would rise,
And a new life shot sparkling from my eyes!
Ah! Faithless glass, my wonted bloom restore;
Alas! I rave, that bloom is now no more!

–Lady Montagu, "Flavia"

*The Sun Monument, erected in 1747 in honor of Lady
Mary by William Wentworth, on the grounds of
Wentworth Castle (Yorkshire, England)*

TO THE MEMORY OF THE
RT: HON. LADY MARY
WORTLEY MONTAGU
WHO IN THE YEAR 1720
INTRODUCED INOCULATION
OF THE SMALL POX
INTO ENGLAND FROM TURKEY

LETTER 25

Breaking and entering into the past

To Muhsin İlyas Subaşı

Dear Lady Mary,
Like you, I enjoy visiting sites and discovering the cultural riches of Turkey, and I have taken many of the same excursions that you did. You traveled up the Bosphorus in a *caique* and observed the waterfront wooden mansions, the gardens, forests, and mosques, stacked like a *"curio cabinet adorned by the most skilful hands."* You visited the Selimiye Mosque in Edirne, you explored the streets of Pera dressed in mufti, and you bargained in your newly-polished Turkish with merchants in the Grand Bazaar. Your descriptions of those Bosphorus sites, the Topkapı Palace, Hagia Sophia, the Süleymaniye Mosque, the Hippodrome, and the Blue Mosque of Sultan Ahmet read as sharply as in any modern tourist guidebook. You even visited a dervish lodge and related the ceremony of the whirling dervishes.

It was the letter that you wrote from Edirne at the beginning of your stay that particularly caught my attention. You told about your visit to an Ottoman *han*, a commercial warehouse, and spoke of your astonishment at the animal you saw inside it, the camel: this *"stag kind of animal, a great deal higher than a horse, and so swift that they far out-run the swiftest of horses... ugly creatures, more clumsy as an ox."* You provided a detailed description of the building, and stated: *"I own I think these foundations a more reasonable piece of charity than the founding of convents."* Those han buildings, now minus those camels, have captured my attention as well, to the point that they have become an important part of my life over the past 30 years.

Ever since I first gazed at the Gök Medrese in Sivas on my initial trip to Turkey, I have continued on an almost obsessional treasure hunt for golden stones. I have traveled yearly to hunt them down, spending much time, effort, money, and energy in the process. I too, adopted mufti dress to wear along the road and to set me apart from the casual tourist. Perhaps not as elaborate as yours, but one nonetheless composed with attention: a practical, rather than fashionable, outfit of sturdy shoes, ankle-length skirts and long sleeved shirts, with sunglasses and headscarves to protect against the beating sun and indiscrete glances. The outfit is accessorized by a sturdy shoulder bag crammed with essential expedition gear (flashlight, tape measure, notebook, pens, pencils, camera batteries and lenses, the ubiquitous water bottle, guide books, papers, a few Ülker biscuits, sketches and old photos dug up from dusty books, etc.) For you see, Lady Mary, the hunt for golden stones is a bit more complicated than a sweet caique ride up the Bosphorus, as it entails enduring the blazing heat of the Anatolian plains, dust, dangerous roads, objectionable lodgings, and perplexing situations. Yet the call of those stones was always stronger than any inconvenience I endured, and the glow from them has illuminated my life in unexpected ways.

However, it wasn't just any golden stones that I sought, but those of the monuments built during the Seljuk Empire. And it wasn't just any monuments, but the forefathers of that very building you saw in Edirne: the *caravansarais* of the vast Anatolian plains built on the roads radiating from the Seljuk capital of Konya.

I have written to you previously about the eternal question of *"Why Turkey, and for heaven's sake, why Turkey for every year for the past 30 years?"* I told you in that letter that I went there initially to quench an obsession to view a building that haunted me since I first glimpsed a slide of it during a class lecture. I have also tried to explain to you in many other letters why I keep returning each year: that hospitality, those TTs, the peaches, and the similarities with the people I grew up with. Yet if truth be told, the obsession with that building in Sivas and its ilk was a driving force to return each year. Turkey may be filled with friendly Turks and beautiful scenery, but it was the magic of those stones that pulled me back each year, as strongly as any magnet.

To explain the pull of that magnet is often difficult, and at times I just shrug and say to others (as much as I do to myself) that it is just because it is, with no explanation possible. There are certitudes in life that you just do not question: how you take your coffee, why your heart beats faster when you approach your front door, or the one look it takes to know that you have found the love of your life: these things cannot be explained with scientific phenomena. They just are. And so it is with the appeal that the Seljuk era exerts over me. Actually, it is actually two-fold, this fascination with the Seljuk era: the first aspect is the society and culture of the era, and the other is the art it produced.

So who were these Seljuks and the empire they created? Like the Etruscans or Celts, they can often appear remote and unimportant in the great march of history, but to me, they represent a glorious moment of civilization. The Seljuk sultans led an exceptional period of politics, commerce, and art from their glittering capital of Konya. It was a very short but golden era, flourishing from the 11-13th centuries and sandwiched in between the two world-altering events of the Crusades and the Mongol invasions. Yet, in a mere 200 years of existence, from 1077 to 1307, they managed to exert an influential economic and cultural impact. Most importantly, the Seljuk period produced some glorious architecture and decorative arts.

These Seljuks were the founders of the Turkey we know today. They were the last of the great waves of Turkomen tribes that had been slowly migrating westwards since about the ninth century from the area around Lake Baikal in Siberia, looking for fresh pastures, new homelands, and promising possibilities. They were a group that split westward from the Seljuk Turks already settled in Iran, known as the "Great" or "Eastern" Seljuks. Leaving the region of Transoxiana (the area between the Aral Sea and the Caspian Sea) and Khurasan (the area of Northwestern Iran), this branch of the Eastern Seljuks reached Anatolia in the early eleventh century. Previously Shamanists, the Seljuks slowly started to convert to Islam on their march westwards. Although they kept certain elements of their former culture, the Seljuks embraced Islam with fervor and became devout defenders of the faith. They gradually took control of almost all the cities of eastern and central Anatolia, and when they defeated the Byzantines at the key battle of Manzikert (Malazgirt) in eastern Turkey in 1071, the floodgates of Anatolia were opened to them.

These people were builders, in both stones and government. My own country, the United States, has done much of the same in its own 200 years, and I thus feel a kinship with the dynamic endeavors of these Seljuks. They were fighters and survivors: they battled Byzantium to create their empire, they had to fight off the Crusaders who stomped across their lands and pillaged their cities all throughout their existence, and finally, they had to confront the Mongols for their very survival, losing it all to them in the end. Yet despite all those upheavals over 200 years, they managed to create a culture that shone brighter than those of Byzantium, the Crusaders, and the Mongols put together.

This bright civilization shone in many aspects. Look at those golden stones, and you, too, will see it. Look, too, in the cultural traces they left. The Seljuks were responsible for reviving the Muslim caliphate, polishing its crown once again with prestige and respect. They encouraged religious life and developed a particular form of mysticism known as Sufism. They invigorated the scientific and literary realms as well, bringing a new breath of inspiration to the cultural life of Islam. Determined to carve a prominent place for themselves in the world order of the day, the Anatolian Seljuks re-energized the Islamic world due to their governance structures, keen sense of social justice, strong leadership style, religious traditions, entrepreneurial attitude toward trade and commerce, and their devotion to education. Above all, their tolerance towards multiculturalism was a significant component to the success of their society: they accepted the diversity of the other faiths that they found in the lands they conquered: Latins, Greeks, Armenians, Provencals, and Jews. This tolerance has proven to be an effective and enviable societal model for others to emulate, from the Ottomans to the Americans.

Yet in my eyes, the greatest cultural legacy of the Seljuks was the innovative building program they undertook. They erected monuments that were noteworthy by their size, variety, and craftsmanship. In architecture, the Seljuks were fast learners, absorbing lessons from all the design traditions they observed in the areas they crossed. In doing so, they created a building style as rich as the savory stews they cooked on the campaign campfires during their march westwards. They started with the rich stock of their Central Asian roots, then enriched the pot with the meaty lessons learned in their contact with Persian architecture, and seasoned it with the rich vocabulary of Abbasid and Arab monuments. They developed a so-phisticated construction system of load-bearing vaults, and the 4-*iwan* (4 open vaulted halls around a central court) plan they saw in the mosques of Iran strongly influenced everything they built, becoming the universal de-sign plan of the Anatolian Seljuks for their hans, *medreses* (centers of high-er learning), palaces, and hospitals. To this style stew they added a dash of their own particular spice mix of innovative decorative features, techniques, and building styles.

These were not just pretty monuments to look at. The Seljuks under-stood that useful and practical buildings could directly foster the goals of the empire they wished to build. Smart they were, those Seljuk Sultans of Konya! They realized that economic prosperity was the cornerstone for the society they wished to build and that this depended on the free flow of commercial goods throughout the kingdom. They understood that by pro-moting trade and commerce, they would engender prosperity, which in turn, could stimulate intellectual and artistic growth. To achieve this vision, they needed to support trade and incoming revenue by encouraging the transit of goods throughout their lands.

So how were they to go about attracting merchants to bring their goods to Anatolia and to leave with those produced on the plains packed in their bags? The Sultans needed to foster a favorable terrain for trade, one that provided a safe and attractive area in which to do business. And so they rolled up their sleeves and came up with a commercial plan with the same determination they showed on the battlefield.

One after the other, the Seljuk Sultans of Anatolia set out to conquer the important coastal cities they needed to establish sea-to-sea, kingdom-wide trade routes: Antalya in 1207, Sinop in 1214, and finally Alanya in 1221. The next step in this vision was to repair the existing trade routes which had served merchants for generations. The sultans were sharp enough to understand that to make money you had to spend money, and their hands-on approach to building their kingdom involved investing in the construction of a solid infrastructure of bridges and roads. The existing roads and bridges, having been neglected and fallen into disrepair during many years of constant warfare and earthquakes, were repaired, solidified, and new ones were built. The old east-west Assyrian, Persian, and Roman trade routes were dusted off and new links were created between the north and south to connect the newly-conquered ports on the Black and Mediterranean Seas. The country was now open for business: the existing Silk Road, linking China to the Mediterranean, now fed up to Konya, and from there, the "Long Road" led across to Kayseri. From there the road split to lead either northward to Sivas or Erzurum, the Black Sea or the Caucasus and eventually Northern Iran, or either southwards to Diyarbakır, Mesopotamia, and Southern Iran.

The last step in their concerted business plan was to create an infrastructure for the merchants themselves. All along the trade routes they established, they undertook the construction of over 200 merchant way-stations, known as *hans* or *caravansarais*. This network, built to serve the needs of the major cities of the empire, was largely responsible for the expansion of both domestic and international trade. These way-stations were built at regular intervals along the most important trade routes, at a daily camel's pace distance apart (every 40 miles or so). Their architecture answered every need of the traveler: strong protecting walls, depot spaces for goods, guard rooms, stables, rooms for sleeping, kitchens, latrines, mosques, and vaults. These hans served as both trading posts and overnight inns. To use a modern comparison, hans were actually a combination of a truck stop, a motel, and a warehouse. As a truck stop, they offered a place to refuel, which in those days meant resting the animals, watering them, shodding them, and tending to any illnesses they may have picked up. It allowed the merchants the possibility of eating a cooked meal, taking a break from the road, and easing the loneliness of the journey through socialization with fellow travelers. As a motel, hans allowed the merchants to rest for the night in fairly reasonable and comfortable quarters. As a warehouse, hans gave them the opportunity to unload their gear in a safe environment, to store it, sort through it, repackage it if necessary, and prepare for the next arduous leg of the journey.

The building of hans with their adjunct array of social services represents one of the most liberal institutions created by the Seljuks. Hans were established as charitable foundations. Every traveler, whatever his nationality, religion, or social status, was entitled to three days free lodging with food, medical care, and other services, all at the expense of the State. The

Sultan, other court members, or private wealthy individuals established foundations for their construction, ongoing operating expenses, and up-keep. These hans will long be remembered for this generosity of services and the non-commercial role they played, just as you noted in Edirne, Lady Mary. Merchants could meet with the other travelers in the han, forming commercial alliances and new friendships. Hans also served another impor-tant, non-commercial feature: they helped to spread news and information throughout the empire. People from all areas and countries came together, related events, shared situations they had experienced in a Babel of languag-es, and told of news from their home regions. This news was then passed on to the local villages and towns. In this sense, hans served as an informa-tion hub, local news center, and a sort of oral public library. Anyone who travels on the long roads across Turkey today can see the descendants of these hans, in the form of the elaborate roadside rest stops *(tesisler)* that provide services for truckers and travelers alike.

Once the state coffers were filled with the money earned from the use of these hans, the Seljuk Sultans turned to the construction of the other in-novative architectural buildings for which they became famous: *medreses* (universities), hospitals, and mosques. The Anatolian Seljuks built in stone, to last, abandoning the use of brick that was the practice of their Iranian forbearers. They devised buildings adapted to the needs of the empire they wished to create, one of growth and dynamic energy. It was in the form, function, and character of their civil buildings that the Anatolian Seljuks showed their brightest talent, starting with the development of the *me-drese*, which become a focal point for the city. The medreses applied the 4-iwan design plan to construct a campus building able to provide spaces for classrooms, lodging for students, study halls, and annex services. Hospi-tals and medical centers used the same plan as well, with ever-present wel-coming twin minarets framing the portal. These medreses and hospitals are some of the most beautiful monuments to be seen in Turkey today, such as the Karatay and İnce Medreses in Konya, the Hatun Medrese in Kayseri, the Daruşşifa medical school in Sivas, and the Gevher Hospice in Kayseri.

All of this was extremely fascinating to me, for it seemed so practical, founded in good sense, and so vibrant at the same time. Since my universi-ty days, I have enjoyed studying the arts of Islam. Islamic art took things from many cultures, mixed them up, and put their own spin to create something unique: in many ways like the culture of the United States. I was also attracted to the otherness of Islamic art, and I wanted to go beyond my garden gate of the Western European canon and see how others think, believe, and build. I wanted to pursue a dialog of artistic differences. Of all the eras of Islamic art, the Seljuks of Anatolia spoke to me the loudest. In addition, the thirteen century was one of great development, all over the world. Who can remain insensitive to this period, the era that witnessed the Crusades and Genghis Khan, Dante, Provençal troubadour poetry, the Magna Carta, and the High Gothic Cathedrals in France? This was a remarkable time to be alive, and the Seljuks were in the midst of it all, participating in their own fashion to the greatness of the century. I was especially drawn to their spirit of tolerance for all the peoples that they found when they came to Anatolia. I was attracted to their hands-on industriousness and will to forge a new social identity that respected the people before them, but also one that put forth an agenda they wanted to create. I was especially impressed by their association of architecture with social improvement, and how they understood that art and architecture could and should help build not only an ideal but ensure the well-being of its citizens. I wanted to get to know these people and their society better.

Above all, I wanted to get to know their architecture better. Of all the buildings the Seljuks created, the hans seemed to be the most innovative and pertinent. I was intrigued by this practical set of buildings that united such a utilitarian purpose with such a particular attention to beauty and detail. Vetruvius, the famed Roman architect and engineer, gives us a definition of architecture as *"firmness, commodity and delight,"* and these hans offer a perfect example of a very felicitous union of these three traits: firmness because they certainly stand up well, commodity because they served the purpose to encourage commerce, and delight because such attention was paid to making them beautiful. And quite simply, hans corresponded to my taste: hans are big, powerful, rigorous and gutsy; traits I admire not only in architecture, but in people, food, literature, and arts. I decided then and there that I wanted to study them in detail.

And so I have spent the past 30 years on the trail of the Seljuks, hunting up their monuments, learning about their history, reading their literature, absorbing their religious and scientific traditions. I have learned much about all of these and have come to greatly admire the Seljuks for many unsuspected reasons. In addition to the entrepreneurial and dynamic attitude that they cultivated, I deem that they laid the basis for all the humanist values that inspired the Turkish culture to follow: tolerance, freedom, love, friendship, hospitality, multiculturalism, neighborliness, patriotism, and respect for others. At the same time they built their roads and hans, they laid the foundation stones for the development of the cultural values of progress, education, economic advancement, long-term planning, expansion, intellectual pursuit, justice, and free speech. Their leaders bettered the lives of citizens by building schools, mosques, hospitals, and observatories. Their scientists and scholars stimulated evolution in medicine, chemistry, law, and astronomy. Their folk writers, poets, and mystics sung the ideals of love, intimacy, hospitality, and spirituality in their creations. Their hard-working farmers plowed to prosperity the black earth beneath them. Their merchants skillfully and honestly developed their markets. Their architects and artists built monuments whose beauty and details sung these ideals across the Anatolian plains for all to hear.

All the architectural treasures that have come down to us today from this period became possible because these visionary sultans ordered buildings to stoke the commerce machine, which then fed the creation of other types of buildings designed to reflect their cultural aspirations. Somehow, all of this sounds very familiar to those observing or living in modern Turkey: the dynamic tigers of Turkey today are none other than the grandchildren of the Seljuks of Konya. I firmly believe that if the Seljuks had not done such a worthy job at this initial empire building, there would perhaps have been no Ottomans or no modern Republic of Turkey to follow. It is not for nothing that Atatürk returned to the geographical and idealistic core of the Seljuks to establish his capital at Ankara and from there to radiate his vision for Turkey and to reinstill a sense of pride in hard work, progress, and industry as the values of a successful society, values that we are seeing laid with renewed vigor in today's Turkey.

Because so many hans still stand, it was possible for me to study them and formulate certain generalizations about them, such as their plans, patronage, road networks, and their decoration. The librarian in me enjoyed studying, classifying, and comparing this distinctive and unified group. I set out on a systematic concerted plan, region by region, to visit every year as many of these hans as I could. I would plan the trips ahead of time with great care and attention and would visit several hans in a specific area on each trip. The adventures I had along the way were often as interesting and intriguing as the monuments themselves.

To find a han, there were often aggravating challenges: mismarked maps, non-existent roads, no signs, etc... but the most frustrating was the fact that few local Turks were able to help me when I asked them for directions. The combination of my poor Turkish, foreign accent, and differences in local dialects often made asking for directions a challenge. Another complication is that a Turk is reluctant to admit to you that he does not know what you are talking about or that he doesn't know where it is. I have learned that Turks hold honor over truth, and sometimes have difficulty distinguishing between theory, the desire to be helpful, and practice. They will tell you that something exists (or is even just in the planning stages) just to make you happy. Taxi drivers do not always know where they are going either but seldom admit it, often driving around in circles. They will also refuse to show you something they think you should not see, much like the waiters in restaurants who will not allow you to eat what you want if they do not think it is in your best interest. When the locals do know that old pile of rocks I am referring to, they scratch their head in disbelief when this foreign woman is asking directions to see it. Sometimes I envy you, Lady Mary, in that you always had a *valet de place* guiding you on your outings in Constantinople: such was not my fortune.

Yet I would not have given up these frustrations for all the kebabs of Kayseri. Being a pioneer may have led me on some complicated, round-about trails to find a han, but in doing so, I had the opportunity to spend time chatting with people and learning local lore that I would not have learned had I arrived directly in front of my destination. So my golden rule has become to be patient: not to rush, not to get upset that you cannot get the immediate answer to your questions, to accept that the answer given may be embroidered, and to use this moment to pursue some interesting interchange. Ask directions from 5 people and take the majority view, say a prayer that after traveling 500 miles to a hot and arid place, lo and behold, eventually, you should be able to find your han. For, in the end, a Turk will never say "*I don't know*" and leave you stranded: that you can be assured of. A Turk will never say "*no*" to a request for information and will spend a whole day with you trying to help you find your treasure, for a Turk is always an optimist.

An example of this optimism was seen in my search for the Altınapa Han. I had read in many texts that it existed, and I had seen old photos of it in dusty books. Yet it proved impossible to find it on the road outside of Konya at the spot where it should have been located. I stopped my car to ask directions at a roadside tea garden, and a typical chaotic *alla turca* scene ensued, with 6 Turks and 6 different semi-answers. First, I approached a 50-year-old Turk, thinking he would have some knowledgeable idea about the area in which he lived. He paused for a moment and replied, "*Well, yes, I have heard of it; yes, well, let's think, well, that's right, there is a han around here somewhere....*" He did not seem to know, but in a typical positive Turkish fashion, did not wish to appear unhelpful and continued to talk around an answer as politely as possible. A second Turk showed up, entered into the conversation and piped up, "*I think I can help! I am sure my friends will know!*" He grabbed me and took me around to a charming set-up of picnic tables overlooking the lake created by the Altinapa dam. Sitting there were three Turks, enjoying the view over the water, smoking cigarettes, and drinking tea. The third Turk put down his tea and pointed across the lake. "*See that grove of poplar trees over there? Well, it is behind them. You can find a road that will go over there.*" His friend, the fourth Turk, interjected: "*Oh, no, abi, it's not there at all, that han has completely fallen down and no longer exists!*" The tone started to rise. In piped up the fifth Turk: "*Oh, my brothers! You have got it all wrong; it is lying at the bottom of the lake!*" A heated discussion with much hand-waving, yelling, pushing, and poking ensued, with another round of tea ordered to bring counsel. The sixth Turk, who appeared to be the umpire in the situation, concluded the discussion by saying: "*Well, wherever it is, I'm sure it is just fine. Now, don't you worry about it, my Lady Visitor, you will find lots more old hans in this area if you want to see one, and after all, what was so special about that particular one? I'll help you find one you will like just as well!*" In reality, the fifth Turk had it right. One of the tragic victims of Turkey's vigorous dam construction projects was the Altınapa Han, which was flooded over when the dam was built in 1967.

Another time, I had difficulty locating the Kırkgöz Han, located near Antalya. A similar scenario as the Altınapa show ensued when I stopped to ask directions: 5 Turks came running over and started to argue among themselves, each one offering two opinions. The discussion among themselves got so heated that I began to fear the results, and sure enough, before I knew it, they got so worked up that they started pushing and shoving each other. Fearing a fist fight, I started to pull away, but one chivalrous knight would not leave me in the lurch. Even though his buddies didn't believe him, insulted him, and even punched him, he persisted and told me exactly how to get there, giving me very vivid landmarks to look for along the way. His unusual clarity inspired confidence in me, and off I went, from landmark to landmark (military police station, tree with three branches, house with the green door...) and sure enough, he was right! Only a Turk would take such pains to help a stranger, to the point of risking a black eye.

As I mentioned previously, I learned, after much experience, that people are not always aware of the historical riches in their midst, or even in their neighborhoods. That glorious historical piece of architecture you have traveled 5,000 miles to see is often only an old pile of rocks to them. Locals would try so hard to understand my request, but many times, they would just shake their heads and say they did not know what in the world I was talking about. I did learn a valuable trick, however, that has served me well: come well-armed with photos or sketches if you can. I once planned a trip to Eğirdir to visit the Gelendost Han which I had read was located about 30 miles north of the town. I approached the municipal taxi stand next to the bus station and approached the 15 or so taxi drivers who were sitting on a low wall passing the time drinking tea, playing backgammon, reading newspapers, chatting, jiggling prayer beads, and smoking. I decided to pin my hopes on one fellow, knowing that in any case, all 15 of them would soon join in on the transaction. I asked if he knew the han and if he would take me there. I could tell instantly that he did not know, but in typical fashion, would not betray the fact. A major conferral session ensued, with all 15 drivers giving their opinion, not one of them aware of the location of the han. The tone rose, they started to wave hands about and argue, and I feared yet another fistfight. To calm things down, I pulled out a photocopied picture of it from an old book and showed it to them. Bingo! He indeed recognized the pile of rocks, even though he had no idea what it was. Off we went, and he had no problem locating it, and I took immense pleasure that afternoon in explaining to him the history of the building and why it was more that just a pile of rocks. I am sure he went back and told the other 15 drivers, who in turn returned home to tell their families. Since then, I have found that a photograph, when I have one, is a valuable finding tool when in the field.

After the thrill of the han hunt was over, I was never disappointed by what followed. The emotion was always the same when I stood in front of a han: I would gaze at it like a star-struck teenager in front of a movie star. Like snowflakes and cats, each han is different: the stones were always of a varying hue, the portal decoration was more or less elaborate, the setting either arid or wooded, the location in the middle of a field or beside the road. I always like to stand in front of them for a long time, to absorb all these differences, to sense the history of each of them, to imagine the energy that went in to their creation 800 years before. I want to memorize their face and personality, and to "make friends" with the han before respectfully entering.

Yet entering these hans often proved problematic, presenting me the second trial on my pilgrimage journeys. The possibility of visiting the interiors of hans was never a given proposition, and the challenge of gaining entry was always an adventure in itself. It was always a disappointment and frustration to have spent much money to get to Turkey, so much effort to trek out to the Anatolian plains, and then much energy to find a han... only to find a huge iron chain and padlock on the door.

But remember, this is Turkey. Nothing is impossible here; everything can be accomplished with a little help from friends who will do anything to satisfy your request in any way they can. And the country of Turkey is full of friends, especially for a woman who wants to enter a han. When I arrived in front of the Durağan Han, my heart sank, as once again the door was shut tight with the dreaded padlock and chain. As if possessed with ultrasonic ears that could hear my sigh, a vegetable merchant from across the street came running over before I knew it and told me to stay put. He ran, not walked, down the street and grabbed a municipal street sweeper who had a bunch of keys on a chain. The poor fellow could not understand why the shopkeeper was pulling him by the arm, yanking the straw broom out of his hands, and dragging him back up the street. The vegetable man argued and argued with him and finally the poor confused soul gave in, pulled the key off his chain and opened the door for me to step into this han, which had been completely restored as a shopping center. None of the stalls were rented, however, and the place was totally empty. Afterwards, I realized that the greengrocer was not being unkind or had not meant any disrespect to the street cleaner. He knew instinctively that the man, even in his modest state, would feel important to have helped someone from so far away and that I would give a tip to him to thank him for his time and effort. And so in this way, he accomplished a two-for-the-price-of-one act of charity for the both us, and I got to see my han.

Another time, I arrived at İncesu to visit the Karamustafa Paşa Complex and notably its vast Ottoman han. As usual, the han was locked up tight and my heart sank. A Turk who saw me standing on my tiptoes trying to look into the high windows came over and told me to come with him. When we got to a far corner of the outer wall of the han, he asked me to wait there and then disappeared. Before long, one of the stones on the wall started to wiggle, and then fell inwards. A hand reached out and pulled me though a small hole so that I could gain access to the interior of the han. As I squirmed out into the vast courtyard, there was the man, grinning from ear to ear and bursting with pride at his exploit.

However, there have been other countless times when I met with a chained and padlocked han located in a totally deserted area, and no Turkish magic hands to mysteriously appear to pull me through secret passages. In this case, my good old Yankee "*just do it!*" attitude clicked in, emboldening me in ways I would never dream possible at home. I have squeezed my rather large frame though doors ajar, or have hoisted myself up over walls by grasping chinks to secure footholds to climb up and plop myself over into the courtyard like a cat burglar. If the wall was too high, I have piled up rocks to create a ladder to give me a boost over the top of a wall. I have run and taken leaps from piles of dirt like an Olympic pole jumper. Squeezing in through tight door spaces and scaling over walls has been worth all the resulting scraped knuckles, broken nails, bleeding hands, bruises, twisted ankles, and bloodied knees. I will never forget the emotion of my first visit to the Pazar Han, where I dared to force the door open and crawl inside, despite the angry squawking of the gaggle of geese standing guard outside. As I made my way through the wild underbrush and overgrown grass and listened to the fluttering pigeon wings in the arcades, I was able to look past the tumble of rubble and fallen stones to see something else. I discovered a han laid out in a perfectly powerful plan, with exquisite decorative elements of fine craftsmanship. More than that, I sensed the evocation of the space. I felt the message of history talking to me, and I knew from that moment on that I had to make the story of this han, as well as that of so many others, come to life.

Although I have been extremely creative and very athletic in my approach to visiting the interiors of hans, I have never officially broken a lock or a door to gain entrance. No, for breaking and entering, I could count on the Turks to lead the way.

Yes, once again, I have seen in this way how Turks will stop at nothing to help you out, to render service, to make sure you get your interest satisfied, and this often in rather dramatic ways. As you may recall, Lady Mary, I told you about that colorful visit to Siirt in eastern Turkey where I survived the attack of the rowdy mob of street urchins. After escaping them, I persisted in my desire to visit the Ulu (Great) Mosque of the city, one of the oldest in Turkey, built in 1129. Like a guardian angel sent from on high, a man came out of a neighboring house and took me under his wing. Alas, the mosque was shut tight with chain and padlock, and he shook his head in regret. A few seconds later the grimy face of one of those street urchins, still tagging behind me, peered up at me. As if to ask forgiveness for the unfortunate incident with his buddies, he said he would help me. This little rogue proceeded to pull out of his pocket a very long piece of metal that looked like a broken knife blade, and started to jiggle the latch and pick the lock with it with the experience of a seasoned burglar. Before you could count to ten, he had sprung the lock and proudly opened the door for me to enter, offering me the guilty pleasure of contemplating the interior of this impressive mosque. Both guardian angel and rogue came with me inside, partners in crime at the service of a visitor and of art history.

Nothing quite prepared me for a few of the other dramatic unorthodox entries I have had along the way. One of the oddest was at the Zazadin Han outside of Konya. The han is in a fairly deserted area, in the midst of sown fields. As I approached the han and saw cows grazing in front of it, I flashbacked to the scene when I first gazed upon those golden stones of the Gök Medrese in Sivas 10 years prior. I walked across a deserted field of rubble and thistles to reach the impressive main portal. Of course, it was padlocked. My heart sank as heavy as that cursed lock: how unfair to be frustrated after such a hot trek across that prickly field, which had torn my hem and bloodied my ankles! Except for those cows and the buzzing flies around my head, there was no sign of life or hope of helping hands. The walls of the han were extremely high, so I knew I would not be able to achieve one of my Mt. Everest repelling expeditions. Frustrated, but still determined to get the best out of the visit that I could, I resigned myself to walking around the perimeter of this vast han to observe its fine outer walls, which were decorated with numerous carved stones reused from Byzantine churches. As I stood there sketching the design of one of these recycled blocks, I sensed the presence of someone by my side. Silently and seemingly out of nowhere had appeared next to me a strange-looking, dark-haired man with wild eyes, dressed in grimy khaki fatigues, combat boots... and carrying a long, black 12-gauge hunting rifle. I took a deep breath and wondered how I was going to extricate myself from this situation with my life intact. He stared at me, glanced over at my notebook and started to speak, his ebony eyes flashing in the bright sun. Although I had a bit of trouble deciphering his garbled speech, I came to understand that he was a nomad living off the land and that he had come here to shoot birds. As he explained it, the han was full of many kinds of plump game birds that he could easily bag. *"Come, I will show you!"* he stated, and although I was still more than uneasy about it, I followed him. Would I ever have followed an incoherent, wild-eyed homeless man with a shotgun in a deserted field in America? Not on your life, but this was Turkey, and somehow I trusted that this was not going to end tragically. We came around again to the front of the han, and, without a moment's hesitation, he lifted his shotgun and took aim. After a flash of light and a roar, the padlock was history. Swinging by its singed metal bits on the frame of the door, it was no longer an impediment to my entry or to his bagging of dinner. And so, in this rather unconventional way, I gained entry to one of the largest and most impressive hans in Turkey, which was indeed filled with game birds. When my hunter started after them, I left and wondered if I would ever have such an eventful visit again.

Of course, I should have known that I would have other unorthodox entries. A few years later, I pulled up in front of the Karatay Han after a rather difficult time of locating it and spending two hours stuck in the car in the middle of a flock of sheep on their way to market. Once again, there was an impressive flock of geese standing guard in front, very high unscalable walls, and... a chain and padlock that looked as if it should have been attached to the door of the Topkapı Palace, rather than this empty han. Not again, not another futile attempt to visit a han! I kicked the cursed door in frustration and tried to lift the chain to feel how much it weighed, as I don't think I had ever seen one so large. A little boy, no more than 5 years old, came up to me, stared at my frustrated face, and understood my unhappiness from the universal language of my sighs, scowl, and kicks. He ran away, and after a few minutes, I heard in the distance a hearty yell of "*Halloo! I am here to help you!*" I looked up to find a Turk running towards me, waving, and smiling with the little boy scurrying behind him to catch up. As he got closer, I saw that he was carrying an axe in his right hand. This was no small hatchet, but one that could fell a redwood. "*You want to go inside, I take it? Don't worry, I am here to take care of you! Just leave to me!*" With the little wide-eyed boy standing next to him, he lifted his mighty axe and proceeded to take on the dragon in the form of the giant chain. Pleased to show off his masculinity in front of the damsel in distress, my chivalrous knight whacked away at the chain with impressive grunts. It took him no more than four whomping thuds to split one of the links of the chain, freeing the padlock. He pushed the large creaking wooden door open with much effort, and then turned to me. With a smile on his face as wide as the entry passage itself, he gestured me to enter with a dramatic sweep of his arm, as if I were none other than Alaeddin Keykubad himself. And for one small moment, I felt as if I were indeed the good Sultan.

All this breaking and entering has been worth the danger, for the moments of pleasure at the discovery of these hans has been priceless. Favorite moments include walking across the 13-arched bridge next to the Kesikköprü Han, one of the longest in all of Turkey, listening to the gurgling water of the Kızılırmak River swirling below it and the shrieks of the young boys bathing in its currents. I enjoyed spending an afternoon inside the Issiz Han near Apolyant, now used as a depot for farm produce. I sat among the gigantic mounds of onions stored there, dizzy from their heady odor, pitching in to help the village women who were sorting them into piles by size. They laughed and laughed at me when I hesitated, or perhaps about my funny accent or clothes. But laugh we did, and together we shared a moment of feminine solidarity, despite our differences. I remember going early one morning to visit the equestrian statue of Alaeddin Keykubad at the entry to the city of Alanya. As I stood in front of it, I reflected on the life of this sultan who captured the city for the Seljuks in 1221 and who was responsible for building so many of these hans I seek. Out of nowhere appeared a municipal worker who then disappeared into the base of the statue and turned on all the fountains of the surrounding garden, in order to heighten my moment of historical recognition. It was once again an example of those wonderful thoughtful gestures I told you about, Lady Mary. I lived a very impressive han experience in Doğubeyazıt, in the shadow of Mount Ararat near the Iranian border. As I stood on the balcony of my hotel room located across from the Sim-Er truck stop at 7:30 one morning, I listened to the deafening rumble of international freight trucks idling for departure. I then watched them as they pulled out of the parking lot in a convoy, all 57 of them, one after the other, much as I imagine the merchants and their camels did as they departed each morning from the vast portals of the Seljuk hans, ready to set out in all directions to deliver and trade their goods. The Seljuk roads of commerce are indeed still alive and well today.

Everyone always asks me what is my favorite han, and I cannot select one in particular, just as I cannot choose a favorite poem, painting, or friend. But I have some that I remember above others, mostly due to those colorful breaking and entry adventures, or for their setting, their architectural singularities, their historical evocation, or for personal reasons. I am in awe when I see the Şarafsa han perched like an eagle on its dramatic site over the Mediterranean Sea. I marvel at how well the massive towers of Karatay han reflect the power and severity of its patron, the Vizier Celaleddin Karatay. I admire the Ağızkara and the Sarı hans for the shimmering caramel hue of their stones and the Kayseri Sultan han for the magical dragon snakes carved on its courtyard kiosk mosque. I am touched by the lonely isolation of the Kargı Han and overwhelmed by the elaborate ensemble of the Kesikköprü Han and that unforgettable bridge nearby. I am humbled by the immensity of the courtyard of the Kırkgöz Han, and I am inspired by the evocative decoration on the portal of the Evdir Han. I am intrigued by the origin of the sparkling stones reused from Byzantine churches that punctuate the walls of the Obruk and Zazadin Hans. One thing is certain: in all of them, I can hear the voices of their creators echoing in the arcades: Alaeddin Keykubad, Karatay, Mahperi Hatun, and Gıyaseddin Keyhüsrev.

As you can see from the stories above, visiting those hans taught me as much about the Turks as it did about Seljuk architecture. I saw that although no two hans have the exact same plan, they are all either rectangular or square in shape, with or without a covered section to the rear of an open courtyard. I learned to appreciate how their tall and thick walls were built with finely-hewn blocks of honey-colored local limestone. I passed through spectacular monumental entrance gates, decorated with some of the finest examples of Seljuk stone carving. I walked around their perimeters to see the massive, fortress-like towers of the outer walls. I stood in vast courtyards, surrounded by cells, and tried to imagine the cacophony of braying animals and the Babel of languages of the merchants as they unloaded their goods. When I peered in their dark cells, I tried to imagine their use: were they used as storage cells, baths, repair shops, or granaries? I imagined I felt the heat of their braziers and the flickering light from their candles dancing on the walls. When I entered the large covered halls beyond the courtyard, I could still detect the heady odor of the animals stabled here. I imagined hearing the call to prayer as I climbed up stairs leading to rooftop platform mosques or the upper floor of a cube mosque in the middle of the courtyard. The total silence in most of these deserted hans made it easier for me to imagine what must have been the noisy roar from the staff, merchants, and animals inside.

Once back home in the reading rooms of libraries, I read everything I could on the Seljuks, their culture, and their architecture. I learned that the leading export products for the Seljuks were refined sugar and alum, the most important mordant for dyeing wool. I learned that major trading originated in the cities of Konya, Sivas, and Kayseri. I learned about the many items unloaded from the backs of camels coming from Egypt, China, Central Asia, Georgia, Syria, Iraq, and the Caucasus that were tethered at the end of day in the courtyards of the great Anatolian hans: spices, arms, cotton, woolens, silks, musk and perfumes, glass, cobalt, gun powder, porcelain, pearls, gems, pepper, gold and silver, pharmaceutical products, and furs. I learned what those caravans took back from Turkey with them to their countries: tin, alum, sugar, borax, lapis, leather, mohair, timber, apricots, olives, wheat, textiles, carpets and salt, not to forget mail and official government documents that were also transported along these routes.

All of this information was fascinating to me, and I enjoyed making notebooks of my sketches, photos and research. I could revisit each of these hans as often as I wished on their pages, and I was thrilled to have my own personal guidebook to the discovery of Seljuk art and architecture. Yet one day, I realized that this information should not be kept in piles of notebooks on my desk. The librarian in me felt the obligation to diffuse the information that I had collected and organized, and the amateur of Turkey that I am wanted to make this architecture better known to the world. I also saw that there was little available information on the topic of Seljuk hans in the West, and I hoped to fill in that blank. And so, in 2000, at the start of the internet explosion, I decided to share my notebooks with the world via this most democratic of venues. The overarching aim of my website was to educate people and to generate a greater appreciation of the art, history, and architecture of the Seljuk period. My objectives at the onset were simple: I wanted to create an information resource in English that would serve as an introduction to the Turkish han, furnish a descriptive list of hans currently standing, and provide resources for those who wish to study the architecture of hans, or even to visit them. I was unsure at that time if anyone would care about these hans, or would visit the website, but I decided to create it anyway. I designed it entirely on my own, and I will never forget the joy and sense of accomplishment as I uploaded it live for the first time.

However, underlying these clearly stated public objectives, I had several fundamental personal objectives. I also wanted to convey this information to all potential user groups, not just specialists in the field or academics. I wanted this site to be a serious study, but transparent enough for the average, non-academic user to enjoy at his level. I chose the format of a *catalogue raisonné* (a detailed description of each han) to do this, rather that long essays on the subject matter. Above all other motivations, I wanted to share my love and admiration of Turkey with the world. Much like these letters I am writing to you, Lady Mary, I wished to convey my sensitivity and affinity for the country of Turkey: its people, its landscape, its history, its art, its architecture, its hopes. As a person who has devoted her career to cross-cultural relations, I felt this website was a way for me to explain my interests and to further mutual understanding and respect.

Along the way, my website, *www.turkishhan.org*, has offered me much happiness. Organizing the photos, writing the text, determining how

I wanted to present the information, and designing the layout have all given me immense joy. It has also given me other delights, such as the impetus to continue my research and to speak to students and journalists about my work. The greatest reward, however, has been in observing the reaction of Turks to what I have to say about their architecture and history.

When I tell Westerners that I am interested in this tiny slice of history, I spend much time explaining to them the particulars of the era and why I admire this civilization. Yet I find that I spend a lot of time explaining the same thing to Turks, who often are not aware of the richness of this time of their history. The Seljuk era has been completely overshadowed by the Ottoman period, the one of glory and fame for the Turks. The Seljuks are mostly reduced to a brief section in textbooks, and the farther one lives from the Konya-Sivas-Kayseri triangle, the more remote they seem. It has given me much satisfaction and reward over the years to share my enthusiasm of the period with the Turks, and the joy I see on their faces as they come to share my passion is more rewarding to me than feedback I have received in the West.

I have been interviewed on Turkish television, and I also was fortunate enough to be the subject of a full-page article in a Turkish newspaper, complete with photos of me, hans, and an interview about my work. This "strange American lady" rebaptized "Kadriye" proved to be of interest to the Turks. I started to receive letters from all corners of Turkey about this article, telling me how they enjoyed reading it and learning more about this era. It was in these letters that I learned that many Turks came to discover this period through my website. Turks told me how they were now planning to take their family vacation to visit the hans, they sent me photos, books, poems, and invitations to visit them. It was a magnificent display of that Turkish kindness and respect I have often spoken about to you, Lady Mary. I have since visited some of the people that wrote to me, and friendships have been made on the basis of this mutual respect for history. I have seen how this simple website has done much to fill Turks with a pride in their heritage, and this warms my heart more than anything I could have imagined when I first set out to create it.

I have also learned from the reactions to my website that the Seljuk decorative arts, although long overshadowed by Ottoman arts, have started to appreciate in value in the eyes of Turks. Seljuk art, like any art at the base of a culture, seeks to confirm or express in each artwork man's spirit, physical structure, and relation to society and nature, combined with attention to detail, advancing techniques, mastery, and elegance. So what does their art say about the Seljuks? It says they are confident, strong, in charge, solid, and turned to serving both society and God.

Turks have not lost sight of the fact that these arts must be preserved in order to ensure an important sense of cultural independence. Two new carpet museums have been created in Istanbul, the London Islamic salesrooms at Sotheby's are full of Turkish bidders, and the famed Paşabahce glassworks has come out with a spectacular collection of glass that imitates medieval models: all of this signifies a renewed interest and pride in their culture.

I remember distinctly when I went to Turkey in 1978 and wished to buy a carpet. Unfortunately my student budget would not allow me to buy the carpet of my dreams, so I lowered my sights to a *heybe* saddle bag, one of those small universal bags that stored everthing from salt to spoons. I kept asking my Turkish friend to help me find one, and he looked at me perplexed. He just could not understand what I was asking for, and both of us were getting more and more frustrated. Finally, I saw one in a back alley and showed him. He stared at me in disbelief and said, *"A donkey bag! You want a donkey bag?! Are you crazy? Whatever would you want to do with a rotten, dirty old bag full of fleas and horsehair?"* Today there would not be such a reaction to that request, for I believe that Turks have gained respect and pride in their heritage. Their crafts now allow them to connect to the past, something very important to them. As Turkey forges ahead at breakneck pace to a new future, this is one area that can provide a reference point to connect with their families and their ancestors as a whole.

Along these lines, one of the unstated motivations of my website on Seljuk hans was to sensitize people to historic preservation. From my first visit to a han, I have witnessed a tremendous change in the way they are maintained and used. Gazing upon the carved zodiac stones of the façade of the Gök Medrese in Sivas in 1978, I had to step around cows peacefully munching grass in front of the medrese. Now, it has become engulfed in modern construction. So it is for many hans. It is important to make sure that the hans currently standing are preserved for future generations. Not just for future generations of architects who will come to study them, but for the children of Turkey, who, by coming to visit them, will "read" the memoirs of their civilization.

Ottoman-era monuments have been opened as museums or skillfully renovated for adaptive reuse in the major tourist cities of Istanbul and Ankara. Ottoman medreses have been skillfully turned into health clinics (Bursa Yıldırım, Eyüp Sokollu, Üsküdar Mihrimah), libraries (Istanbul Şemsi Paşa, Üsküdar Mihrimah Mektep), or warehouses for businesses (Ulukışla Öküz Mehmet Han, Edirne Han). The houses of entire Ottoman towns, such as Safranbolu, have been preserved. The monuments of the Seljuk period have received attention as well: the spectacular medreses and mosques of Konya, Sivas, Alanya, Antalya, and Kayseri offer the interested student of Seljuk architecture much material for observation. Hans, too, form an architectural heritage worthy of the same consideration. When I first started to hunt hans in the early 80s, only a few had been preserved and turned into museums by the Turkish government, notably the two spectacular Sultan Hans of Alaeddin Keykubad, one on the Aksaray-Konya road and the other on the Kayseri-Sivas Road. Since that time, several other hans have been opened as living museums by the Turkish government, notably the Ağzikarahan and the Sarı Han.

Next to these spectacular examples, others stand abandoned and falling into ruin. It is estimated that almost ½ of the hans originally built have been lost, which is not surprising in this land trampled by Crusaders and Mongol hordes and shaken by seismic horrors. Yet many hans have not been destroyed by them but by the hands of unthinking modern citizens. Many hans were demolished for profit, with their stones being sold for building materials or as collectible antiques, a phenomenon common in Europe. Another tragic consequence was the disappearance of a han due to the flooding of a dam, as was the case of that mysterious Altinapa Han on the Konya-Beyşehir Road.

Happily, many hans remain in good condition. Often they have been "adopted" by the village in which they are located and serve as municipal storage or farm co-op buildings to store farm machinery, goats and sheep and crops, a use not unlike their original intent. Over the past 5 years it has been the policy undertaken by the Turkish government to subcontract the restoration of a monument to an outside company or vendor who then runs it as a business once the restoration is completed. The Seljuk medreses of Sahibiye, Avgunu, and Seraceddin in Kayseri have been turned into bookstores, and the Sivas Darüşşifa and the Kayseri Hatun Han have been turned into shopping centers and tea gardens. The same practice is now being applied to hans, which are being modified to suit contemporary needs. The Durağan han is being used as a commercial shopping center, the Horozlu and Niğde Saruhans are now tourist restaurants, the Kesikköprü Han is used by the local municipality for civic events and weddings, and the Sarı Han is now a mixed-use cultural center for tourists. The Alara han now offers numerous merchant stalls to sell artifacts and handicrafts to busloads of visiting tourists from Alanya. There are less usual reuse programs: the Kadın Han is a furniture store, the Şarafsa Han has transformed into a discothèque, and the Tercan Han has been turned into a sports gymnasium. The construction ribbon was cut in 2007 to completely renovate the Zazadin Han by the municipality of Konya. It is odd for me to think that its front door, so dramatically blown open by my shotgun-toting friend, will now be opened to all to enter. There are also projects, such as for the Hatun, Ezine, and Hekim Hans, where the sites have been cleaned up and leased but without firm projects determined.

Turks are becoming more and more culturally aware in their daily lives of this need for historic preservation of their architectural monuments. Over the past few years, there has been an increasing production of high-quality books with elaborate photos and documentation. The Turks have for many years published ethnographic-style books on the various regions of Turkey, with black and white photos of local historic monuments, the fleet of fire and garbage trucks, local crops, and costumes. These books, complete with local dialect terms, folk sayings, and songs, are *catalogue raisonné* snapshots of a proud community. They are becoming increasingly sophisticated and are now accompanied with CDs, DVDs, and interactive CD-ROMs containing photographs of professional quality. I have met 3 famous photographers in Konya – Ahmet Kuş, İbrahim Dıvarcı and Feyzi Şimşek – who have set out on a mission to publish spectacular high-quality photographs of all the cultural monuments of Konya and Turkey to ensure that there will be a record of their heritage. Turks are awakening to their cultural richness and are promoting awareness of it.

It is commendable that an effort is being made by the Turkish government to preserve these hans. It is unrealistic to expect that all buildings should remain frozen in time and retain their original profile and use. Life marches forth, and in historic preservation, one must encourage new life for a building. A building, like the civilization in which it sits, is an evolving, living organism. In this vein, it is encouraging to see that these hans are being creatively adapted for use in the twenty-first century. By encouraging their use in a contemporary social function, it is certain that their preservation will be assured by bringing them into the life of a modern world. In May, 2008, a joint wedding ceremony for 35 couples was held in the newly-renovated Zazadin Han in Konya, as magnificent a start for the new life of this han as it is for these lucky couples. Respect for cultural patrimony is an integral part of becoming a modern nation, and it is to be hoped that Turks will continue to be as compassionate for preservation as they are in the other aspects of their lives.

So you see, Lady Mary, how hans have enriched my life: their study has taught me about architecture, brought me cultural awareness, provided me fanciful adventures, shone light on the Turks themselves, and has shown me the debt Turks owe to their Seljuk forebearers.

And a significant debt it is. It is obvious to me that the leaders and citizens of Turkey today are using the same tactics as the Seljuk sultans to create their empire for the twenty-first century. The Seljuk strategies of globalization, international commerce, free trade on safe roads and ports, improvement of infrastructure, respect for civility and dialogue, and the creation of an atmosphere of tolerance and cultural development are being copied with success. The Seljuks established a sense of identity for the Turks and gave them the confidence to be generous with foreigners, to share their food, land, and culture freely. They created a confident people, proud of what they have and what they can do. It is not hard to see the traces of the Seljuk spirit in the hardworking Turks of today: with their sleeves rolled up, they are tackling the building of a country with the same drive, gumption, and determination.

How proud the Seljuk sultans would be to see how their kingdom is now woven with a web of concrete roads based on their trade routes, and yes, how proud they would be of those dams and the resulting economic prosperity they bring! Although the Seljuks lasted only some 200 years, the stones of their monuments and their cultural keystones laid the basis of the Turkey we know today, confidently capable of supporting the future that Turkey will build in the twenty-first century.

Ars longa,
Kadriye Branning

Aksaray, Taş Medrese

The double-headed eagle, symbol of the Seljuks

Ticket to caravansarai, Ağzıkarahan village

Niğde, Hudavent Hatun Tomb

Sivas, Kesik ("Cut") Bridge

The Seljuk spirit lives on...   *Tomb of Melik Ghazi*

Tokat, Pervane Medrese   *Konya, the restored Sahipata*
complex, 2007

Diyarbakır

Ezinepazar Han

LETTER 26

Fast and furious knots

Dear Lady Mary,
Another similarity between our Turkish experiences is that we both witnessed the country during periods of significant social and cultural evolution. You lived there during the Tulip Era, a time during which the Ottoman Empire opened up to Western ideas and models. I, too, encountered a period of notable change, especially in the 1980s, when Turkey again looked attentively at Western notions and lifestyles.

Traveling to Turkey every year has allowed me to notice the slight, and not so slight, changes in lifestyle. Enough time passes between visits to allow me to count the number of these bricks of change being laid in the foundation wall of a developing Turkey. Each year certain differences would distinctly jump out at me, and I dutifully noted them, even the most trivial, in my travel journals. Some things, of course, never change in Turkey – the smell of lemon cologne, the chaos of Eminönü, the sonorous blasts of the horns of the Bosphorus ferries, the muezzin's call, the smell of grilling lamb, the tinkle of spoons in tulip-shaped tea glasses, the taste of Kanlıca yogurt, or the color of the fawn hills of Anatolia – but each year, many new sensations are built upon these eternal foundations.

I have always been struck by the irony that the geographical contours of the country of Turkey follow the same golden rule proportional system (2:3) that carpets do. In many ways, I see the knotted carpet as the symbol for the modern Turkey now being woven: a carpet in which you can see the patterns of the past and the colors of the future.

The loom of this carpet is the geography of Turkey itself: its mountains, fault lines, forests, and seas; a loom as sturdy as those 500-year-old plane trees you see so often. This loom is strung with vertical warp threads, representing the basic, traditional Turkish societal values of religion, customs, language, and family structure. The horizontal red wefts passing through these warps are the shoots of innovation and progress that keep driving this Turkey rug upwards to completion, and which also hold each successive row of knots in place. Finally, I see the woolen knots tied to these warps and wefts as the particular spin and twist given to this tradition and change. The choice of the colors of the wool and how the patterns of these knots will be designed, interpreted, and embellished remain in the hands and eye of the weaver herself: in this case, the people of the Republic of Turkey. When a weaver sits in front of an empty loom and picks up the wool for her first row of knots, she has already laid out the rug's pattern in her mind's eye. Yet, she is also well aware that her intended pattern may not always come out as she planned and that her knotting tension will vary daily. A rug, like life, sets out with firm intentions but is adjusted on the fly.

I have seen months and years of knotted rows climbing up the loom of my Turkey carpet. And right now, the knots are flying fast and furious as this rug strives to reach the top of the loom.

Yet it would seem that there are two sets of hands tying those fast and furious knots. These two pairs of hands belong to two different weavers, each one bringing a different strength, pull and tension to the knotting process. One pair of hands belongs to the craftsmen of modern Turkey and the other pair to traditional Turkey. These two pairs of hands can be seen in the Turkey of slick concrete apartment towers and modest old wooden houses, broad avenues and narrow back streets, exorbitant wealth and dismal poverty. They are seen in the struggle between East and West, the desire and the necessity for change and economic survival in the globalized world versus a certain nostalgia for the traditional Turkish way of life, in the strong attachment to the Muslim faith versus an admiration for the European Christian world, and in the faithful connection to the culture of Atatürk versus the perceived need for a more modern democracy. Yet in this tug of war, I believe that the dignity of the Ottoman Turkey that you knew, Lady Mary, still lies under the surface of the young, Westernized Turks of today. Just scratch a bit and a Turk will always be a Turk, no matter how much his world changes or how sophisticated his outlook becomes. The people of Turkey, a country sitting on two continents, have always had the rare opportunity to see the world with two sets of eyes, Eastern and Western. They peer out from behind a pair of double-vision bifocals, always tilting their head to adjust to the view of the moment, whether it be up-close and immediate or one far-reaching into the distance.

And so, Lady Mary, I would like to share with you some of the rows of knots I have seen woven into this carpet. As you gave us insights into the daily life of the Tulip Era, I would like to describe to you some of the things I have witnessed in four distinct growth eras in my 30 years of travel to Turkey. I relate them, not to serve as a political or historical analysis, but as descriptions of everyday life. These four periods are my own categories, and I beg forgiveness to those historians, economists, and sociologists who would disagree with my classification. Starting with my first trip in 1978, these periods are: the dark years of 1978–1985, the wake-up decade of 1985–1995, the break-through-the-gate consumerism era of 1995–2000, and the drive to modernity from 2000 to the present – and beyond.

As I have told you, Lady Mary, my first visit to Turkey was in 1978 at a time I now look upon as the "dark years." I call these difficult times the "dark years" not just because times were indeed tough, but because they literally were dark: there was not a light bulb to be had in all the country. My friends and family (especially my worried mother) would say to me at this time, *"Why in the world would you travel to a country with such problems, apparent danger and instability, not to mention all those earthquakes?"* And right she was, my mother: the 1970s were a tough period for Turkey.

In the years preceding my first visit, Turkey had gone through a decade of confusion, political conflict, violence, and bleakness – all seemingly bent on undermining Turkey's sense of purpose and Atatürk's secular identity. From the outside, it looked like it was a society on the road to self-destruction. The year I arrived, martial law was instigated in the Kurdish areas. There were fights between the left and the right, political violence on the streets, constant government changes, boycotts, clogged courts, strikes, arrests, unemployment, rampant inflation, insufficient social and educational opportunities, bleak jails, skyrocketing oil costs, and internal friction with Sunni Alevis and Kurds. Nothing seemed to be going right.

In France, where I was living at that time, these difficult political times were reported in the press, but there were also signs of it closer to home. Between 1975 and 1981, Armenian gunmen went after and killed Turkish diplomats in Paris on three occasions and bombed the Turkish Airlines office on the Champs-Elysées not ten minutes after I had passed in front of it on a leisurely stroll down the avenue. If this were not enough, the most devastating incident was the accident of Turkish Airlines flight 981 on March 3, 1974. I will never forget hearing the news of it over the radio as I awoke on that bright spring Sunday morning. Crashing in the forests of Ermenoville, just north of Paris, the accident killed all 346 on board. This crash was by far the worst air disaster in all history and did much to sully the reputation of Turkish Airlines and the country of Turkey, who came off looking incompetent and irresponsible.

But the worst attack onto Turkey's image came from the arts. The film "Midnight Express" was released in 1979. This film by Alan Parker, depicting the torture and violence prevalent in Turkish prisons, turned into a national hate film, bringing the West's worst fears and prejudices concerning Turkey to the forefront. It closed horizons and has left lasting scars on the image of Turkey until this day.

All this midnight darkness led to the military coup of September 12, 1980. Entitled "Operation Flag," this day led to a period of three years of military rule from 1980–83. Tanks rolled into place at street corners, soldiers with machine guns stood on every street, internal communications were cut, a 10-p.m. curfew was installed, and there was a ban on foreign travel.

I stayed in Turkey during the early period of the coup, for the month of December, 1980. Unaware of the gravity of the situation, I decided to visit a friend for a week and discover what life in Istanbul was like in the winter... little did I realize what was in store for me. What I had read in the papers about the coup had led me to believe that life was continuing as usual. In many ways things were normal, but daily life was anything but easy. The first thing that struck me was the presence of soldiers with machine guns everywhere: on the runways of the airport, in every public space, on every street corner, in front of every large shop, constantly patrolling back and forth. Grave-sounding public announcements blaring from electronic megaphones assailed you on the street: as my Turkish at that time was non-existent, it was impossible for me to understand their gist, but the tone was enough to let me know that they meant business. The intolerable smell of lignite coal, used for heating, added to the dismal streetscape. It was cold, very cold, and one evening the snow started and did not stop falling for three days, covering the streets with a brief moment of beauty before the mud churned it back into a dismal mess. I am not sure if it was the terrible cold, the snowfall, or the fear and uncertainty, but an eerie silence reigned on the sidewalks of Istanbul. The talking, laughing, and boisterous chaos of normal Turkish street life was silenced. Inside Turkish homes, it was hardly any warmer. A state of penury reigned, and everyone tried their determined best to confront the situation without complaint. It was an example of that strong commitment to social cohesion I spoke about earlier, Lady Mary: the ancestral clan spirit of Turks comes to the surface and bonds them together in times of challenge and hardship. The most difficult hurdle of all was the lack of heat. There was no fuel oil, and as is always the case in such trying times, that winter passed with unforgiving bitter cold. Lady Mary, you spoke once about how you sat in your sunny Pera garden on a January afternoon and enjoyed the mild and sweet weather, but I can tell you this was not the luck of the climatic draw this January. A very creative ritual was inaugurated to ensure survival during this time. Every evening, the extended family of my friend would gather together in one of their homes, rotating from home to home each night. They would turn on the precious rationed heat so that everyone could benefit from some warmth for at least a few hours. Wearing multiple layers of sweaters, gloves, scarves, and socks, we huddled together in one room chock-a-block on the low couches, drank tea, chatted, and watched television for updates on the situation. Night after night was spent like this, with no other activity possible, as most normal activities were suspended during the coup. The oddest thing, though, was the lack of light bulbs. In each home, there was usually only one light bulb to be had, and like a magical talisman, it was ceremoniously unscrewed and screwed into the lamp of the room where needed, forcing everyone to stick together to see or read. Night fell early, around 4 p.m., and the streets became so dark that you were forced to return to an equally dark home. In the late afternoon, there was not much to do other than sit quietly in a room in the shadows, bundled in your overcoat with a rare candle for company. Not only was there no fuel for heat… but there was none for hot water, so bathing became a brisk challenge. There was food, but no butter or coffee or much soap. Restaurants were completely empty, museums were closed, and the opening hours of shops and banks were unreliable. When it came time for me to leave, I went to the airport for my flight only to discover that the airport had been closed, and all flights were suspended until further notice. So what had been planned as a simple week getaway turned into a month-long trial before I could finally find a flight to take me home to Paris.

Although a mood of despair and depression reigned, those Turks never lost their enthusiasm for life during the coup. It was during the coup that I traveled over the Bosphorus Bridge for the first time in that rattle-trap car, and my friend's aunt, who was studying classical Ottoman dance, gave me dance lessons each afternoon. Faced with my clumsiness, her laughter was as endless as her patience. Her delight and sense of grace when she danced was a symbol for me of all the optimism of Turkey, and I was convinced that the people of Turkey would help the country dance through this period of darkness and cold.

I have strong memories of these dark years of the coup from subsequent visits. The very darkness itself, for example. Even after the coup and the return of light bulbs, there were often no lights in banks or public buildings, and power outages were frequent. Many a dinner was eaten around candlelight not to enhance romance but out of necessity. The streets of Istanbul were congested by lumbering large American cars of the '50s which operated as *dolmuş* (communal taxis): old de Sotos, regal '58 Chevies, and imperial purple Pontiacs. Lovingly kept in top form by this nation of skilled tinkerers, these thoroughbred modern stallions dabbed flashy highlights of color on the blue Bosphorus canvas. Swarming the streets of Istanbul were flocks of itinerant peddlers, hawking sesame rings, freshly-cut cucumbers, milk, single cigarettes, water, newspapers, *boza* (a fermented winter drink), and lottery tickets in singsong chants. In the teeming commercial areas of Beyoğlu and Eminönü, *hamals* (porters) bustled around, carrying merchandise on their backs like human camels, weaving around the dense Bazaar neighborhoods more efficiently and quickly than could any truck or cart. I once saw a *hamal* (porter) carrying an entire dining room set, complete with table, credenza and chairs, on his back! They have all disappeared now. Public writers and scribes set up their tables in most parks and market spaces, pecking away at their typewriters to produce everything from official petitions to municipal authorities to love letters to distant sweethearts for the villagers who clustered around them.

Despite the traces of its Ottoman imperial glory and memories of the picturesque streets depicted in the novels of Pierre Loti, much of Istanbul remained a tumbledown town during these years. There were abandoned buildings, crumbling walls, littered open areas, and backstreets full of vines and garbage. Dilapidated wooden houses, their door and window casings out of whack, leaned so precipitously forward that you were frightened to walk down the street for fear they would fall on you. Adding to the urban challenge was the beginning of the invasion of rural peasants and the growth of *gecekondu* slum areas. In 1978, when I first visited Istanbul, the population was 4 million; by 1998 it had grown to 12 million.

Cigarette smoke was everywhere. The clouds of cigarette smoke coming from the back deck of the Bosphorus ferries were as impressive as those coming from their smokestacks. Clients and shopkeepers puffed away while making transactions, and bank tellers blew smoke at you while they counted out your lira. I was even examined in 1979 by a doctor who held a cigarette in one hand while he felt my swollen glands with the other. My nurse friends in Eyüp smoked in front of their work stations. It was an unavoidable part of Turkish life, drenching you with its odor in taxis, shops, airports, post offices, busses, and restaurants. The most surprising smoker I ever encountered was a librarian who chain-smoked with the greatest of ease while cataloguing rare books.

They were perhaps ramshackle, those streets, but they teemed with life and joy. These were the days before plastic bags and plastic bottles, when every purchase was neatly wrapped in newspaper or a sweetly-designed wrapping paper, tied with string so that it looked like a present. Purchases at the pharmacy, even one as small as a box of aspirin, were wrapped in paper to insure discretion. There were cats everywhere, hundreds of cats. Scrawny, dirty, limping, one-eyed gaunt mousers with notched ears, bloodcaked noses, crooked tails, and matted fur... or every once in a while, an absolutely gorgeous angora cat enthroning in the doorway of a shop as regally as any Sultan on his dais. In restaurants or in shops, you always felt the swish of fur weaving around your ankles.

In cities outside of Istanbul, a rural atmosphere persisted. On my first visit to Sivas, the road in front of the hotel was not paved, and cows grazed peacefully around the Gök Medrese in town. There were more horse carts than cars in those days on the streets of Anatolia.

The dark years were obvious to tourists as well. As hard as the Turks tried to put on a good show, it was not always possible to cover up the stained and lovingly mended bed sheets, the dust balls in the Topkapı palace, the plague of mosquitoes in Laleli hotels, or the showerhead that sprayed the whole room, toilet included. No wonder rooms were built with a big drain in the floor and came with a pair of plastic sandals by the bed. Back home, you never saw glamorous articles in the newspapers or magazines on travel to Turkey, and there were perhaps only 2 guidebooks to Turkey in print. You stood out in airports and bus stations with your matched luggage sets, alongside the Turks who traveled carting bundles, sisal sacks, cardboard boxes tied with twine, and duffel bags. Restaurant tables had blue plastic buckets filled with sliced bread and aluminum pitchers with fountain water. Despite the time-consuming torture of changing money, you avoided changing too much at a time because the inflation rate varied wildly from day to day. Bus rides across the Anatolian plains were made insufferable by the cigarette smoke and the lack of air conditioning in the bus coaches.

Yet, Turkey survived that martial law period and those problematic years, and in many ways, it was the last time that Turkey would ever remain dark and cold, for after this time, Turkish society experienced an opening towards a brighter future. Despite the political turmoil, I kept returning, convinced ever since that first ride across the Bosphorus Bridge I told you about, Lady Mary, that this country was destined to be something big. A new constitution was written in 1982, the Southeastern Anatolia Project (GAP) dam project was inaugurated, and coffee beans made an appearance once again in 1981, if only for the tourists. That year also was designated as the "Year of Atatürk" (for the centennial anniversary of his birth), and the flurry of schools and parks opened that year all bore a proud "YUZYIL" ("100 Years") in front of their names. Yes, after this period, there was no looking back: Turkish society experienced an opening to the future and took off like an airplane down the runway to a new horizon.

Around the year 1985, the promise of a bright future started to become a reality: Turkey opened up to the world via trade and tourism. Bent on erasing the bad memory of those dark years, the horses broke forth from the starting gate at an amazing pace. I look at the decade from 1985-1995 as the "wake-up years." After the Constitution was rewritten in 1982, a political force named Turgut Özal came upon the scene with his newly-formed ANAP (Motherland) party. This reformist leader opened up the Turkish economy to free trade, removed heavy dependency on foreign aid, and released the pent-up energy of a young and ambitious generation of entrepreneurs. His vision coincided with the computer revolution, with technology beginning to drive all sectors. Factories popped up in every corner of Turkey and exports increased, notably in textiles and foodstuffs. For a country that counted wheat and hazelnuts as its major exports before his arrival, Turgut Özal's program was a revolution. Overnight, Turkey became too big for the blue jeans it now famously exported to the world market, splitting at its seams from the rapid growth and change brought on after the dark years. Upwardly striving in earnest, Turks became business-minded on a big scale and proved to themselves and to the world that their richest natural resources were not oil, minerals, or diamonds, but hard work, determination, and scrappiness. The "Turkish Tiger" cub was born.

Tourists today see a Turkey of promise and sophistication, but that was not always the case. I witnessed the opening of the Turkish stock market, the integration of Turkey into world markets, and the privatization of industry. In daily life, I observed the birth of civic associations and foundations and the creation of media, satellite TV, and private TV stations with open advertising. Stores were flooded with imported goods and services... including computers. I remember walking in Çekirge in Bursa and seeing a sign advertising classes for "Knowledge Counters" and being puzzled at what this was. It was only later that I realized that this was the Turkish neologism for "computer." And most importantly, Turkey courted Europe for the first time: the Prime Minister Özal, in an improbable romantic lead role, applied for membership in the European Commission in 1987.

The biggest change for me during this time was the explosive building projects that rocked the country like an earthquake. Turkey literally built itself up from the ground overnight. Like the Seljuk sultans before them, Turkey's leaders and businessmen rebuilt the entire infrastructure of the country. Roads were repaired, airports built, and electrical pylons improved. The dreadful airport serving the capital of the country at Ankara was thankfully rebuilt. In 1987 there were only two 5-star hotels in Istanbul; today there are more than 20, and they are filled to capacity. The shores of the Aegean and the Mediterranean Seas, which were virtually empty after World War II, now saw a total ribbon development. The country experienced an intended policy of decentralization, with cities such as Bursa, Kayseri, and Adana coming to the forefront to compete with their big brothers of Ankara and Istanbul. The Atatürk Dam, the centerpiece of the Southeastern Anatolia Project (GAP) of 22 dams and 19 hydroelectric stations, was completed in 1990. GAP began churning forth irrigation water and electricity to arid southeastern Turkey, reinforcing the power of another Turkish natural resource: water. GAP is one of the largest development projects in the world, and it put Turkey on the map not only for its innovation, but also for its controversy, as it flooded historical sites and diverted the water supplies of downriver neighbors.

Istanbul benefited from a major facelift during this time. The leather-curing tanneries located outside the city walls at Yedikule were displaced between 1985 and 1991, and thankfully you were no longer subjected to their stench as your first impression of Istanbul on the drive in from the airport. UNESCO declared the Byzantine city walls of Istanbul as a World Heritage site in 1985. This led to an earnest preservation and parks program, but also to the demolition of many of the older buildings nearby. The stagnant waters of the Golden Horn were cleaned up, and the narrow coastal roads up the Bosphorus were widened starting in 1983 or so. Unfortunately, they displaced the charming quayside tables of seafood restaurants to the opposite side of the road.

But all was still not perfectly rosy. Prices rose, with double-digit inflation, there was an increase in unemployment, and the rural poor continued their flood to the cities, creating an ever-increasing social cleavage between the conservative Islamic lifestyle and westernized secular elite. There were issues with Bulgarian refugees in the summer of 1989, and the start of Kurdish warfare. Attacks on Turkish companies continued in Paris with the Orly airport bomb attack of 1983, leaving 8 dead. Iraq invaded Kuwait in August 1990, provoking the first of the Iraqi-US wars. And in 1994, a financial crisis and recession halved the value of the lira over a few months and plunged the country into a tailspin. The black market exchange rate continued to offer some 30% difference over the bank rates of 1988.

But Turkey soldiered on to progress in ways other than exports and building. The pint-sized wrestler Naim Süleymanoğlu, lovingly nicknamed "the Pocket Hercules," captured the nation's imagination and pride when he earned Olympic gold medals in 1988, 1992, and 1996. Like Turkey, he showed that the little guy can win big on the world's playing fields.

Politically, too, Turkey was sending messages to the world. Turkey elected a woman prime minister, Tansu Çiller in 1993–1996, a feminism light years ahead of any Western country. The Turkish government started to send cultural exhibits abroad, which proved to be a clever way to stimulate interest in the country to foreign culture consumers. I remember with pride attending the gala opening of the huge "Age of Sultan Süleyman the Magnificent" exhibit in January, 1987 at the National Gallery of Art in Washington, D.C., with dignitaries from all the cultural and political spheres of the world in attendance.

In my own country of America, the same overwhelming political, economic and physical changes were occurring in the 1980's, spurred by the advent of the computer age. When I think how our lives were changed by those "knowledge counters," it makes the rapid changes of Turkey seem all the more dizzying. After Özal woke Turkey up in the 1980s, it seemed that everything of the old regime was thrown out the window. It was during this time that I both marveled at the progress at the same time I began to be filled with a certain nostalgia. Everyone now wanted to live in concrete block apartments or suburban developments instead of wooden homes, which were now turned into hotels for tourists. No one wanted to shop in the covered bazaar but in the "market." No one took pride in wearing traditional clothes and jewelry. Plastic bags replaced hand-woven saddlebags.

These changes impacted foreign travelers such as myself. I was happy to see that new taxi meters were installed in cabs, putting and end to haggling, arguments, and profiteering. I was pleased that I no longer had to stay in dingy hotels and that toilets and showers worked. I was relieved that citizens could now travel efficiently and cheaply on the subways of Ankara and Istanbul. I was eager to discover Kurdish music starting in 1991, when the ban against the sale of music cassettes of this distinctive music was lifted. The favorite gift to bring Turks still remained American cigarettes, lighters, and vitamins, largely unavailable at that time. The first-ever US check-in counter of Turkish Airlines (THY) at Newark airport still resembled a bus terminal in the heart of Turkey, full of pandemonium, travelers lugging microwaves in cardboard boxes, and burlap bags wrapped in tape. There was not even a permanent sign for THY over the counter: a piece of cardboard hand-written with black marker and attached with twine swinging over the check-in desk did the job. There were no direct THY flights from the United States to Istanbul or Ankara, with stop-overs necessary in Brussels.

The streetscape also changed. Starting around 1989 and especially after the fall of Communism in Russia in 1991, the Laleli neighborhood became invaded by Eastern Europeans. There were still no street signs, but I began to see dogs kept as pets (French poodles!) for the first time. There were fewer stray cats, and my favorite Kayseri İskender Kebab salon became equipped with air-conditioning and fancy pink window blinds. Towns such as Niğde and Afyon, which seemed lost in the infinite dusty plains on that first trip in 1978, now seemed like built-up metropoli. All over Turkey, massive building projects were undertaken, yet countless sites stood half-completed and deserted. Major museums remained closed for renovations, posted with signs saying they would reopen at a date 2 years previous to the day you were standing in front of their doors.

Perhaps the biggest change of all for me was in the city of Antalya, which exploded with the appearance of a series of flashy 5-star hotels in 1991, such as the Falez and the Sheraton Voyager. When I first went to Turkey in 1978, Antalya was a bustling town with a stunning historic inner harbor full of Seljuk monuments and fishing boats, with its neighboring seafront undeveloped. I stayed in a small motel on the Lara Road to the east of town, very rundown, but full of charm due to its impressive corniche setting. The centerpiece of this modest motel was a large plane tree on its cliffside terrace, perhaps some 300 years old. It had a distinctive shape, with long horizontal branches that stretched all the way over to the edge of the cliff, as if it wanted to offer as much protection as possible. It was under the shade of those wide boughs and their broad leaves that I ate my meals, caught the cool breezes, read, lounged, and contemplated the perfect view over the Antalya harbor. That tree provided a haven of total peace, love, and quietude I have rarely felt. Years later, in 1991, fleeing those impersonal, modern hotels, I decided to return for a stay in that unpretentious spot to savor once again that quietude under its tree. My heart sank when I arrived in front of the entry road to the property and saw that the grounds were boarded up and surrounded by barbed wire. A sign was posted on the fence: "*Construction Site: No Entry: Dangerous demolition in progress."* My tree! My beloved tree! Was it being bulldozed over into the sea? I became very sad that day and was left to wonder if Turkey understood that progress had certain responsibilities to heritage and tradition, without which evolution becomes an empty promise.

Starting around 1995, once Özal's race horses had left the gates, they started to pound down the track as if there was no reining them in. Another societal change occurred in Turkey that lasted for about five years. Something had snapped; things started snowballing to a point where there was no turning back. The door to consumerism had been thrown wide open by Özal, and Turks, with their love of progress and change, ran right through it. Turkey was on a committed path to modernism, racing to become bigger and better than anything in Europe or America, and in some ways, it succeeded. In a period of about five years, the slumbering giant that woke up in the previous decade took its place on the world stage and shouted, *"Get out of my way, here I come!"* Like a teenager, Turkey started to seek its way, stretching, growing towards adulthood, all through a swift and explosive integration into the global culture of consumerism. Daily life changed beyond recognition, even in the short period between my visits. If I had returned to Turkey after an absence of 20 years, instead of every year, I would not have believed my eyes. This period of rapid evolution coincided as well with the arrival of the internet and the World Wide Web as an explosive global driving force. It was an era of more and more conspicuous consumption, driven by a new elite rising from meritocracy and education, just like the Janissaries had under the Ottomans.

A big year driving this change was 1996, the year of the United Nations Habitat II Conference in Istanbul. In order to show that Istanbul was a player on the world's cultural stage, the city was seriously gussied up: street signs were hung, public transportation improved, and many stray dogs and cats were eliminated from the streets overnight. Familiar neighborhood signposts disappeared at the same time those street signs were being put in place, and in many ways, this purified Istanbul lost much of the mystery that so intrigued Pierre Loti. By 1996, the population of Istanbul had grown from the 4 million when I first went there in 1978 to over 12 million. The density of the city had become palpable.

One of the characteristics of this period to me was the evidence of a new wealth, visible in many ways, especially in the building boom of houses, apartments, and urban commercial centers. Luxurious gated communities in the Levent area of Istanbul, called "*site*" (pronounced as the French "cité"), provided a complete living environment with homes, roads, individual lawns and gardens, movie theaters, shopping plazas, health clubs, tennis courts, and pools. At this time, Turkey witnessed a rapid growth in the construction of shopping malls, planned as the forums of social life. In the late 1990's they popped up everywhere, starting with the Galeria (1988), Akmerkez, and Kanyon in Istanbul; Metro and Atakule in Ankara, and the 42-floor Site Kulesi in Konya in 2006. The male-dominated atmosphere of the bazaar now flipped over to the more women-centered atmosphere of these malls, and I saw women as sales clerks for the first time. The shiny, polished marble floors of these malls did not resemble the muddy streets of the old city centers, and you usually had to reach them by car, not on foot: another increased sign of consumerism. Malls came with food courts filled with Western restaurant chains but also with some reassuring kebab stands. Foreign retailers rushed in to populate the stores of these malls from Starbucks to Harvey Nicols.

In addition to the malls, this period saw the complete transformation of the corner "*bakkal amca*" grocery store ("uncle" store) to the market, to the supermarket (such as Ismar), and finally to the "hypermarket" (Migros and Carrefour). The hotel building boom continued as well, now with a focus on luxury or boutique hotels, the more lavish the appointments the better. All in all, this building boom reoriented the urban grid: the glue of the three traditional cohesive elements of the Ottoman town – the neighborhood, the market, and the local mosque – was now coming apart to be reshaped in a different pattern. Little children no longer grew up in the Sultan Ahmet neighborhood of Istanbul, which turned into a stage set of Ottoman homes for tourists.

I witnessed these changes to communication, fashion, food, and leisure in ways large and small, yet it was always the fever of consumerism that characterized this era in my eyes. Everyone had to obtain a cell phone, a car, and had to now shop at the supermarket. Istanbul had always been a commercial gateway, and now outsider Europeans and Westerners knocked at its door to sell not just their products but their lifestyles to an eager society. Despite the zeal for progress and consumerism, there still remained a vast discrepancy between the great wealth and fortunes flashed by the new rich of Istanbul and the hopeless poverty of the rural areas, usually in the East.

Consume, they did, those Turks, but produce they did as well. It was during this period that Turkey surprised the world with its technological savvy and advances at home and abroad, becoming a cutting-edge player with its telecommunications industry. When the new ultra-modern Terminal 1 opened at JFK airport in New York in 1998, THY stepped up to be one of the five international airlines signed on as tenants next to the prestigious Air France and Lufthansa. THY flights to Istanbul became non-stop, with every seat filled. The bus terminal atmosphere of the past at the check-in process was replaced with slick, elegant, and swift service...and Turks now traveled with designer luggage. In a show of the astonishing technological innovation appearing at this time in Turkey, I used an automatic cash machine to withdraw money for the first time in my life in the dusty farm town of Afyon, not on Wall Street in Manhattan. Again, for the first time, I used the energy-saving system of key-activated light switches, not in Las Vegas or Paris, but in a Kayseri hotel, and cooled myself with efficient, above-window air conditioners in Aksaray. In 1999 the Taksim to Levent subway opened, and I waited for a red light to change in my car while counting down the seconds on an LED display counter for the first time, not in New York, but in a small town on the Black Sea coast. The "Silver Bullet" fast tram from Sirkeci to Eminönü roared down Istanbul's historic Divan Yolu on its inaugural voyage, down the very street where your Janissaries once marched, Lady Mary.

The streetscapes changed rapidly as well. I began to see street push carts selling Western foods such as corn on the cob, hot potatoes, and popcorn. Dogs were paraded on leashes and fancy cars parked in front of old wooden houses. Natural gas replaced the slow-burning lignite coal that gave the distinctive smell to Istanbul in winter. Internet cafés sprung up everywhere after 1995, and satellite dishes on the rooftops of houses blossomed as fast as the geraniums in the olive oil cans at their doorsteps. Bicycles started to appear in 1996 at the same time as baby carriages, something never seen before in Turkey, a culture where women held their babies up close, in their arms or on their hips. The Sultan Ahmet area was refurbished in 1997, with the creation of a new park and the remaining litter cleaned up. A discrete railing was put around the sunken stargazing pool of the Konya Karatay Medrese as a concession to clumsy tourists. A new floor was laid in the Covered Bazaar in 1998.

Not only were new products and patterns of consumerism flooding into Turkey, but also came globalized images, names, pop stars, foods, and life patterns via satellite TV and the media. Turkish youth started to adopt the international dress code of jeans, tee-shirts, sports shoes, and baseball caps...and tattoos. Chubby children became more common. Sparkling magazines flashed forth on the newsstands: Turkish versions of Cosmo, Marie-Claire, as well as decorating journals and glossy fashion magazines battled cheek-to-jowl for attention. Turkish designers strutted down the international fashion runways, starting in the mid 1990's with Rıfat Özbek and Atil Kutoğlu creating imaginative collections with an Oriental flair and imagination...at the same time I noticed imported Turkish blue jeans and polo shirts for sale in my local K-Mart store.

Turks interpreted the Western consumer yuppie lifestyles *alla turca*: Women started to focus on their bodily health and beauty, not only in the articles from those fancy fashion magazines, but also articles in the general press, advertising, and with the arrival of international beauty products. As unbelievable as it may seem in this country of the nargile and whose name is synonymous with tobacco, the Turks enforced smoking bans in public places far earlier than Europe, right behind the Americans. Cafés and fast-food restaurants appeared, and new food products appeared in Turkey before I saw them in New York. Cell phones became universal. Chocolate cakes, cubed sugar, and nescafé became the status symbols of the day.

The Turks not only acquired consumer goods, but they also sought to attain better educational opportunities for their children. Private universities appeared on the educational horizon at the same time that Turks fled in record numbers to attend institutions of higher learning in America, as the possession of an American diploma was deemed the passport to success in Turkey. Like the Ottoman princes sent to the provincial towns to learn their trade with a tutor, the contemporary heirs-apparent were sent to the USA to attend the finest schools and to rack up the highest diplomas.

This change did not take place just in Istanbul, but all over the country. However, it took a different spin out in Anatolia, where there was an even more concerted effort to reject the past in favor of Western lifestyle patterns to prove their modernity. Practical and perfect items replaced traditional house wares: old hand-beaten copper pots were tossed out in favor of aluminum sets given away by newspapers, innox cutlery replaced hand-carved wooden spoons, wall-to-wall carpeting took the place of hand-woven kilims and rugs, and ornate couches and chairs replaced the traditional low *sedir* banquettes that you so enjoyed sitting on, Lady Mary. On a visit to Konya in 1981, I was almost run over by the confusion of hundreds of horse carts in front of the Sahip Ata Külliyesi, an area for repair shops and replacement parts. There was not one car there in the midst of those hundreds of carts. But when I returned there in 1995, the entire area was empty, with not one horse cart in sight.

Of course, change willy-nilly brings unintended consequences. The most regretted change I have noticed in Anatolia at this time was the appearance of roadside visual pollution. It used to be that you could travel for hours and not see one billboard, only miles and miles of pure countryside – countryside so pure that you felt detached from the world and could stretch your eyes and imagination to the horizon and beyond. Now, billboards popped up everywhere, full of vulgar and unnecessary information. Not only were these billboards polluting the countryside, but so was garbage, notably those indestructible plastic bags and water bottles. Garbage was *never* seen on the roads of Turkey. Now it is everywhere. I witnessed another regrettable change in Konya in 1996. The sparkling rainbows of hand-woven prayer carpets that covered the floors of the Alaeddin Mosque had been removed and were replaced by a monotonous sea of teal blue carpeting. This royal mosque, the most famous and sacred of all the Seljuk mosques, with its famous carved walnut mimbar from 1155, its mihrab of spectacular underglaze turquoise tiles, and its original carpets ordered by the Sultan Alaeddin Keykubad himself, was now stripped of its aesthetic historical glory by the laying of that industrial carpet – all in the name of progress.

In the consumerism and change during the years of 1995–2000, it was perhaps the evolving political scene that is the most lasting legacy of this period, the one that will have the largest impact on the future of Turkey. These five years witnessed a country struggling to come to grips with change that was often too dizzying to absorb. Western consumerism had left a large part of society, especially those outside of the urban centers, feeling excluded. Not unexpectedly, many turned to something more reassuring, more familiar, and more in tune with their value system and sought a tolerance of different lifestyles and economic stability. It should not have appeared as a surprise to anyone that Turkey elected Necmettin Erbakan, its first Islamic Prime Minister, in July 1996, ushering in a new tone of government.

The fourth and final period of evolution I witnessed took place in the years 2000 to the present after the shattering events of the 1999 Izmit earthquake and September 11, 2001 in New York. Turkey and the world have not been the same after these two events, and they led the final frantic drive to modernity that Turkey wished to achieve. In my eyes, this period is characterized by a massive tourism flood, an intense drive to woo Europe, a sentiment of anti-Americanism caused by the second Iraq war, the emergence of religious political parties as a power, and the arrival of Turkey on the political and economic world stage front and center.

The political atmosphere changed rapidly and saw the abolition of the death penalty in 2002. Although the Kurdish insurgency ended in 1999 with the emergency rule lifted in November 2002, it was still very common to see machine-gun carrying soldiers in hotel lobbies and public spaces through 2004, the year that the TRT state television broadcast a Kurdish language program for the first time. After a financial crisis in 2001 caused Turkey's currency to lose half its value, the country introduced IMF-inspired reforms that were doggedly maintained. As a result, Turkey has not only experienced impressive GDP growth but rid itself of the hyperinflation that plagued it for most of the 1990s.

The changes of the previous decade continued to steam forth. The building boom persists, with vast housing construction projects in progress on plots of land outside of cities such as Kayseri, Malatya and Konya, and office building towers in Ankara and Istanbul, and even more shopping malls and hypermarkets all over the country. The roads crisscrossing the country are now on a par with those of Europe. Technology continues to steam forward: 2001 witnessed the opening of a new subway in Ankara and an international airport in Istanbul. In a sign of the times, mosques now post notices saying, "*Lütfen cep telefonunuzu kapatınız*" (please turn off your cell phones) and, in a small town outside of Tokat, a LCD zip banner sign on the local mosque announces the prayer times in glaring red letters. On January 1, 2005, Turkish currency dropped six zeros and the new "YTL" currency was released. With astonishing efficiency, I was able to withdraw my first bills of "new Turkish lira" from an ATM at 10am that morning: never did I expect that machine could be capable of spitting out the new currency, but all went smoothly, much more smoothly than Europe when it changed over to the euro. No advertisement appears now without its internet site address, and WIFI connections are more universal and reliable than they are in America and are certainly far ahead of Europe. Turkey has become aware of the green movement, continuing to tidy up urban areas, creating new gardens, parks, and pedestrian malls (such as the Istiklal and "French" streets in Istanbul) and planting traffic strips on approaches to cities. It is now common to see "expat" workers from Western countries living in Istanbul, and some 300,000–400,000 people emigrate to Istanbul each year. The Silver Bullet train is now comfortably air-conditioned.

International market development continues, with Turks exporting 90% of their cars to Europe. In April, 2007, I saw a bottle of Turkish Efes beer for sale in the tiny corner grocery shop on the street where I live in New York. The departures board at the Istanbul airport now has every conceivable destination posted, far from that cardboard sign at the THY counter at Newark.

But the biggest change of this period is the massive tourism that has hit Turkey. You cannot walk the streets of Istanbul anymore without being jostled by foreigners: Istanbul is the new Rome. Ever the hospitable hosts, the Turks are doing their utmost to welcome these tourists. Turkey has developed an excellent transportation system with sophisticated intra-city busses, trains, tramways, ferry boats, sea buses, taxis, and a newly-developing underground. Railroads and major highways are undergoing upgrades, with many 4-lane highways and toll roads in place to ease their travel. There are multi-lingual smiling policemen to ensure their safety. The Tourist Information booth in Sultan Ahmet is a marvel of efficiency. Historic Ottoman homes and hans in Safranbolu, Diyarbakır, and Amasya serve as guesthouses. Starbucks awaits tourists on the Divan Yolu and Istiklal Streets, should the traditional little glasses of tea, nescafé, and Turkish coffee not be to their fancy. Ice machines are appearing in hotels. Tourists can dance to international hits and Turkish rap in the countless *jeunesse dorée* discos opened for them.

A felicitous offshoot of this opening of Turkey as a world cultural destination is a heightened awareness in the presentation of their national heritage. In addition to improvements to the outstanding state museums in Ankara, Istanbul, and Antalya, a series of privately-funded museums (Kadir Has in Kayseri, Koç, Sabancı, Pera, and Sadberk Hanım Museums in Istanbul) have opened their doors to greet foreigners and Turks whose interest in their cultural identity has been awakened. Turkey is becoming a world cultural player with these museums, especially with the new (2004) Istanbul Modern, the first of its kind in Turkey to showcase contemporary art. The traditional arts are not neglected, however, with plans afoot in Istanbul to create a museum dedicated to flatweave carpets. Tourism and museum brochures, formerly riddled by the most egregious of language mistakes, are now slick and linguistically polished. Audio guides impeccably present visits in numerous foreign tongues. Guide books are published in every language.

The people of Turkey are also becoming more culturally aware along with the tourists. Book production is more sophisticated, with artistically-designed colorful covers and quality white paper – a vast improvement over the dull jackets and grainy newsprint paper of yore. Previously, approximately 10,000 books were published each year in Turkey. In 2006, some 30,000 went to press. Fancy bookstores are popping up everywhere, with window fronts presenting engaging displays of graphically-appealing titles. Spurred by the declaration by UNESCO of nine properties in Turkey as World Heritage Sites and the resulting interest of world scholars in archeological digs, there is a greater consciousness in Turkey that traditional legacies must be saved, valued, and appreciated. Turks are becoming more and more aware that their culture is one of vast richness that must be cherished and preserved with attention and professionalism.

I note many changes to my guideposts. Good bread is getting harder to find. Ayran now comes in sterilized cups, not homemade in pitchers. This year, for the first time, I hear police and ambulance sirens on the streets. Old wooden houses and strolling lottery salesmen have become rarities. Fruit juice comes in cardboard boxes, not in tiny, colorful, cone-shaped glass bottles. You cannot get a drink of water anywhere without it coming out of a plastic bottle, as if those cool aluminum pitchers on restaurant tables or the glasses from itinerant peddlers are now deemed unsanitary. Babies have become fussy; children sassier and fatter. The Spice Bazaar is losing its integrity, with its famous mountain peaks of colored spices fading to a blur of tourist trinkets and tee-shirts. Jewelry shops are even crawling in: this year one with an obtrusive glassed-in front appeared, in total disrespect to the architectural integrity of this historical monument.

In all this change, I pray that the local individuality of each region in Turkey, so rich and distinctive, will be able to withstand globalization and its international standardized stamp of uniformity, for this regional diversity is one of the great resources of Turkey. Local customs and costumes, folk songs, dialects, accents, foods, music, and artistic patterns must stay vibrant. I want Konya to look differently from Şanliurfa; I do not want grey Erzurum to resemble golden Ankara, nor do I want the regional accents to disappear from speech. I want to hear Alevi music in Elbistan and eat gummy ice cream in Kahramanmaraş and marvel at the Blue Mediterranean in Antalya and the fawn plains in Niğde. In this march to progress, I especially hope that the unspoiled sweetness and spirit of the Turkish people will never be lost. Thievery will happen, burglary will happen, mobsters will happen: elements coming in from the West risk influencing traditional values. When I visited Isparta in 1991 and locked the car, the parking lot attendant laughed and mocked me saying: *"Foolish woman! You do not need to do that here; this is Turkey where no one steals from one another!"* How I hope he will always be right.

Yet these are but minor pebbles along the hurtling highway of progress. I, too, hop on board with all the same excitement as the Turks to this great Bosphorus ferry steaming towards the future. Two major projects are planned for the Bosphorus, and they remind us of how far Turkey has come since Süleyman the Magnificent dreamed of building a bridge across the Bosphorus. The "Marmaray" project, planned for completion in 2012, will link the European and Asian sides of Istanbul by a 13 km undersea rail tunnel across the Bosphorus, which will become the world's deepest immersed tube tunnel. A third bridge over the Bosphorus is planned for then as well. With this type of development, it is going to be soon very hard for France or Austria or anyone else in the world to ignore Turkey. A new generation of bridge crossers are currently hard at work drawing up the construction documents for these projects, and I can only hope that their experience with Turkey will be as rich as mine has been since the day I first worked on those translations for the Fatih Bridge.

Are you dizzy reading all of this, Lady Mary? Please do not worry, for despite the changes I have just described, many of the impressions you enjoyed during your stay in Turkey will not change on this road to progress and change. There will always be those tiled walls of the Selimye in Edirne for you to admire, that view from the heights of your Pera window, the pleasure boat rides up the blue Bosphorus, the charming women with diamonds large as hazelnuts, those Black Sea hazelnuts themselves, an obsession with children, a love of families, and those carpets laid out for picnics.

I deeply admire the city of Kayseri, Lady Mary, and how I wish you could have visited it. I think that one of the reasons that I admire it so much is that it symbolizes the parade of continuity and change in such harmony. When I stand in the main square and look around me in all directions, I see the full scope of the history and power of Turkish progress: the volcanic Mount Erciyes represents the beginning of time, the bustling market echoes the footsteps of Assyrian and Hittite merchants, the stone city walls are testament to Rome and Byzantium, the Mahperi Hatun and Sahibiye Medreses showcase the importance of this Seljuk capital, Sinan's Ali Pasha Mosque encapsulates the grandeur of the Ottoman Empire, the ideals of the Republic ride along with Atatürk on his equestrian statue in the center of the square, and the Turkey of European dreams glitters in the glass façade of the new Hilton Hotel, itself designed to mirror the profile of the majestic mountain of Erciyes across from it. I hope that every citizen of Turkey can look around him in his town and feel the same pride in this impressive march of history and progress.

I have every confidence that the giant "Turkey Rug" now being woven, 1000 miles long and 300 wide, will become a magic carpet for the entire world to admire. I hope that the Turks will reflect upon the fact that the plain, teal wall-to-wall carpeting now in place in the Alaeddin mosque in Konya will not be remembered as are the rugs woven during Sultan Alaeddin Keykubad's time that originally graced its floors. The good Sultan's rugs have gone down in the art history books as some of the finest examples of woven art. They are now the crown jewels of the Islamic Art Museum in Istanbul, drawing millions of visitors yearly. And so, this is what I wish for Turkey: that she and her people continue to weave a shimmering carpet of country, of great individuality and distinction, original in design and executed with the finest workmanship.

I never forgot my tree in that run-down motel in Antalya. It has haunted my memory and my dreams ever since that day when I feared its destruction behind that barbed wire fence. And so this year, I went back to Antalya, determined to find it. I was convinced that it was still alive, for I had trouble believing that something that precious and noble could have been bulldozed during a construction project. I walked down the Lara Road to the point where I sensed it had been and entered the grounds of a modern hotel now built there. Just when I was about to give up hope of finding it, suddenly, there in the maze in front of me, it stood. Not only had it been spared, but it had become the focal point of the entire land-scaping design of the hotel. A sweet terrace veranda had been built around it to showcase its majesty, and it stood just as it had been before, still welcoming people to sit under its sheltering shade to enjoy its peace and the magnificent view over the Antalya bay. And so I would like to think that Turkey will share the same destiny as my tree: eternal yet changing, grace-fully evolving with time, adapting, always able to stand tall and proud, with its roots firmly planted in the ground for generations to come, as its branches reach for the moon and stars.

Sincerely,
Kadriye Branning

The Çınar Hotel, built in 1958, one of Istanbul's first 5-star hotels

Soğuk Çeşme Street, Istanbul, 1978

Soğuk Çeşme Street, Istanbul, 2008

Vintage bus, Tokat

Drop those zeros!

Construction in progress

Wall-to-wall carpeting in the Konya Alaeddin Mosque, ca. 1996

Konya knotted-pile carpet, ca. 1220 from the Alaeddin Mosque,
Türk ve İslam Eserleri Müzesi, Istanbul, Inv. no. 681

Kayseri Gevher Medrese, 1985

Kayseri Gevher Medrese, 2004

Eyes on the street and fur at your feet

Sahip Ata Külliyesi, Konya

Old and new in Beyşehir

Refurbished Byzantine city walls, Istanbul

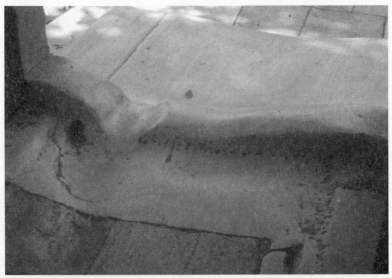

Pilgrim-worn threshold to the entry to the Tomb precinct of
Süleyman the Magnificent, Istanbul

Restoration, Külliye of İsmail Bey, Kastamonu

*Ottoman public water fountain, Istanbul, now dispensing
coca cola and bottled water*

Public scribe

In the lee of Mount Erciyes: the Kayseri Hilton, built in 2002

The new caravansarai of the Anatolian plains: the Konya Hilton, built in 2002

The plane tree of Motel Antalya, Lara Beach Road, 1981

LETTER 27

A bouquet of tulips

Dear Lady Mary,

If you could only see how this country has grown since you were here! You would not recognize Turkey today, so different than the one led by that warring and self-absorbed Sultan you knew – this country is a peaceful one, no longer bent on external conquests but on an internal battle for a political, financial, social, and moral standing for its citizens.

And Turkey certainly is growing: its youth, by its sheer numbers (70% of the population is under the age of 35) is now in charge. They are enthusiastic, they look both East and West before crossing the street, and they want to be happy and educated. They want to share the European vision of access to social advances, justice, freedom of speech, technological progress, and financial opportunity. They will be the masters of this country in a few short years, heirs to a very rich legacy, left to them by the Seljuks, the Ottomans, and their descendants who formed the Republic. They will not be afraid to break free of the past, to make sacrifices, and take chances. From their masses will rise the new Alaeddin Keykubads and Süleyman the Magnificents who will determine the profile of Turkey's future, a country which could become one of the most surprisingly successful nations of the twenty-first century.

In a letter to Alexander Pope on February 21, 1717, you describe passing through the battlefield of Karlowitz, site of the Austrian General Eugene de Savoie's great victory over the Ottoman Turks on September 11, 1697. The view of the field, still strewn with skulls and carcasses, prompted you to make some rare political comments. But you soon stopped, saying "*I won't trouble you with them, but return in a plain style to the histo-*

ry of my travels." Indeed, it is often difficult for a foreigner to make commentary without appearing to be judgmental of issues where they perhaps lack deep knowledge. This is one of the toughest lessons of crossing bridges: when to hold your tongue.

In these letters to you, I have held my tongue on the "shadow zones" that exist in Turkish culture. Perhaps you think that I have painted too idealistic a picture of this country and have glossed over the rough spots. As you stated in a letter dated August 30, 1716 from Ratisbon, "*...I think it very prudent to remain neuter,*" and I have chosen the same path. I am, like you, a traveler, not a journalist or an experienced political scientist. I leave the issues of societal differences and problems with politics, religion, culture, and ethnicity for them to analyze.

You, too, lived in a time when underlying problems were casting a shadow on society...but on the surface all appeared as the joyous Tulip Era of Ahmet III, devoted to parties, poetry, and tulips. Yet the taxation he imposed to feed his lush lifestyle caused a popular revolt that led to his downfall from the throne in 1730, twelve years after you left Turkey.

But who remembers those social problems of his era now, after some 280 years? What the world *does* remember are those tulips, with their bright colors and dancing stems. Appropriated by Holland, the entire world now looks at them as the symbol of springtime renewal and joyous hope. This is how I will always look at Turkey: as a country bearing a big bouquet of tulips to the world.

When I speak of Turkey to people around me, I often have a hard time getting past the darkness cast by the "shadow zones" they read about in the press and which seem to influence their firsthand perception of the country. Every culture, race, and country has these shadow zones, which are darker or lighter according to your viewpoint. I can clearly see the ones in Turkey, as many of them are the same that face my country. Traveling to Turkey and observing its struggles with these very same questions has helped me to see my own country and its institutions in a different light. Dealing with shadow zones is not a question of being ashamed of them, but confronting them, researching them, discussing different perspectives, analyzing the issues, and then moving on, so as to not repeat them.

Turkey has now reached a level of maturity that calls for responsibility, and the country is ready to make some remarkable changes. The adolescent country has grown up and is able to make its own decisions. Adult Turkey is striving to decide what form its democracy will take and how it will be nourished. I have every faith that the Turkish people with what they have learned, with their intelligence, strength, determination, and societal values, will always be able to select a path worthy of their brightest dreams for the future. Turkey will stand with pride on the world stage in the eyes of the citizens of the world.

Before I end my series of letters to you, I wish to express, Lady Mary, how much of an inspiration you were to me while writing them – and also how their lessons help me to better cross bridges. One of the things that I admire most in your letters – besides their cheerfulness, optimism, and the downright charming way in which you express your thoughts – is how you were so natural and open-minded about all that you saw in Turkey. A gifted writer, you were able to vividly describe your surroundings in a way that makes us feel right there at your side. But I think the real gift of your letter-writing is that you never placed yourself above what was going on around you, which never left a place for a scolding or condescending tone. How were you able to remain so remarkably free of ethnocentrism and prejudice like so many of your fellow Englishmen? I also appreciate how you framed your thoughts in a careful style, respectful of the sensitivities of all potential readers, no matter what their moral position. I also value how you chose your stories with great attention to illustrate a point to your cultured friends back home and to dispel the negative or slanted opinions they had of the Turks. Your letters are not just empty chatter relating your everyday activities, but offer meaningful and lively insights into the world around you. As you wrote to Lady Rich: "*I am now got into a new world, where every thing I see appears to me a change of scene.*" Instead of seeing only the change of scene and the differences, you understood the commonality between cultures, and when you did identify differences, you chose not to depict them with a judgmental attitude. You saw yourself better, you perceived your culture more clearly, and you led us by the hand to do the same. "*Tis as for them as tis for us,*" you wrote. For all of these reasons, I do not think I am alone in saying that people read your letters with as much eagerness today as when you first wrote them. It has thus been a pleasure for me to write these letters to you, Lady Mary, and to have had the opportunity to express not only my appreciation to the country and people of Turkey that we both love and respect so much, but also to you.

Although I will heed your advice to remain neuter, I will leave you in closing with certain of my beliefs, with the assurance that you, Lady Mary, a woman so enlightened, will share most of them. I believe in science and its potential to incite progress and well-being in the world. I believe in law and its authority to ensure equality. I believe in education and its power to help people see things larger than what is in their own imaginations and to avoid the pitfalls of ignorance, folly, and prejudice. I believe that it can light our human darkness and can create the catalyst for empathy, under-standing, and change. I believe that the message of wisdom is gleaned from many sources and in many fashions. I believe in community and the capa-bility of men to come together in society and governance to create a just world for its citizens. I believe that there is an invisible hand that always pushes people in the direction they need to take to make the proper deci-sions. I believe that this influential hand can emanate from heavenly mes-sages or from the stock market; it may come from medicine, it may come from a courtroom, but it always comes to a people of democracy. I believe that each meeting of two people, each small conversation, each glass of tea shared is a chink in the wall of intolerance. And glass after glass after glass of tea, perhaps the world of my dreams will one day become a reality.

Does such a world exist? Perhaps not for now. But tyranny never wins in the end. Human rights will always rise to the top. A love of freedom al-ways prevails. My dream is that Turkey – its citizens, politicians, lawmak-ers, military, and religious leaders – will cross a few more bridges towards these goals and cultivate a garden as lovely as the ideal one they depict on their tulip-strewn İznik wares. For above all things, I believe in the people of Turkey.

Sincerely,
Katharine Branning

LETTER 28

Maşallah

Dear Lady Mary,
You certainly survived some dangerous scrapes on your travels, both on route to Turkey and on the return trip home to London. In your letter of November 21, 1716, you relate a hair-raising crossing of the Alps on the journey to Turkey:

> "...We passed by moonshine the frightful precipices that divide Bohemia from Saxony, at the bottom of which runs the river Elbe, but I cannot say I had reason to fear drowning in it, being perfectly convinced that, in case of a tumble, it was utterly impossible to come alive at the bottom. In many places the road is so narrow that I could not discern an inch of space between the wheels and the precipice. Yet I was so good a wife not to wake Mr. Wortley, who was fast asleep by my side, to make him share in my fears...I have been told since 'tis common to find the bodies of travelers in the Elbe; but thank God that was not to be our destiny."

Later, despite the horror stories of potential travel hazards that awaited you on the road, you fearlessly plunged ahead from Vienna:

> "...if I am to believe the information of the people here, who denounce all sort of terrors to me; and indeed the weather is at present such as very few ever set out in. I am threatened at the same time with being froze to death, buried in the snow and taken by the Tartars, who ravage that part of Hungary I am to pass..."

As if you hadn't gone through enough on the way to Turkey, the penultimate leg of your journey home to London proved to be another tough crossing, this time over water instead of snowy mountains:

"I arrived this morning at Dover after being tossed a whole night in the packet boat in so violent a manner that the master gave us notice of the danger. We called a little fisher boat, which could hardly make up to us, while all the people on board us were crying to heaven, and 'tis hard to imagine oneself in a scene of greater horror than on such an occasion..."

I, too, have experienced some dangerous incidents along the roads of Turkey. I have seen huge transport trucks topple over on their sides on the edge of perilous night highways. I have risked being taken, like you, by potential ambushers on remote stretches in Eastern Turkey during the Kurdish difficulties. I have both dodged and witnessed the most atrocious of car crashes. I have seen impacts that have thrown people in the air like raggedy-dolls; and in one particularly horrid incident in Southern Turkey, I witnessed, from below, a car carrying a family of four plummet over the corniche cliff and land mangled practically at my feet. All of this reminds me of your thanksgivings of *"arriving safe...so much tired with fear and fatigue that it is not possible for me to compose myself to write..."*

But I would like to relate to you the story of a different type of difficult travel experience I had, one of an eventful return to my homeland after a stay in Turkey. Unlike you, however, I was not left alone and afraid in a carriage with a helpless and sleeping husband. I had an entire country at my side during this hardship, and it is a story that in many ways resumes the nature of the Turkish people and the Republic of Turkey.

This trip started out on a warm and crisp late summer morning in Istanbul. It was the last day of a glorious voyage to eastern Turkey, where I saw some of the wildest beauty known to man: from the white snowy peak of Noah's Mount Ararat to the deep cobalt blue of Lake Van and to the intense dark emerald green of the Kaçkar Mountains. It was a day when I felt particularly blessed because I had been lucky enough to witness such stunning examples of nature, God's most loving gift to man. It was a day when I was looking eagerly forward to heading back to the devoted embrace of my husband and to the warmth of my colleagues at my library. It was a day with a crystal clear sapphire sky and bright sun. It was the morning of September 11, 2001.

The return trip home announced itself like so many others before it. I traveled the familiar road to the airport filled with an infinite sadness to be leaving Turkey at the end of an intense time of learning, joyful play and living history, mixed with anticipation of the happiness of being reunited with loved ones at home. Candy, halvah, lokum, and Turkish coffee were purchased in the duty-free shop; last copies of the newspaper *Hürriyet* were tucked into my carry-on bag, and left-over Turkish lira coins were exchanged for *bonjuk* blue bead trinkets. As I passed through the first, second, and third security checkpoints, I commented to myself how thorough these Turks were when it came to ensuring security in this often volatile point of the world. I felt safe.

There was a delay of almost 2 hours before we could leave, due to the proverbial and mysterious "engine problems." We were fed tasty white cheese and tomato sandwiches in the interim. Finally we took off, but after only one hour out in flight, the pilot ("Kaptan") came on the intercom to tell us that we needed to head back to Istanbul because the pesky problem was apparently still not cleared up. The stewardesses stored away the food service carts, seatbelts were fastened, and we returned, deplaned, and waited another two hours in the same embarkment area. It was starting to become a bit tiring, so we were very pleased when the Turkish Airlines (THY) employee announced that a new plane had been found and that we would be heading out shortly. Once again, off we took, convinced that surely this time, all problems were behind us.

Unbelievably, about an hour out, the Kaptan came back on the intercom and stated in Turkish that we needed to return to Istanbul yet again. The entire cabin groaned and grumbled, and I began to doubt that I would ever get home that day. Only this time, his voice sounded odd, and he said, very vaguely, that we needed to return because "*All American airspace has been closed.*" I was immediately seized with panic, for I knew that something very, very terrible must have happened, for American airspace has never been closed in our entire history. I started to cry out of unknown fear, for I could not imagine what this issue could be, only that something very serious must have happened. A little Turkish boy came up to me and asked me why I was crying, and I was totally helpless to tell him of the foreboding I felt. Not wanting to frighten him or the other Turks on the plane, I said that I was crying because I was so sad to leave my friends in Istanbul.

About a half an hour later, the Kaptan came back on, still in Turkish, and said that it looked like the problem was that a "*big building in New York City has suffered some kind of attack.*" And then I knew in the pit of my stomach what that "big building" had to be: it could be none other than the one I see day and night from my window of my apartment, standing like a sentinel for the whole world to see: the Twin Towers of the World Trade Center. And I knew somehow that the assault was not a mere accident, but had to have been a terrorist attack.

At last the plane landed back in Istanbul. The cabin hostess made an intercom message requesting that everyone remain in their seats. The Kaptan came on and gave a message in Turkish, and then made another one in English so that the few Americans on the plane would be able to finally understand what was going on. He spoke very clearly and slowly, not because his command of English was weak, but because he was searching for the right words to communicate his message as gently and carefully as possible. In a voice obviously trembling with emotion, he said: *"Dear Ladies and Gentlemens. I must inform you of some very sad news. There has been a terrorist attack on the big building in New York City, the World Trade Center. It is very, very bad, and many people have been hurt. To all the American people on this plane, I want to say I am so so sorry for you and your country today."* And then we heard him sob. To hear that sob made me realize how intense it must have been for him to announce that news to us, this ever-gracious Turkish host, to his "guests" in his aircraft home. The Kaptan must have felt devastated that a plane, object of his livelihood, had been used as an instrument of destruction. He choked up too, as he probably had been trained as a pilot by American flyboys and because he had probably been to America so many times on this route, circling around those distinctive endpin towers of Manhattan Island for his job. He was surely heartbroken, too, because he already knew the terrorists were fellow Muslims. His soft sob made the imagined bang of the crash in my ears all the more loud, and the whole incident became very real for me, although at the time, I had no idea that the Towers were to fall and that the terrorists were allegedly Muslims.

Because of those engine problems, we had been saved the fate of so many others who were flying home to America that day. Instead of being stranded, the few Americans on that Turkish Airlines flight that day had the great fortune, in the midst of all the ensuing chaos, to be returned to a country that would open its arms and take care of them.

When we stepped off the plane and came into the airport terminal, there stood in front of us a platoon of people of all kinds, lined up in total silence. The entire airport staff had gathered there to wait for us: some were officers dressed in suits and ties, some wore THY service uniforms and ties, some were baggage handlers in their grey tunics; there were the char women in their pink aprons standing attention next to their cleaning carts, police officers with their thick black leather belts, food service attendants in their white paper hats, security clerks in their black blazers, and so many others in a blur of colors and clothes. It seemed as if the full airport had come forth to form this very human wall to surround us with their protection. After that point everything became a slow motion blur, as if I were about to faint or as if I were underwater, with people moving towards us but no sounds coming from their mouths. But I do remember clearly all the hands coming forth – those famous magic Turkish hands that appear whenever there is a need – taking us by the elbow and guiding us to the baggage claim area. I do not recall what was said to me at this point; all I remember were their eyes – and it was the sadness that I saw in those eyes that made me realize the gravity of the situation. I distinctly remember, however, a grey-haired, handsome man in a charcoal suit with a walkie-talkie in his hand, who came up to me. In perfect English he said, "*Please do not worry, you are being taken care of. We will be taking you by a van to a nearby hotel to stay. It is very beautiful and nice, do not worry. You will stay there for the time it takes for things to normalize and for you to go home again. Do not worry. We will take care of you. But know that when you go into your room and turn on the television, you will see images of a brutality never before seen, and that you will be very upset. There will be someone at a table in the lobby, a health worker, who will be there for you to speak with if it all becomes too much for you. Good luck and God bless you.*" And to this day I can still see the sharp dark features of the unshaven face of the skinny man in a ragged black suit coat who stuck out his hand to whisk away my suitcase and to load it in the van for me.

Who was this "we" that was taking care of us? Obviously Turkish Airlines, but it seemed like everyone else in the country was joining in as well. How could a country reputed to be so disorganized have managed, in the space of under two hours, to mount such a relief operation, complete with lodging, transport, and a psychologist set up at a table? How was it that they could be so professional and calm, so seamlessly helpful in order that we could better focus and deal with our own emotional horror? I was too numb to register it all. When the few Americans on that flight arrived at the hotel, we were ushered to our rooms with the hushed consideration usually reserved for funeral services. After I entered that room, in that indeed very beautiful hotel, sat down on the edge of the bed and saw those images on the television screen, I knew that the grey-haired man had not exaggerated. I learned of the story of the *"attack on the big building in New York."* I learned that in was done in the name of Allah, the most Merciful and the most Compassionate.

I stayed there for a week, unable to get personal news of the tragedy, with only the droning reports of CNN and those never-ending images of the impact of the crash played over and over as if one time was not enough to gouge it in your memory forever. Was my husband safe? Was my assistant, who crossed under the Towers every morning on her commute in from New Jersey, lying flattened under the tonnage? How was everyone in my downtown neighborhood, now closed off from the world, coping with the tragedy? Over and over again as I saw those images of that hole ripped in the sky, I felt as if a hole had been ripped in my heart. When I saw those crushed beams, I felt as if my own bones had been crushed. After a few hours, all became a haze, as if time had stopped and as if my breathing had as well. But I do clearly remember the next morning when I went out of the hotel to get some air, there fluttering in front of me on a giant flagpole was the Turkish flag – its red color symbolizing the blood of its own fallen – at half mast. It was then that I understood that this tragedy was not one that had just struck my city, but it was affecting the entire world as well.

Turkish people greeted us everywhere on the street, with sadness in their eyes, with a word of encouragement, a wan smile, or a touch on the arm from all of them. So many of them spoke about the tragedy that they had suffered on a hot summer August day two years earlier: the Izmit earthquake. A mere 40 seconds during the black night of August 17, 1999 were enough to kill an estimated 40,000 innocent people in their sleep. A mere 5 seconds in 2001 were enough to kill 3,000 innocent people at their work desks. The parallels between the two horrific incidents were not lost on the Turks, who knew the pain of imagining loved ones trapped under crushed beams, with dust in their lungs instead of sweet air.

One night that week when I couldn't sleep I got up to write a thank you letter. I did not know exactly to whom I should address it, or how I would get it to them. But I just felt that writing a letter would help me in that moment of stress, for putting emotions to paper seemed the only possible outlet for my grief, as the shock of it all had pushed my tears way down deep inside of me. At least for that moment in time, I could control something in the world: the flow of words onto paper in my own proper universe.

One morning about eight days later, the hotel staff called to say that we were to be ready to leave in an hour: the US airspace had opened and that we were being sent home. We were to be picked up at the hotel by a special THY van and taken to the airport.

Before leaving, I went to the front desk of the hotel to ask what I owed them for all the expenses I had incurred staying there: the luxurious room, the breakfasts, the vain phone calls, and faxes home. I did not know the protocol of such a situation, but I wanted to make sure I had taken care of everything. The young woman at the front desk just looked at me, bowed her head, and whispered, "*You owe us nothing.*" It was as if she could not bear to look at me, knowing how much pain I must have felt while staying in her "home." And I could not bear to look at her, overwhelmed by the hotel's charity, the intensity of this tragic event that I knew I would read in her eyes and my incapacity to thank her for the role she played in my well-being. I could not speak but handed to her the envelope with the letter I had written on that night I was unable to sleep. She looked at the addressee, visibly moved, and then back at me, and quietly said "*Thank you.*" And it was only then that my tears started to fall, as if all the immeasurable solace and tender consideration provided over the past week made the horror of the event suddenly too much to keep inside.

We piled in the busses and arrived at a still-hushed airport and boarded the flight to New York City, mirroring the same steps of a week prior. The same triple checkpoints for security, the same attention to protocol, and the same efficiency. No one talked much on that 11-hour flight home: everyone was either too frightened to be in the cursed skies, in one of these apparatus now associated with an instrument of mass destruction, or quite simply because we were all apprehensive about what we would find once at home. The city I found when I arrived that night was as quiet as the plane.

The former glorious view onto the World Trade Center from my Greenwich Village apartment was now filled with a billowing, yellow-grey cloud, glowing in the day from the sun reflecting off all its dust and in the evening from the giant high-intensity lights set up at the site. The furnishings of my home were covered, that day and for many months to come, with the pulverized dust of those fallen Twin Towers and the ashes of its 3,000 victims. Each day as I cleaned it away, day after day for months, I ceremoniously repeated prayers and recited Scripture for all of those innocent souls reduced to the dust I was wiping away.

New York City healed, the United States healed, and I healed. We are still living the consequences of that ignominious event up to this day, some small, some large, some local, some international. In many ways, I wonder if the recovery from that day was for me harder than most Americans. Although I personally suffered no loss of life in the crash, I still felt a tremendous loss to my city and in my faith in my fellow man. I felt betrayed by Islam, this faith that had earned a special respect in my heart; I felt betrayed that several fanatics of this religion I considered so pure and so noble had tarnished it beyond apparent forgiveness. I could not believe that the Islam I knew, through my studies, though my life shared with Muslims, through the many Muslims I had met in Turkey, those who believed in a *God, the most merciful, the most compassionate* – could be anything like those who had done this act. When I saw the dangerous turn my grief was taking – veering towards doubt, bitterness, and deception – I knew it had to stop. It was then that I made a vow. I perhaps could not control the outcome of all the events in the world, I reasoned, but I could control my immediate sphere, the orbit around me that I influence. It is said that perhaps everything in life happens in order to help us live. And so from the horror of that day, I told myself that I needed to recommit my efforts to support understanding between people and religions and that I needed to continue more than ever my dedication to fostering cross-cultural relations. It made me realize that if a person like me, who had such respect for Islam, was feeling such negative emotions against Muslims, what must the average American be thinking? I needed now to be a bridge-builder more than ever.

The Turkish part of my 9/11 story has one last chapter. About five months after the incident, I returned to work after my lunch break one day, and the front desk receptionist handed me a very large wooden box. A

THY envelope with my name on it was taped to it. My heart stopped and I was overcome with all the memories – good and bad – of that week in Istanbul that came flooding back to me. I waited to open it at home, in private, for I knew it would be something special, yet again another bit of Turkish kindness graced upon me. The letter was from the New York director of Turkish Airlines, extending his wishes for my well-being and telling me that he desired to offer this token of appreciation on behalf of the THY staff for *my* letter, the one I had addressed "*to Turkish Airlines and the People of the Republic of Turkey*" and left at that hotel desk months before and which had finally come into his hands. It was inconceivable to believe that after all that had already been done emotionally and materially for me, that the warm arms of the Turks were continuing to surround me with compassion and goodness.

Inside of that giant box, encased beautifully in an elegant walnut and glass frame, was a large, oval plaque in silver. On this plaque, inscribed in fine cursive calligraphy, was the iconic message "*Maşallah*" which translates as "how beautifully God created" and is used by Turks to mean "may God protect you from all evil."

Yes, Turkey – this magnificent and most generous of nations – has shown me that I must never doubt the infinite goodness of my fellow man.

Sincerely,
Kadriye Branning